DECOLONIZING FEMINISMS

Piya Chatterjee, *Series Editor*

AXIS OF HOPE

Iranian Women's Rights Activism across Borders

CATHERINE Z. SAMEH

UNIVERSITY OF WASHINGTON PRESS
Seattle

Axis of Hope was made possible in part by a grant from the UC Irvine Hellman Fellowship Program, supported by the Hellman Foundation Fellows Fund.

Printed and bound in the United States
Composed in Minion Pro, typeface designed by Robert Slimbach

23 22 21 20 19 5 4 3 2 1

UNIVERSITY OF WASHINGTON PRESS
uwapress.uw.edu

LIBRARY OF CONGRESS CATALOGING-IN-PUBLICATION DATA
LC record available at https://lccn.loc.gov/2019010533

ISBN 978-0-295-74630-2 (hardcover)
ISBN 978-0-295-74632-6 (paperback)
ISBN 978-0-295-74631-9 (ebook)

Cover design by Katrina Noble
Cover illustration by Hedieh Javanshir Ilchi

The paper used in this publication is acid free and meets the minimum requirements of American National Standard for Information Sciences—Permanence of Paper for Printed Library Materials, ansi z39.48–1984.∞

To my parents, Abbas Sameh and Stephanie Sameh, who taught me about justice, and my sister, Sarah Sameh—border-crossers all

CONTENTS

ACKNOWLEDGMENTS

The production of knowledge is a deeply collective process, one that sustains me during many solitary hours of writing. I wouldn't be here without the support, generosity, and love of many.

I am grateful to Larin McLaughlin, Piya Chatterjee, and everyone at the University of Washington Press for the enthusiasm, labor, and skill they have brought to this book. It has been an absolute privilege and delight to work with such an incredible team. I am deeply appreciative of the three anonymous reviewers of the manuscript. Their astute suggestions and generous comments greatly improved the book. Any flaws and omissions are surely my own. Thank you to Amy Smith Bell, who copyedited the manuscript, and Eileen Allen, who provided the index. Hedieh Javanshir Ilchi has elevated this book in allowing her exquisite piece, *Across Solemn Distances #12*, to be used on the cover. I am honored and grateful.

Early research for this book was made possible by generous funding from the Association for the Sociology of Religion. My deepest gratitude goes to the Hellman Foundation, whose generous funding enabled the completion of the manuscript. I am immensely grateful to the One Million Signatures Campaign activists and Mahboubeh Abbasgholizadeh, who so generously gave me their time and trusted me to tell some of their stories. Their persistence in the face of many odds inspired this book, and I hope I have not let them down. I am grateful, too, for the opportunity to work with the wonderful students at the University of California–Irvine (UCI), who are hungry to talk and think about the issues raised in this book.

Chapter 1 was developed from an article, "Discourses of Equality, Rights, and Islam in the One Million Signatures Campaign in Iran," which appeared as part of a special issue on new directions in feminism and human rights in the *International Feminist Journal of Politics* (12, nos. 3–4 [2010]: 444–63). Chapter 2 grew out of an article, "From Tehran to Los Angeles to Tehran: Transnational Solidarity Politics in the One Million Signatures Campaign to End Discriminatory Law," published in *WSQ: Women's Studies Quarterly* (42, nos. 3–4 [Fall–Winter 2014]: 166–88). A small portion of the introduction builds on ideas explored in "Political-Social Movements: Feminist: Iran," in

Encyclopedia of Women and Islamic Cultures, edited by Suad Joseph (first published online in 2017).

This project began when I was in the Department of Women's and Gender Studies at Rutgers University, where I was fortunate enough to have some of the best scholars in the field as advisers, mentors, and friends. My deepest gratitude goes to Ethel Brooks. Her support and encouragement during the early stages of this project were unfailing. I thank Ethel for her patience, kindness, good humor, and—not least of all—her beautiful and much needed scholarship. I am grateful to have worked with Jasbir Puar, who pushed our cohort to think across fields and frameworks. My thinking has greatly benefited from her brilliance. I am grateful to Joanna Regulska for the comparative perspective she has brought to my work. I will forever admire the ease with which she accomplishes so much. I am so fortunate to have worked with Ousseina Alidou and participated with her in "The Culture of Rights, The Rights of Culture" seminar held by the Institute for Research on Women in 2009–10. Our conversations on gender, rights, and Islam were truly inspiring, and I continue to marvel at her exquisite work. During my time at Rutgers, Ed Cohen, Mary Hawkesworth, Dorothy Hodgson, Mary Gossy, Leela Fernandes, Elizabeth Grosz, Leslie McCall, Yana Rodgers, David Eng, Mary Trigg, Lisa Hetfield, and Harriet Davidson also provided support and tremendous inspiration. I was fortunate enough to learn from Beth Baron and Samira Haj at the Graduate Center of the City University of New York. Samira in particular greatly influenced my thinking about religion, secularism, gender, and Islam, which ultimately shaped the direction of my research.

While finishing my PhD, I was lucky enough to land a dream job at the Barnard Center for Research on Women (BCRW) and work with the incomparable Janet Jakobsen. Janet was and continues to be an incredible mentor and friend, and I learned so much from her about how to do whatever it takes to build and sustain feminist and scholar-activist spaces. Janet really does know everything. At Barnard, I worked with a team of brilliant and wonderful people who will be my co-thinkers and friends forever. In addition to Janet Jakobsen, Christina Crosby, Elizabeth Castelli, Rebecca Jordan-Young, Collen Thomas, Betsy Esch, Hope Dector, Anne Jonas, Pam Phillips, and Nicci Yin provided much inspiration. I had the deep pleasure of working closely with Yvette Christianse, Shayoni Mitra, Hilary Link, Jane Bennett, Attiya Ahmad, and the late Alison Bernstein on a transnational feminisms initiative. I learned so much from our endeavors to build transnational networks of feminist scholars and activists.

Moving from Barnard to the Department of Gender and Sexuality Studies at UCI, I gained an incredible set of colleagues. Thank you to Laura Kang, Lilith Mahmud, Jeanne Scheper, Jennifer Terry, and Emily Thuma for the soft landing into a fabulous new job. A special thanks goes to Laura Kang and Jennifer Terry for their mentorship and for their invaluable comments on parts of this manuscript. Outside of my department, Nasrin Rahimieh has been an immensely supportive colleague at UCI, and I thank her for her helpful feedback on some of this manuscript. Arlene Keizer, Christine Balance, Touraj Daryaee, Adria Imada, Glen Mimura, Cecelia Lynch, Kaaryn Gustafson, Jonathan Alexander, Heidi Tinsman, Michele Goodwin, Victoria Bernal, Roxanne Varzi, and Patty Pierson have also provided much inspiration and collegiality.

I am lucky to have an amazing network of friends who have sustained me through this project from its beginnings to completion. A special thanks to my New York family, Ilana Berger, Eli Dueker, Kim Gilmore, Stephanie Luce, and Erin Small, who have given me some of the best years of my life. In our twelve years together, Erin provided encouragement on the project and created a life around us of big ideas and big pleasures. In our friendship we have only gained. Special thanks to Hannah and Rosie for the joy they bring to 248. Thanks especially to Arlen Stahlberg, Jennifer Terry, Surina Khan, Laura Kang, Arlene Keizer, Adria Imada and Glen Mimura (and their children, Naia and Saku), Paula Chakravartty, Amy Hartford, Denise Small, Casey Ruble, Rosie Bruno, Janet Jakobsen, Christina Crosby, Elizabeth Castelli, Hope Dector, Anne Jonas, Pam Phillips, Nicci Yin, Neal Terry, Henry Rasu, Laura Stahlberg, Treva Swersky, Nesve Yaylar, Jesse Levin, Johanna Brenner, Bill Resnick, Carolina Banks Munoz, Pam Galpern, Chloe Tribich, John McGough, Dean Spade, Craig Willse, Jan Haaken, Denise Morris, and Adam Rhynard and Mimi Martin (and their children, Iris and Arlo) for friendships old and new. I have thoroughly enjoyed and benefited from thinking and being together with Azza Basarudin, Sherine Hafez, Sondra Hale, and Khanum Shaikh. A special thanks to Monica Zimmerman for her love, encouragement, and sense of humor, and for hanging in there with me, and to Julia Olsen and Tori Fornaciari (and their children, Celia and Neve) for support and lots of fun. I am grateful to Nargess Fassih for all of her support.

Nothing in my life would be possible without my family. Sarah Sameh has offered love, humor, support, and encouragement in everything I do. I thank her dear partner, Jay Reeck, for his kindness and laughter. Judy Sameh has given so much love and inspiration. From my parents, Abbas Sameh and Stephanie Sameh, I have learned what a gift it is to be alive. They model what it means to live lives defined by compassion, generosity, humility, empathy, service, tenacity, tenderness, and deep joy. I am grateful for everything they have given me.

ABBREVIATIONS

CEDAW Convention on the Elimination of All Forms of Discrimination Against Women
CISADA Comprehensive Iran Sanctions, Accountability, and Divestment Act of 2010
GWOT Global War on Terror
IRI Islamic Republic of Iran
MENA Middle East and North Africa
MERIP Middle East Research and Information Project
NGOTC Non-Governmental Organization Training Center
OMSC One Million Signatures Campaign to End Discriminatory Law

AXIS OF HOPE

INTRODUCTION

To Think of and Be With

> In the past thirty years, the main target of the government was women. Now, women are there not because of their husbands, not because of their sons. They are there for themselves. They're there to fight for their own rights. This is very important. During 1979, they were there for nationalism. But now, they're there because they want their own rights.
>
> —FAKHRI, ONE MILLION CAMPAIGN SIGNATURES MEMBER

> As a women's leader, when you leave your country, it's distance. But more than distance, it's loss.
>
> —MAHBOUBEH ABBASGHOLIZADEH

ON A WARM SUMMER DAY IN 2018, I SAT WITH MAHBOUBEH Abbasgholizadeh, an Iranian women's rights activist, in her Brooklyn apartment. I had first met her approximately eight years before that, and we had met on several occasions to share ideas about and histories of activism. The quotation above comes from oral history interviews I collected from Mahboubeh over that summer. In these conversations she wrestled with the different personas, or personal and political identities, that comprise her sixty years, the majority of them as a women's rights activist in Iran. Exiled since 2010, Mahboubeh described, in that particular moment, the difficulties of being an activist outside of Iran and of sustaining connection to a community she built her life around. She spoke of the debates and tensions, and the shared histories and divergent pathways, that define many activist communities but that become particularly pronounced and poignant when the contours of home and community shift dramatically, and not by choice.

Referring to no one in particular, Mahboubeh, an accomplished media maker, set the stage for this scene, as if directing a film sequence.

> Say, for example, we had this long history together. We were in jail. We were friends. And now, after ten years, we have different points of view. We are different, totally. And sometimes, we are on the opposite sides and arguing. So, normally I don't go to see your TV interview. But, after a while, I say, "You should do it because this is part of the movement, and you should just listen to what she says." And then you feel, "I know this tone. I know this kind of talking. I know this way she's using this sentence. She's very under pressure. I feel it." Cut. And then, you go to sleep. And then, in your dream, you see that, all of that. For example, in your dream, you see her daughter, who is no longer a kid. Now, she is like a young woman. And she's coming to you, like an aunt and says, "Hey, I am very worried about my mom." And you say, "Okay." It's kind of like a connection, a connection by your dream and family and history. And so, your reaction shows there is no distance. Because you have memory. You have history. You have a lot of emotional history.[1]

Mahboubeh brings into sharp relief the shuttling between connection to and disconnection from Iran, neither as fixed or stable states, that characterizes her life as an Iranian women's rights activist.

As she talks about the importance of memory and history, Mahboubeh goes back to this dreamlike state. What defines women's rights activists in the diaspora, she says, is that "even if you don't have any connection [to activists in Iran] at this time, we had the same history. And still, we are, in our dream, in that different part of us, living with them." For Mahboubeh, history and memory become embedded in her unconscious. When she finds herself in the persona of, in her words, "immigrant Mahboubeh," who is being criticized by, again in her words, "activist leader in Iran Mahboubeh" for not being in Iran, for assimilating into New York life, she draws on this unconscious as a resource. When "activist leader in Iran Mahboubeh" tells "immigrant Mahboubeh" that her time as an Iranian activist is "finished," Mahboubeh surfaces what has defined so much of her life. "If you want to interpret the connection between the women's movement in the diaspora and inside, it's not just because of my memory or because I have social media to connect with them. It's many, many things in between—identity, story, unconscious, post-trauma." She pauses. "And also, commitment."

This book examines the commitments, stories, discourses, practices, visions, and organizational cultures of Iranian women's rights activists—those inside and primarily outside of Iran. I trace a partial and modest history of decolonial feminist world-making through the narratives of women's rights activists in the One Million Signatures Campaign to End Discriminatory Law (OMSC); interviews with campaign members living in Southern California; two memoirs by human rights lawyer and Nobel Prize–winner Shirin Ebadi; and the life story and activist project ZananTV of Mahboubeh Abbasgholizadeh. In rendering an account of activist struggle, joy, sorrow, pride, pain, and labor, I attend to what it means to partake in daily, year-after-year thinking, writing and doing of changing one's society and the world, particularly when notions of homeland and diaspora, inside and outside, are insufficient to convey a beloved community.

Within the online, print, and oral narratives gathered throughout this book, an overwhelming life force and politics—a collective voice—emerges that I distill as decolonial feminism. Considered together, the expressions of friendship, love, solidarity, patience, and inclusivity; the commitments to nonideological and nonhierarchical practices; the critiques and rejections of past and current epistemic and political violences; and the shared investments in a political project of fighting for women's rights on these activists' own terms point to what Sahar, an OMSC campaign activist in Southern California, calls "the power of unity, the power of thinking of the other and being together."[2] Through building local and transnational projects, and by creating and sustaining networks along axes of feminist solidarity, friendship, love, and shared community and commitment, Iranian women's rights activists have cultivated ways of *thinking of* and *being with* each other that rupture the relentless difference-making and violence of coloniality.

Axis of Hope locates Iranian women's rights activism within the long-standing tension between Iran and the United States, intensified in the post-9/11 period by the Global War on Terror (GWOT), and the ongoing demonization, isolation, and economic strangling of Iran through decades of sanctions.[3] From 2001 to 2009, the long years of the George W. Bush administration, the US government amped up the rhetorical war against Iran and committed to a policy of isolation, sanctions, and containment. This fueled repression against reformers and activists inside Iran. When reform forces were barred from Iranian Parliamentary elections in 2004, the state's more conservative forces began to consolidate their control, after a long period of relative openness and the expansion of civil society under reform president Mohammad Khatami. With Mahmoud Ahmadinejad's election in 2005 the reform movement suffered another blow. Surveillance and repression of activists, including women's rights activists, became more frequent, and any political activity that challenged the state was labeled as a "national security threat." Women's rights rallies and protests were shut down in 2005 and 2006, and many student, labor, and women's rights activists were targeted over the next several years. Under Ahmadinejad the state's repressive forces were emboldened enough in 2008 to arrest Esha Momeni, a dual citizen and women's rights activist living and attending graduate school in the United States, while she was doing research in Iran.

In December 2008 and January 2009, I traveled to Iran to visit my large extended family in Isfahan, Kerman, Shiraz, and Tehran. I offer a brief snapshot of that time: It is six months before the 2009 presidential elections in Iran and just a few months after Barack Obama's historic election to the presidency of the United States. Despite the incredibly high inflation, massive unemployment, and choking pollution in the major cities, people are in decent spirits. Jokes about Bush fly from Iranians' cell phones and emails, and hope springs eternal for a change in United States–Iran relations. The reform campaigns of candidates Mehdi Karroubi and Mir-Hossein Mousavi are heating up, and people are eagerly anticipating the June elections. "You must come back for the elections," everyone says to me. "It will be a historic time." Iranians of all ages, genders, and classes are tired of Mahmoud Ahmadinejad. He certainly did not put Iran's oil revenues on people's tables, as he promised. Many are excited about Obama and watched as he swept into victory in November 2008. They celebrated his win as a sign of hope for their own futures. "Obama" is loosely translated into Farsi as "oo ba ma": he is with us.

When Ahmadinejad was fraudulently declared the winner of the June 12, 2009, elections, a massive and peaceful protest movement erupted in the streets, coined the Green Movement. The color of Mousavi's campaign (green) is associated with the Prophet Muhammad and Shia Islam's history of resistance, repurposed in this new uprising. The security forces would soon repress the movement, arresting, beating, and jailing protesters. On June 18, Supreme leader Ayatollah Ali Khamenei endorsed the election results and vowed to squash the movement. On June 20 protester Neda Agha-Soltan was shot dead by a sniper, among a dozen who were killed and the many thousands beaten. Her dying and death were filmed with a cell phone, and the video circulated around the world.

Before the Green Movement erupted, scholars had examined how Iranians used new media technologies, considering the ways in which clerics, students, artists, women—indeed those from a variety of social locations and political persuasions—accessed new media as readers and content creators, ultimately extending the arenas for political discussions, debates, and movements.[4] The OMSC, a networked on-the-ground and online campaign to reform Muslim family law from a gender equality perspective, is one such example. The OMSC, like the Green Movement, used hybrid forms of resistance and would share characteristics of the many political eruptions that followed, including the Arab Uprisings of 2010 and 2011, the Occupy Movement of 2011, the fightbacks against austerity in Greece and other European countries, the 2014 student protests against tuition hikes in South Africa, the 2016–17 protests against President Park in South Korea, and other movements including #BlackLivesMatter, #saynotothememo, and #MeToo.[5] Nearly every social movement and uprising is now mediated through the innovative uses of multiple broadcast and communication technologies. In considering the mediated and networked characteristics of contemporary social movements, I point to how cyber technologies *extend* rather than mark the *beginning* of political movements. The moments of eruption on the ground and online are made possible by the years, often decades, of sustained political organizing by activists, whose bodies and labors are often eclipsed by the spectacle of media.

Scholars have explored the networked nature of some of the recent social movements in the Middle East and North Africa (MENA) and elsewhere.[6] Others have considered the particular ways in which new media has facilitated women's activism and enlarged conceptions of the political in the Global South writ large (Alidou 2011; Sreberny 2015). Some scholars have examined the porosity of national borders through the mediated connections between those "within" and "outside" of the nation (Bernal 2014). Still others have considered how digital technologies are shaped by and used to maintain geopolitical structures of domination (Hussain and Shaikh 2015; Khiabany 2015). As Gholam Khiabany (2015) has noted, these promising technologies have also been promoted and endorsed by the US government and development organizations as a tactic of regime change in Iran. *Axis of Hope* situates Iranian women's rights activism and network-building within these contradictory uses of technology and the multiple (and often counterpoised) understandings and practices of mediated resistance.

Ayatollah Khamenei and others in the Iranian government "sought to portray their country as the true genesis of the Arab Spring political uprisings" (Gladstone 2012) and performed support for the Occupy Movement by staging a "rally" of stern-looking, black chador–clad Iranian women with "The End of Wall St" signs.[7] In making connections between Iran, the Arab uprisings, and the Occupy Movement, the cynical maneuvering by Khamenei was flimsy indeed. More robust are the actual connections between the horizontalism and leaderless structure of the feminist networks in Iran and the Iranian diaspora, the Green Movement, many of the Arab Spring uprisings, the Occupy Movement, and the struggles against neoliberalism in many European countries, South Africa, South Korea, and many more places. Such movements and moments continue to animate scholars and activists who sift through and theorize these innovations in online and on-the-ground activism as well as the mediated techniques and technologies of repression and control. This book is not a study of new media per se but considers its role in the formation of transnational activist communities.

The repression of the Green Movement and the crackdown on activists and citizens that followed created new conditions for women's rights activists inside Iran who had long committed to reforming their society from within. Many of these activists were forced into exile. *Axis of Hope* considers the narratives of two of these women: Shirin Ebadi, Nobel Prize–winner and human rights lawyer, and Mahboubeh Abbasgholizadeh, women's rights activist and founder of ZananTV. As with the OMSC activists living in the United States, Ebadi and Abbasgholizadeh draw attention to what it means to live and work outside of Iran, in the heart of empire, and the nuanced ways in which each navigates questions of identity, belonging, home, and community.

Sadly for Iranians, the Obama administration only exacerbated worsening internal conditions. I offer a second snapshot from Iran: It is January 2012, Obama's fourth year in office, and my cousins have just come to the United States from Isfahan to settle their daughter into graduate school. Over breakfast they tell me that before they left Iran, the supermarkets were empty of food, as people, panicked about the economic sanctions, snatched up all the food they could carry home. My cousins recount that on their flight from Tehran to Europe, Iran Air had to land in Ankara, Turkey, to refuel, as sanctions prohibited the airline from buying fuel from European airports. They tell me people are scared—scared of sanctions, of the threat of war. As sanctions policies toward Iran, Iraq, South Africa, and many other places have shown, it is always ordinary people—not regimes or individual leaders—who suffer. So-called "targeted" sanctions target everyone. They are war by other means. Obama and Secretary of State Hillary Clinton did little to improve US-Iran relations. In his first term Obama signed into law the Comprehensive Iran Sanctions, Accountability, and Divestment Act of 2010 (CISADA), a far-reaching and punitive set of sanctions.

In his first presidential bid Hassan Rouhani campaigned on the promise to improve US-Iran relations and deliver an end to sanctions and geopolitical isolation. Rouhani's surprise victory in 2013 gave new hope to reformers and activists for more political freedoms and to citizens for relief from the crippling effects of sanctions. In 2015, Obama and Rouhani brokered the Iran Nuclear Deal. The United States eased up on some of the sanctions against Iran, but Obama did not lift them unilaterally. In June 2016, Canadian-Iranian scholar Homa Hoodfar was arrested in Iran, charged with meddling in "feminism" and "security matters," and spent 112 days in the notorious Evin Prison. After her release in October 2016, Hoodfar told *The Guardian* that she believes she was "a pawn in [the] struggle" between Rouhani's reform government and more conservative factions of the state who control Iran's Revolutionary Guards (quoted in Kassam 2016). In the spring of 2017, Rouhani was reelected for a second term as Iran's president. Iranian activist Reihane Taravati campaigned for Rouhani on Instagram in part because of his work to increase the country's Internet speed and freedom. "We are our own media now," Taravati claimed after his victory, pointing to Rouhani's facilitation of social media activism and its capacities to influence political movements and results.[8]

By all accounts, Rouhani's reelection was a victory for reformers in the state and a reflection of the democratic participation and majoritarian desires among the populace for a softer, more reform-minded government. Forty-one million people voted—more than half of Iran's population and two-thirds of eligible voters. But in May 2018, President Donald Trump pulled out of the Iran Nuclear Deal, and by August he had reinstated a horrific sanctions program that has exacerbated a failing economy and high inflation. Another round of US-Iran standoffs is unfolding, as Iranians are squeezed by the massive devaluation of their currency.

(RE)LOCATING RIGHTS TALK

Under decades of severe internal and global conditions, Iranian women's rights activists have not shrunk from demanding their rights and crafting notions of sovereignty on their own terms. The poly-vocality of rights talk and contestations in interpretation signify not only Iran's historically rich culture of debate but also the ways in which activists and citizens have produced particular understandings of the meanings of gender equality. When women's rights activists articulate their desires for women's equality under the law, they seek not to necessarily instantiate a "progressive" people against an "authoritarian" regime nor rights only for an elite group of women at the exclusion of ordinary citizens. Instead, women's equality has become part of the national discussion about what constitutes a just state and a good society. Women's rights activists and ordinary women have acquired fluency in making claims for what they see as not only possible but rightfully theirs: full legal and undifferentiated equality within a contemporary Muslim country. *Axis of Hope* explores the effective and affective politics of Iranian women's rights activists, theorizing beyond the failures or successes of legal reform to the more dynamic ways in which these activists have socialized institutions of authority into some of the normative desires of everyday Iranians for gender equality. Forms of women's rights activism can loosen the women's rights instrument from its neocolonial trappings.

Abundant and indispensable critique has been devoted to explicating how the human rights instrument has been mobilized to "save brown women from brown men" (Spivak 1988), wedding Muslim women's rights to American and Western empire and military intervention. Feminist scholars have debated women's rights discourses and practices, with particular attention to their recruitment by and operability within empire. Some critics have argued that as an offspring of development discourses, women's human rights regimes can consolidate the epistemic authority of the West (Grewal 1999) and strengthen imperialist aims (Basu 1995; 2000). Others have argued that women's rights discourses often work to stabilize the category of "woman" through universalizing discourses; focus on "culture" as the perpetrator of human rights violations; reify North/South binaries; and cohere US feminist subjectivity through rescue and savior narratives (Abu-Lughod 2002; Grewal 1999; Narayan 1997). As Inderpal Grewal (1999, 346) has argued, "Global feminism constructs 'American' feminist subjects in the US in particular ways and enables them to become agents in the practice of 'rescuing' victims of human rights violations." Similarly, Tani Barlow (2000, 1103) has maintained that through human rights regimes "students do come to recognize . . . a newly retooled ideology promising unmediated access to women from other countries."

Despite such problems and dangers, human rights frameworks remain compelling for feminist activists. Decades of debates—along with new feminist movements, practices, and discourses that have emerged from the Global South—have led to richer conceptions of the human rights framework. As Michael Ignatieff (2001, 15) has written: "If there are human rights movements in developing countries, it is because non-derogable individual rights remain the single most powerful inspiration for all battles against corrupt and tyrannous regimes." In a more measured view, Pheng Cheah (1997, 260, 263) has claimed that "to be a concrete agent in history is, after all, to be contaminated in turn by historically existing ideals and norms, no matter how contaminated these ideas and norms are" and that "human rights are double-edged but absolutely necessary weapons that are given to the disenfranchised by the global force-relations in which they find themselves mired in a given historical juncture." A more positive assessment from Hilary Charlesworth (1994) points to the ways in which human rights are not only taken up by a multiplicity of political actors but are shaped by them. Indeed, many women of color and antiracist feminists in the United States (Roskos 2004; Schulman 2004; Smith 2004) have used the tool of human rights to level powerful critiques against US policies at home and abroad.

Dorothy Hodgson's explication of the different iterations and circuits of rights discourse is helpful. "'Women's human rights' is never a static category that an individual or collectivity either 'has' or 'does not have.' Rather, the very terms of the category—women, human, and rights—are always in question, subject to alternative and sometimes competing interpretations, 'vernacularizations,' appropriations, and contestations" (Hodgson 2011, 14). In Muslim contexts in the MENA and also in the larger African continent, in such countries as Indonesia and Malaysia, as well as in the United States, Muslim women's rights activists are claiming human rights discourses as their own, as part of larger reform discourses that recognize the compatibility of women's rights with the tenets of Islam and as part of transnational frameworks that are making links across various global borders. In this sense they are refashioning transnational feminist discourses of women's rights, bringing their particular historical contexts to bear on globally circulating ideas and practices. Working against the bifurcation of culture and rights—in which Islam is framed as an excess of "culture," impinging on universal and ahistorical "rights"—women's rights activists in Muslim contexts are shaping "new human rights discourse" (Maoulidi 2011, 49) and "'multi-culturalizing' the human rights regime" within their particular contexts (Alidou 2011, 199).

Axis of Hope pivots on this robust archive of critical scholarship and debate, while articulating the embodied political subjectivity of Iranian women as more than their double-victim status—first, as losers in their religion and societies, and second, as victims of neocolonial feminism. The subjects of this book forcefully intimate that women's legal equality under the Islamic Republic is achievable, desirable, and the highly anticipated outcome of a society that has democratized everyday life and relationships. They argue for women's rights within an Islamic society as part of a decades-long pragmatic political shift, reflected both nationally and regionally. Equally important, they draw attention to the ongoing need for women's rights struggles inside the United States, denaturalizing the Western feminist subject as always already rights-bearing.

Although the feminist critiques of human rights regimes—as constituting and constitutive of a particular neoliberal and neocolonial subject made legible within intertwined structures of war, humanitarianism, state power, and transnational governmentality—undergird my own analysis, I'm interested in thinking beyond the sense of human rights as a dead end. Indeed, given the unevenly distributed yet broad-based deployment of human rights discourses and practices by multiple political actors, the meanings, significances, and effects of human rights praxis cannot be determined a priori. Rather, they must be considered through the particular historical and political contexts in which they emerge. As Lila Abu-Lughod (2011) has argued, women's human rights have a "social life" when they are circulated by and through differently situated and embodied subjects. Building on Abu-Lughod's conceptual framework, I argue that the bottom-up practices of Iranian women's rights activists, as well as the affects and effects of their campaigns, projects, and networks, have political and epistemic significance despite (or perhaps beyond) the thorny entanglement of women's human rights praxis within structures of colonial modernity. Iranian women's rights activists have decolonized feminist and women's rights discourses by casting a spotlight on the complex locations in which they struggle and fashioning practices of solidarity that contest colonial binaries and hierarchies.

ROMANCING THE DECOLONIAL

While never officially colonized, Iran has been subjected to colonial interference by foreign powers throughout the past two centuries. The Constitutional Revolution of 1905–11, largely a movement for political reform of the corrupt Qajar dynasty (1796–1925), sought to establish Iran as a modern nation independent of colonial (British and Russian) influence and intrusion. Autonomous women's groups formed and organized during this period, and some worked against foreign intervention in Iran.[9] Since the early twentieth century, both colonial and anticolonial discourses have deployed gender as a key trope in narratives of resistance, progress, nationalism, sovereignty, modernization, tradition, and cultural restoration, wedding the "woman question" to the national question.

The nation-building era of Reza Shah Pahlavi (1925–41) focused on the establishment of the state as the epicenter of national leadership. As Parvin Paidar (1995, 78–81) has noted, the project of modern statehood—with its economic, bureaucratic, and militarized apparatuses—was a coercive one. This is important for understanding the current Islamic Republic as not necessarily exceptional in terms of its repressive nature but continuous with its secular predecessors. Among the top-down reforms for women established by Reza Shah was compulsory unveiling in 1936. While the right to unveil was a demand of a small number of elite women and reformers for decades before Pahlavi's rule, the compulsory and violent installation of unveiling proved the top-down, coercive power of the state. Police, ordered by Reza Shah, violently removed veils from women who appeared with them in public, creating deep resentment among women who chose to veil. Although there is an abundance of focus on the Islamic Republic's compulsory veiling policies, often forgotten is this period of Iranian history, when violent and compulsory unveiling was part of the modernization process imposed by Reza Shah. Indeed, Iran has a long history of state coercion, with roots in the secular era of the Pahlavis. Embedded in colonial ideas and practices, secular modernity has deeply violent beginnings, with women's bodies as collateral damage.

The modernizing project in Iran cannot be read in simple terms as an emancipatory one. Modern nation-state formation constructed ideas about "women" and "men" as well as "masculinity" and "femininity" in particularly gendered ways. The "secular" eras of the Constitutional period and the Pahlavis enabled and constrained women's possibilities through gendered ideologies and the regulation of women's bodies. The protection of women's bodies and sexuality by men signaled a unified and integral nation, with proper masculine and feminine subjects. Revisiting the Constitutional period, Afsaneh Najmabadi (1998, 183) has argued that "to have envisaged the homeland as a female body, whose purity constituted male honor and who was in need of male protection, created a discursive space within which woman-as-citizen landed in a conflictive domain, at once claiming parity yet subject to male protection."[10]

When the Iranian Parliament voted to nationalize Iran's oil industry in 1951, Britain and the United States overthrew the popularly elected Prime Minister Mohammad Mossadegh in a coup d'état. Ten years earlier, Britain and the Soviet Union had invaded and occupied Iran, fearing Reza Shah's friendliness toward Germany would compromise the British-owned Anglo-Iranian Oil Company. Reza Shah was deposed during this time and replaced by his son, Mohammad Reza Shah (the Shah). The Shah regained national power, supported by the United States throughout his increasingly repressive tenure. The Shah continued the top-down reforms of his father and fortified the repressive apparatuses of the state during his reign (1941–79). The Shah mobilized a discourse of Iran as a "Great Civilization," recalling the era of Cyrus and Daryus, when non-Islamic kings with powerful armies ruled prosperous, Western-style civilizations (Paidar 1995, 148). SAVAK, the secret police, was established in 1957 with support from the CIA and then MOSAD, the Israeli national intelligence (Paidar 1995, 135). The political repression, imprisonment, and executions of those opposed to the Shah were extreme.

Under the Shah a more independent women's movement emerged, one not tied to the state's agenda. However, the largest women's organization, the Women's Organization of Iran, was deeply tied to the Shah's top-down control of political power. Nayereh Tohidi (2010, 384) has asserted that women's associations and presses expanded between the 1920s and 1940s, and by the 1960s more women were publicly active in nationalist and socialist politics. Most of the Shah's reforms in health, fertility, and education benefited middle- and upper-class women. By 1976 the literacy rate among rural women was only 16.5 percent, a mere 15 percent increase over twenty years (Paidar 1995, 162). Even for middle- and upper-class women, ideas about the patriarchal control of women in the family remained dominant. By the late 1970s deep resentment of the Shah's modernizing program, which not only was coercive but also shut out vast sectors of society, characterized the feelings of those in many corners of Iran.

The Iranian Revolution of 1979 erupted as a broad-based oppositional movement against the Shah's corrupt dictatorship. The revolutionary coalition "included an array of political groups (leftists, nationalists, and Islamists) and social forces (women and men of the middle classes, the intelligentsia, the working class, and the urban poor)" (Moghadam 2002, 17). Since the revolution, the demonization of the Islamic Republic of Iran (IRI), regular cycles of war talk, and decades of crippling sanctions by the United States and other Western powers have produced Iranians as de facto colonial subjects. In addition, the deployment of gender and sexuality by colonial powers sets Iranian women up to be "liberated" by various logics and apparatuses understood to be intrinsic to the West. In mobilizing the decolonial as a conceptual framework, I use "romancing" in two ways. First, I myself am romancing the decolonial, eagerly and openheartedly engaging with it as a way of thinking about how my interlocutors "name, situate, and articulate the pluri- and interversals of feminisms, understood as spheres not of unification (or uni-versalization) but of pluralism, plurality, and possible interrelation" (Walsh 2018b, 39). Breny Mendoza (2015, 100) has written that decolonial theory emerged in response to and as part of a legacy of anticolonial thought: "The Anglo academic world has traditionally associated anticolonial struggles with national liberation movements designed to achieve 'independence,' and social justice movements that arise in the context of nation-building after the colonial power has been overthrown." Edward Said's *Orientalism* (1978), Mendoza argues, expanded the historical and epistemic frame of colonialism, shifting the field to postcolonial theory. Decolonial theory, claims Mendoza (2015, 101), emerged from scholars who "emphasized that anticolonial thought originated in the context of a much earlier period, as a reaction against the violence history of Western colonialism inaugurated in 1492."

The field and frameworks of postcolonial theory enlarged with the contributions of postcolonial feminist scholars, most notably Gayatri Spivak (1988) and Chandra Talpade Mohanty (1991). Decolonial theory has been more receptive to feminist scholarship, argues Mendoza (2015, 102), but "gender analytics occupy a liminal space in decolonial theory." Maria Lugones (2007; 2010) challenged these lacunae, theorizing the ways in which coloniality naturalizes gender and heterosexuality. Other feminist scholars have expanded decolonial theory's intellectual purchase by situating women of color and queer feminisms inside the rubrics of decolonial thought for the ways in which they explicate and link racializing, gendered, and sexual logics inside colonial and capitalist modernity.[11]

I have been particularly persuaded by Catherine Walsh's notion of "the decolonial *for*" (Walsh 2018a) or the ways in which the concept can "broaden the spheres from which we can understand decoloniality as action, insurgence, prospect, praxis and project" toward an "otherwise" (Walsh 2018b, 45). In thinking with the activists represented throughout these pages, I engage decoloniality not as a pure and utopian destination but as a relational process. I am interested in how we might think of decoloniality as process and relation, particularly in a postrevolutionary and nonrevolutionary period of Iranian politics. In this sense I take a rather *unromantic* romantic approach. How can we think in more open-ended ways about the gesturing toward the decolonial *for* by examining how, inside a geopolitics very much constrained by coloniality, women's rights activists reject binaries, practice and articulate nonviolence, commit to open and nonideological visions and practices, and build solidarity? How can we understand their investments in their own and their country's sovereignty as challenges to colonial and postcolonial patriarchal and militarized nationalisms?

I also use "romancing" to critically push against the limits of decolonial theory in the particular ways it engages Islamic and/or Critical Muslim Studies and tends to formulate a narrow vision of the *de* in decolonial by collapsing it with precolonial histories. While perhaps open to feminist thought and ideas, and gender as a frame of analysis, decolonial theory often reproduces an exclusionary male voice in key ways. First, although such figures as Ali Shariati and Frantz Fanon are eloquent and important anticolonial thinkers with great relevance for the relationship between colonial and Islamic epistemologies in Iran and MENA, on their own they are insufficient for theorizing the liberation of women and other Others. In their engagement with Shariati as the *sole* decolonial thinker from the Muslim world, important and persuasive decolonial thinkers (Grosfoguel 2010; Mignolo 2018) not only center a masculine voice but also keep decoloniality in the past, eliding the complex ways that feminists are thinking and practicing decoloniality in the troubled present.

The ideological theorists of the revolution mobilized a discourse of gender equality that gave women a key role in the revolution. Ali Shariati, the popular leftist Islamic theorist of the revolution, gave frequent lectures based on his book *Fatima Is Fatima*.[12] Drawing on the founding period of Islam, Shariati argued that women should emulate Fatima, the prophet Muhammad's daughter, who was "the center of a family of fighters. She took on responsibilities and became socially engaged, equally to men but in a different way" (Keddie 2003, 205). Like Shariati, but from a conservative or traditionalist perspective, Ayatollah Khomeini argued for women's freedom within Islam. "As for women," he asserted, "Islam has never been against their freedom. It is, to the contrary, opposed to the idea of woman-as-object and it gives her back her dignity" (in Sanasarian 1982, 117). Khomeini drew on a growing critique of "Westoxification"—the consumerist, sexually exploitative, and individualist trends thought to be promoted by the West. In a speech to a group of women in the holy city of Qom in early March 1979, Khomeini (1985, 264) declared: "We want our women to attain the high rank of true humanity. Women must have a share in determining their destiny. The repressive regime of the Shah wanted to transform our warrior women into pleasure-seekers, but God determined otherwise. They wanted to treat woman as a mere object, a possession, but Islam grants woman a say in all affairs just as it grants man a say." Khomeini's discourse positioned women as key agents in transforming Iranian society. He contrasted women's new role as revolutionary agents with their object status under the Shah, a passive position created by capitalist consumption and sexual exploitation.

Deploying anticolonial discourses, the theorists of the Iranian revolution sought to restore women's dignity, freedom, and rights through a revaluation of her central role in the family and community of Muslims. In revolutionary Iran, Shariati's valorization of Fatima and Khomeini's claims for gender equality under Islam incorporated women into a national vision that promised them equal rights and an important role in defending the revolution but ultimately only within the confines of their role as central family figures—that is, wives, mothers, sisters, daughters. As Minoo Moallem (2005, 3–5) has argued, in the revolution's "return to Islamic culture as an authentic and oppositional identity," women were called to be sisters to their male brothers, framing the "conditions of [their] belonging" in gender differentiated terms. In decolonial theory's romancing of Shariati and Khomeini, women's particular experiences and losses are diminished in favor of romanticizing the postcolonial nation and its particular gendered ideologies. Finally, in looking back to the *pre* (the precolonial, before 1492), decolonial theory often fails to theorize other modes of power that perhaps did not racialize and gender people through coloniality's epistemologies but were not without hierarchical and gendered systems of power. In considering the activist world-making discourses and practices here, I aspire to ground decoloniality in the here and now as well as in the processes and relationalities that gesture toward the decolonial *for*.

EPISTEMOLOGICAL LOCATIONS

Against the backdrop of the Bush, Obama, and Trump presidencies, the Khatami, Ahmadinejad, and Rouhani presidencies, the GWOT, the Iranian state's crackdown on internal dissent, and Trump's Muslim ban, researching Iranian women's rights activism is risky and fraught. Although this book fundamentally critiques the notion of Iran as an inherently repressive space, it also acknowledges the experience of activists and scholars who have suffered greatly from state violence and repression for decades.

Fieldwork with activists inside Iran would have added an important dimension to my research, but I chose not to further endanger those activists or put myself, a dual citizen, at risk. The activists living in the United States that I did spend time with, however, remain deeply connected to life and activism in Iran. They interrupt and offer alternatives to the frameworks that cast nation and community in narrow and essential terms. At the time of my initial interviews with OMSC activists in Southern California over several days in October 2009, some of them were still traveling to and from Iran as they were able. This fact, combined with the heightened repression of activists in the wake of the Green Movement, led to a mutual agreement that I would use pseudonyms. As an activist in exile with a visible public profile, Mahboubeh Abbasgholizadeh did not request this anonymity.

Analyzing my interviews alongside a discursive analysis of the One Million Signatures Campaign, a close reading of a transnational figure like Shirin Ebadi, and the life history of Mahboubeh Abbasgholizadeh has allowed me to "excavat[e]" rich "hidden or unacknowledged" data (DeVault 1999, 55–56). Feminists have long sought to unearth the reality of women's lives—for instance, their unremunerated, gendered, and racialized laboring practices of social reproduction (Glenn 1992; Hartmann 1979; Parreñas 2008). In focusing on feminist activist practices, organizational cultures, strategies, discourses, labors, and desires, I have sought to make visible an important understudied part of the story of Iran, and the story of Iran in the world.

In this approach, however, I do not mean to stabilize the category of "Iranian women's rights activist" by presenting the subjects of my book as singular or unified, without class, ethnic, political, and other kinds of differences, or as an exhaustive representation of the many Iranian women's rights activists organizing today. Nor am I arguing for an essentialized gendered standpoint, extant a priori, that fails to render the historicity and specificity of gendered experiences (Bar On 1993; Longino 1993). Instead, I wish to foreground the ways in which "'subjugated' standpoints are preferred because they seem to promise more adequate, sustained, objective, transforming accounts of the world" (Haraway 1988, 584). While many women's rights activists do their work inside of large nongovernmental organizations (NGOs) and transnational spaces such as UN conferences, most of the activists profiled in this book work from extremely grassroots and nonelite spaces—in homes, cafes, street corners, underground, and in cyberspace.

I also acknowledge my location inside the fraught enterprise of knowledge production about Middle Eastern and Muslim women's rights. I draw heavily from feminist scholars whose work attends to ways in which the discursive construction of the "Third World woman" or "Muslim woman" secures Western—and Western feminist—hegemony.[13] These cautionary tales guide my research and writing. Iranian women became particularly visible during the Green Movement. Images of protesters wearing green hijabs and flashing peace signs were ubiquitous in media coverage, and Iranian women came to signify Iran's struggle for internal democracy. This visibility is a double-edged sword. It had the effect of producing the Green Movement outpouring as a sort of come-from-nowhere moment, with women as the surprise element. There is much to critique about the representation of women in scholarly and popular accounts of protest movements and daily life in Iran, the Middle East, and the Muslim world. Shuttling between a particular hypervisibility meant to take the temperature of (Western-style secular) democracy and an invisibility that renders them absent from many decades of political life, Iranian women's political subjectivities are often occluded.

This book leans decidedly on such critiques yet moves beyond representational critique to demonstrate the central role Iranian women's rights activists have played in their country and the contributions they have made to transnational feminisms. Too much caution can be disciplining. Feminist interventions into Orientalist, xenophobic, and Islamophobic discourses about Iran and Middle Eastern and Muslim people must be made, even as they risk contamination by old and new forms of dominant ideologies. As Elizabeth Grosz (1990) so eloquently reminds us, critique is not enough. The project of feminism must produce alternatives to that which it critiques and create crucial, world-building knowledges that might transform oppressive structures into something new.

To better navigate the challenges, dilemmas and contradictions of knowledge production, feminist scholars argue that self-reflexivity by the researcher surfaces the inherent power relations between her and her subjects, and makes clear the potential intertwining of knowledge production in political processes that might reify relations of inequality and domination (Alexander and Mohanty 1997). Others argue that reflexivity can always only be partial, as "unconscious desire make[s] a fully intentional subjectivity impossible" (Clough 1998, xvii). Still, some degree of reflexivity can help deconstruct the ways that researchers can be both insiders and outsiders. In her fieldwork France Winddance Twine anticipated that Afro-Brazilians in Brazil would embrace her, an African American, as part of a transnational community of African descended people. She found, however, that black Brazilians had very different notions of race and racialization than she, and they resisted her attempts at familial solidarity. Ironically, it was with Caribbean immigrants in England, with whom she did not initially identify, that she found "the transnational black community that [she] had anticipated encountering in Brazil" (Twine 2000, 19). Twine's findings about insiderness/outsiderness were counterintuitive, revealing the degree to which subjectivities or identities are not innate or preformed, but emerge and transform within the production of knowledge. Naheed Islam confronts these issues in her work on Bangladeshi immigrants in Los Angeles. As a "sociologist of upper-middle-class Bangladeshi Muslim origins" living in a multiracial, multiethnic, nonheteronormative community in California, Islam (2000, 42) states that the "multiplicity of [her] belongings raises the question, am I conducting research in my 'own' community when I do research in the Bangladeshi community in Los Angeles?"

Engaging this dilemma, Nancy Naples (2003, 49) argues that "the insider/outsider distinction masks power differentials and experiential differences between the researcher and the researched. The bipolar construction of insider/outsider also sets up a false separation that neglects the interactive processes through which 'insiderness' and 'outsiderness' are constructed." Indeed, as I experienced, political affiliations can create a sense of shared ideas and goals that minimize other kinds of differences between a researcher and her subjects. Furthermore, postcolonial and decolonial feminists have destabilized the West/Other binary that consolidates colonial relations of power, and extend this critique to overly simplistic notions of where researchers and their subjects are located.[14]

Insider, outsider, diasporic, exilic—all of these terms obscure more complex negotiations of identity and home, for my interlocutors and for me. I am an Iranian American, born in the United States to an Iranian father and American mother. My father came to the United States in the 1960s for professional training, never expecting to stay. But after meeting and marrying my mother, my father pursued his US citizenship. Because of the discriminatory legal structure in Iran, which grants citizenship status through patrilineal lines, I have "become" an Iranian national with dual citizenship. I recognize the irony in acquiring this status through the very legal structure my research subjects are challenging. I also recognize my privilege in being able to travel to Iran, at least before 2016, by keeping my activist profile under the radar. So many activists do not have this privilege, including some in my extended family. As many cases since 2008 have shown, dual citizens have become more vulnerable too, and the policies of the current US administration have further curtailed travel options in many directions, for Iranians in Iran and those in the diaspora.

Although I use the term "diaspora," I want to trouble the ways in which it stabilizes otherwise fluid or liminal identities and locations. Along with other feminist scholars who consider the Iranian diaspora critically and in conversation with critiques of gender, race, class, sexuality, nationalism, transnationalism, war, and Islamophobia, I seek to dislodge it from the ways it can, even when critically used, strengthen the oppositional categories it seeks to break down.[15] While it is nearly impossible to get around the term as a descriptive, conceptually and even descriptively "diaspora" is limited, often sedimenting discussions around the revolution to the exclusion of other experiences. Nima Naghibi (2016) examines the ways in which Iranian women's narratives from the diaspora are overrepresented by the affective registers of trauma (revolution) and nostalgia (prerevolutionary past). Indeed, my interlocutors did not identify with these affective registers, particularly as they have been expressed to signal a critique and rejection of the revolution and/or Islam. Nor did many of them describe themselves as diasporic. Rather, they often self-identified as Iranian or Iranian American, or struggled to find a word that fully encompassed them conceptually.

As Inderpal Grewal and Caren Kaplan (1994, 16) have argued, diasporic communities are not homogeneous but "multiply organized" outside essentialist or naturalized ideas of what is home and what is the diaspora. Pointing to a liminal space, Minoo Moallem (2005) conceptualizes the connections between inside and outside Iran as "in between." Amy Malek (2006), building on Hamid Naficy's (1993) deployment of liminality, draws attention to cultural production and the act of writing as modes for negotiating Iranian and Iranian American women's shifting identities. In later work Malek (2015) offers a visual and discursive examination of second-generation Iranian Americans living in Los Angeles, pointing to the ways in which they shatter cultural representations of the Southern California Iranian diaspora as materialistic and superficial, which, as Malek notes, often work in tandem with representations of Iranians as terrorists.

As an activist for several years in the New York Iranian diaspora, and now part of the diverse and ever-changing Southern California Iranian diaspora, the affiliations I share with my interlocutors have guided and informed my thinking about the difficulty and absolute necessity of feminist solidarity praxis as well as the importance of social movements and activism as sites of scholarly investigation. Following Kim Tallbear (2014), I wish to stand and think *with* these activists with whom I share so many political, personal, and epistemological investments. While I take full responsibility for the shortfalls and omissions of the book, I am keenly aware of how collective knowledge is and how much these activists have shaped this project. I am deeply grateful for the opportunity to connect with activists in the Iranian diaspora, with whom I share a political "home," a place to think about and create feminist practices against militarized global patriarchy.

GENDER, FEMINISM, ISLAM, AND RIGHTS

Writing about the relationship between Islam, feminism, gender, and rights surfaces many of my political and affective investments. The very lives and practices of ordinary Muslims, my large extended family included, are under heavy pressure, as their religiosity is scrutinized, held suspect, repudiated, and deemed in need of making over by non-Muslims of many stripes (Mahmood 2006; Puar 2007). As a regime of truth and as a mechanism of power (Asad 1993, 2003; Connolly 1999; Mahmood 2005), secularism has the power to define and subjugate its Other. In its fundamentalist form, secularism violently forecloses the very lives of Muslims around the world, including many who are seeking change from within their own contexts and on their own terms. As I explore throughout the book, religious/secular binaries, which show up in geopolitics as well as feminist activism and scholarship, are troubled and interrupted by the desires and discourses of Iranian women's rights activists.

The Islamization process in postrevolutionary Iran produced contradictory effects, with simultaneous closures and openings for women.[16] The mandatory imposition of hijab (veiling), exclusion from certain occupations and educational fields, and the repeal of women's rights within the family signaled a serious defeat for women who had been promised greater equality under revolutionary Islam. But it was precisely that promise that enabled women to push to exchange the "emblem of Islamification" (Afshar 1998) for actual reforms in society. In addition, in the decade and a half following the revolution, Iran experienced what Valentine Moghadam (2002) has described as contradictory phenomena that opened up political space for women, destabilized the regime, and gave rise to the reform movement. The Iran-Iraq War (1980–88) created employment opportunities for women; the death of Khomeini and the presidency of Ali Akbar Hashemi-Rafsanjani encouraged liberal clerics to support economic liberalization; and a population explosion forced the state to launch a successful family-planning campaign, which gave women access to contraception (Moghadam 2002,

18–20). Overall, the postrevolutionary period saw massive improvements in women's health, education, and life chances.

The economic and social realities of postrevolutionary Iran and a highly educated and politicized population led to a vibrant and diverse reform movement in the mid-1990s, which elected reformer Mohammad Khatami to two presidential terms (1997–2005). Women, students, clerics, and ordinary citizens pushed for and won reforms by challenging the hardliners' interpretations and applications of Muslim law. During Khatami's presidency female MPs, backed by the reform movement, organized to reform the Iranian civil code. For instance, the legal age of marriage for girls was raised from nine to thirteen in 2002. Although thirteen is still quite young, it is important to note that in practice the median age of marriage is twenty-two. As a member of the Women's Faction of the Reformist Parliament (the Sixth Parliament, 2000–2004), Elaheh Koolaee (2009, 58) worked with other women parliamentarians and their male supporters to change "some articles of civil law that were against women [*sic*] rights," such as child custody and inheritance, which favor men. The Sixth Parliament was notable in that it included thirteen women, who campaigned for gendered reforms (Moghadam and Haghighatjoo 2016).

Muslim women activists working within a politico-religious framework, who supported the revolution but found themselves subsequently shut out, were key players in this movement. These activists ranged from conservative Islamist women to self-identified Islamic or Muslim feminists to those who didn't take on any label. Some shared a desire for reforms in favor of women's equal rights, while others were against reforms but still active politically themselves. All of these activists were part of a larger reform period, which ushered in Khatami in 1997 and formally ended in 2005, with the exclusion of reform candidates from the parliamentary elections the year before and the hardliners' rise to power, resulting in the election of Ahmadinejad to the presidency.[17]

Islamicate feminists, like those associated with the most well-known women's journal *Zanan*, (re)entered the public political sphere through a vast and burgeoning press by engaging in *ijtehad*, rational engagement with the Qur'an in the spirit of one's historic context, alongside the "new wave" of religious reformers (Mir-Hosseini 1999).[18] In using the term "Islamicate feminisms," I follow but modify Margot Badran's (2009, 242) definition: "It is a feminist discourse and practice articulated within an Islamic paradigm. Islamic feminism, which derives its understanding and mandate from the Qur'an, seeks rights and justice for women, and for men, in the totality of their existence." As Badran rightly claims, those using Islamic feminist discourses may or may not use "Islamic feminist" to describe themselves. Those producing such discourses "also include religious Muslims (by which is typically meant the religiously observant), secular Muslims (whose ways of being Muslim may be less publicly evident), and non-Muslims" (Badran 2009, 244).

As Roxanne Marcotte (2010, 133) has argued, the definition and political meaning of Islamic feminism has been much debated, making it important to identify different meanings: "While many Muslim women would not endorse the use of the term 'Islamic feminism' to describe themselves and what they do, many of their writings and activities, nonetheless, aim at the betterment of women in Islam and can thus be understood in the first sense of the term." Acknowledging Islamic feminism as a contested term, or as some of my interlocutors told me, a term invented within Western academic circles, I use "Islamicate feminisms" to signal a looser and more pluriversal term, perhaps more able to accommodate this range of social actors. As an analytical framework, Islamicate feminisms encompass various religious and political identities, some of which might seem to be at odds with one another. However, what is clearly more important in understanding Islamicate feminisms is the way in which its constituents share a desire to rectify what they consider the "wrongs or injustices" enacted in the name of Islam (Marcotte 2010, 132). In other words, although they are not the only feminists to challenge patriarchal interpretations of Islam, Islamicate feminists find Islam an essential resource for their feminism. Using this flexible definition also enables a range of activisms in Muslim-majority contexts to come into view.

Many secularly identified women in Iran and the diaspora extend Islamicate feminist discourses as part of a pragmatic reform strategy within the particular context of Iran, even if they don't embrace the label. As Badran (2009, 244) has argued, "The terms religious and secular are porous rather than rigid categories." The transnational circulation of Islamicate feminist discourses has also fundamentally reconfigured transnational feminism by breaking down many of the binaries associated with the religious/secular distinction: Global South and North, traditional and modern, repressive and liberatory; rights-needing and rights-bearing. While not necessarily a novel conceptual framework, increased education and literacy, access to ideas through print and cyber culture, and democratizing trends within their societies have enabled women to make claims and speak with fresh kinds of authority about their lives within the parameters of Islam.[19]

As new "exegetes," Iranian Islamicate feminists reflected the social justice and equality vision of Islam back to those in authority who had promised, but not delivered, such a vision.

Islamicate feminists in Iran, as elsewhere, argued that *fiqh* (Islamic jurisprudence), or human understanding and execution of sacred law, should reflect the social justice vision of *sharia*, the sacred law or will of God as revealed to the Prophet Muhammad (Mir-Hosseini 1999, 2006b). Many drew on a hermeneutics that looked to the ethical precepts of foundational Islam to "unread" past and present patriarchal Islams (Ahmed 1992; Barlas 2002). Islamicate feminisms in Iran proliferated in unprecedented ways precisely because the state's Islamization project, in its failure to provide gender equality, paradoxically pushed women to criticize patriarchal codifications of Islam using the very discourses internal to Islam (Afshar 1998; Badran 2006; Mir-Hosseini 2006b). Moreover, women's high education and literacy rates coupled with an expanding civil society facilitated their new roles as Qur'anic exegetes.

Islamicate feminists, religious intellectuals, and reformist clerics were frequently seen in the feminist press, such as *Bad Jens*, *Farzaneh*, and *Zanan*. Particular attention was paid to Islamic jurisprudence as pliable and the possibilities of women's right to reasoned interpretation. Fluent in the Qur'an, Shahla Sherkat, publisher of *Zanan*, the most influential Islamicate feminist journal, and others argued for women's right to *ijtehad* (Moghadam 2002, 24). Sherkat, like her compatriots around the world, became one of many new feminist exegetes who "commanded considerable respect in the global umma"—that is, the worldwide Muslim community of believers (Badran 2006, 3). The government shut down *Zanan* several times, but Sherkat fought these shutdowns, often successfully. In 2014, she launched another women's magazine, *Zanan-e Emrooz* (Women today). Founded in Tehran, the magazine has a print run of ten thousand copies, with distribution of half of those inside Tehran and half to Iran's other provinces. The magazine has an online version, allowing access to those outside of Iran. As Sherkat (2015, 378) claims, the magazine is "training a new generation of journalists who combine writing and research skills with a gendered approach [*negaah-e jensiyati*]." The magazine is eclectic and broadly focused, moving from theoretical discussions to current news to articles on physical and mental health.

I have not thoroughly analyzed the magazine but several themes emerge from Sherkat's description of *Zanan-e Emrooz*, many of which resonate with the women's rights activists' narratives I consider in this book. First, in discussing the magazine's readership of fifty thousand as mostly students or college educated, Sherkat asserts that a quarter of them are men. This, combined with Sherkat's commitment to broad print and online distribution, points to aspirations of inclusivity and dialogue with different sectors of Iranians inside and outside Iran. Second, Sherkat (2015, 377–78) claims that the magazine's "objectives are to make the government and women aware of and sensitive to gender discrimination [*tab'iz-e jensiyati*]," and that the magazine "must continually prove that [they] are not against family or motherhood. Rather, [their] goal is to comprehend the transformations of the family as an institution and to articulate new definitions of women, men, and parenthood." These claims signal the ways in which Sherkat and her editors are deploying pragmatic and reform-minded discourses that bring shifting attitudes and social practices to bear on the state. Third, *Zanan-e Emrooz* blurs the lines between journalism and activism, organizational culture, and platform. While clearly a magazine with paid staff and defined roles between the editorial board and those in training, the magazine's focus on a new generation, its online presence, and its transnational reach reveal its networked characteristics and effects. Like ZananTV, *Zanan-e Emrooz* hopes to "grasp . . . opportunities" to make interventions around women's issues when there are openings (Sherkat 2015, 376).

In addition to utilizing the ideas of religious reformers inside Iran, Islamicate feminists also drew on ideas and discourses from the transnational feminist sphere. They incorporated notions of individual human rights into their claims for gender equality within Islam.[20] In Muslim countries such as Afghanistan, Algeria, and Iran, activists looked to transnational feminist networks to support and solidarize with local campaigns (Moghadam 2003, 2). Nayereh Tohidi (2002, 9) has pointed to the "international dialogue" between Western feminists and Muslim women: "Women activists in Iran, including many religious activists . . . have shown as much, if not more, curiosity about the discourses, struggles, and achievements of their non-Muslim and nonreligious sisters in the West and in the developing world." As neither "a product of East or West," Islamicate feminism "transcends and eradicates old binaries" (Badran 2009, 245). In the reform period of the late 1990s and early 2000s, Islamicate feminists pushed the post-revolutionary state to live up to its own description of itself as modern and just by honoring international conventions and "proving" that Islam and human rights are compatible. With feminists from around the world, Islamicate feminists from Iran attended international UN conferences for women and participated in the vibrant exchanges that produced what Amrita Basu (2000, 71) has called "global alliances based on collective political goals and a common agenda."

Iranian women pushed Khatami's government to develop "indicators and other planning and monitoring tools for measuring women's advancement in Iran against CEDAW [Convention on the Elimination of All Forms of Discrimination Against Women]" (Paidar 2002, 248). Under Khatami the most progressive parliament to date, the Sixth Parliament, pushed for major changes. As reformist parliamentarian Elaheh Koolaee (2009, 58) has noted, the reformist parliament "tried to change women's legal status by focusing on laws related to issues such as inheritance, divorce, child custody, and insurance. The reformist government ratified and the parliament approved the Convention on the Elimination of All Forms of Discrimination against Women (CEDAW). However, the Guardian Council rejected CEDAW, interpreting it as in contradiction with Islamic values." Despite such resistance, Islamicate feminists inside and outside of parliament pushed the state to honor its own commitment to human rights. In so doing, Islamicate feminisms in Iran have produced new discourses and movements that rupture putative oppositions between religion and secularism, duties and rights, East and West, oppressive and liberatory, backward and modern. The activists profiled in this book draw on and extend the discourses and strategies of Islamicate feminisms, even if they are critical of the term or do not deploy it themselves. In the context of globally circulating and intertwined epistemologies of Islamophobia and colonial modernity, the Iranian women's rights activists considered here build on the recent histories of Islamicate feminisms and extend some of its conceptual frameworks, underscoring its potential to think toward a decolonial *for.*

ORGANIZATION OF THE BOOK

The first two chapters of *Axis of Hope* explore the methods and organizational culture of the OMSC. Before the 2009 presidential election, and the intense crackdown on activists that followed, campaigners went door-to-door and sometimes gathered in public spaces to collect signatures and to talk with people about how to change women's legal status. Campaigners emphasized inclusivity and nonelitism, and built a decentralized, flexible network of activists inside and outside Iran. The discursive frameworks, bottom-up methods, on-the-ground and online spatial politics, and horizontal network structure of the campaign predate the Green Movement, Occupy Wall Street, and the Arab Spring, which makes it a particularly interesting and important movement to study.

In chapter 1, I bring a discursive analysis to the OMSC website, considering it as the activists' collective voice. In tracking this voice, I map how campaign activists framed women's rights within an "Islamic human rights" framework and argued that women's legal status should align with the relatively high status they have achieved through massive gains in education, literacy, health and well-being, and civic participation. I attend to the organizational culture and methodology of the campaign by analyzing the website, interviews with activists in the Southern California diaspora, and a published account of the campaign by one of its founders, Noushin Ahmadi Khorasani. By committing to a grassroots, consensus-building, and nonviolent method, the campaign activists emphasized the indigenous or local character of their struggle; pushed the Islamic Republic of Iran to honor its commitments to rights, equality, and justice; and challenged the many violences carried out in the name of postcolonial, anti-imperialist statehood. While conservatives within the state used the notion of "Islamic criteria" to define women's rights and equality along a "separate but equal" axis, the campaign encouraged the state to evolve its understanding of equality in line with explicitly feminist demands for undifferentiated equality under Islamic law. In addition, the campaign created a transnational network and political culture that remapped the Iranian women's rights community, both spatially and affectively. Campaign activists in Iran and the diaspora negotiated the significance, meanings, and boundaries of identity, nation, and community as they attempted to create relations of solidarity and mutuality from their different locations. In these different geographical and social locations, activists reimagined themselves as a borderless and shared community.

Chapter 2 considers the vibrant political affiliations and modes of solidarity produced through the transnational network of the campaign. Through the narratives of this small but determined group of Iranian feminists, I explore what it meant for Iranian activists living outside Iran to have participated in the campaign, particularly as they negotiated several distinct phenomena: their location in the United States vis-à-vis their counterparts in Iran, attention from Western feminists, ongoing anti-Iran prejudice in the United States (including but not limited to Islamophobia), and the persistent elision of Iranian women's agency within human rights frameworks as well as among Western feminists and Iranians themselves. I investigate the dilemmas and opportunities that emerge in feminist solidarity work, showing the important ways in which Iranian women's rights activists have practiced and sustained decolonizing notions of solidarity and feminism through their ideas and organizational practices, and reimagined notions of home, diaspora, community, nation, and belonging. By detailing the ways in which these activists critically engaged Western feminists, I point to the possibilities of "downsizing" Western feminism from universal signifier to particular site.[21] I place the campaign in proximity to other recent social movements that have mobilized new media and organized themselves in similarly decentralized and horizontal networks. I hope to give the campaign its rightful place in the narrative of the latest global social movements, whose innovative organizational structures and use of new media technologies challenged geographical, political, and epistemic borders.

In chapter 3, I examine the two memoirs of Nobel Prize–winner Shirin Ebadi, locating them within a decolonial feminist episteme that has been largely neglected in the theoretical examinations of Iranian resistance. Ebadi has been undertheorized, in part because she has consistently articulated a nuanced critique of the coloniality of the United States and other Western powers alongside an engagement with and critique of the Iranian state. Her narratives do not fit with other Iranian women's memoirs that cast Iran in more narrow and caricatured terms—that is, as an essentially permanent cage—and the United States as a site of unmitigated freedom, especially for Muslim and/or Global South women. Instead, Ebadi attempts to make sense of Iranian politics and social life within a larger and more complex geopolitical frame and historical context. Her political analysis and life's work underscore a decolonial feminism marked by a politics and practice of nonviolence as well as a belief in an indigenously determined feminism that is committed to (but not subsumed by) transnational engagement.

Like the OMSC activists, Ebadi presents an alternative to the hegemonic framings of Islam and women's rights as mutually exclusive and irreconcilable frameworks; she articulates a feminist politics that challenges the militarized and patriarchal nationalisms of both Iran and the United States. As a political thinker and activist, Ebadi draws her readers to the intertwined fates of the United States and Iran, developing an analysis of Iranian sovereignty that is not antagonistic to a peaceful relationship between Iran and the United States. She consistently gives voice to women's human rights as they emerge from within Iran, and Iranian feminism as part of a nonviolent and decolonial movement for democracy and self-determination. Exiled from Iran after the post-2009 election repression, Ebadi reckons with but does not concede the loss of her country.

Mahboubeh Abbasgholizadeh, another longtime women's rights activist in Iran who was exiled after 2009, is the subject of chapter 4. After her exile she founded ZananTV, an independent, alternative Internet-streaming television channel in Farsi and English. Launching it in Zuccotti Park in Manhattan, the heart of the Occupy Wall Street encampments and protests, Mahboubeh crafts an affiliation between Iranian women's rights activists and the burgeoning Occupy Movement. An activist over many decades, she has spent years thinking about, among other things, how to build grassroots feminist networks and organizations in Iran, the complexities of geographical and social location, the relationship of the Iranian diaspora to Iran's social movements, and the ecosystem of new media platforms, activism, and social movements. I explore ZananTV and Mahboubeh's life story as a way of opening up the limited categories of homeland versus diaspora, activist inside Iran versus activist outside of Iran. While these distinctions are often meaningful, they can also shrink the space for thinking more generatively about feminism as a world-making and boundary-breaking endeavor. Echoing some of the themes of chapter 2, I draw attention to the ways in which Western support for Iranian resistance becomes a means of geopolitical domination.

Considered together, the discourses, stories, hopes, aspirations, visions, projects, and practices emerging from the OMSC, its diasporic members, the memoirs of Shirin Ebadi, and the life narrative and political projects of Mahboubeh Abbasgholizadeh bring into sharp relief the importance of theorizing decoloniality from the lives, ideas, and practices of activists who continue to build feminist projects within the complex geopolitical processes that delimit them. Crucial in countering both the modes of despair and cynicism about Iran as well as the dangerous interventions by Western powers "on behalf" of Iranians, the narratives of Iranian women's rights activists have tremendous pedagogical currency in the particularly urgent present. Their stories are particularly germane in these precarious times, marked by war, isolation, sanctions, and the intense demonization of Iranians and Muslims as well as by the authoritarianism, militarism, and patriarchal nationalisms that have come to define more and more parts of the globe. I offer this book as a contribution to decolonial feminist strategies for remaking the world and each other through coalition and solidarity.

CHAPTER 1

WE SANG THE SONGS OF EQUALITY

> In what way can social movements alter the states and political elites into society's sensibilities?
>
> —ASEF BAYAT

> Ronak and Hana, who were arrested because of their participation in the One Million Signatures Campaign and volunteering to collect signatures, have committed no crime but that of seeking gender equality. Their crime is that they do not want their husbands to marry other women; their crime is that they say God has created men and women equal and has given them equal rights, so why is the law so biased?
>
> —SHIRIN EBADI

> It is pretty exciting when I see the power of unity, the power of thinking of the other and being together. I can be part of amplifying women in Iran, my sisters in Iran.
>
> —SAHAR, ONE MILLION SIGNATURES CAMPAIGN ACTIVIST IN SOUTHERN CALIFORNIA

MODEST AND HARDWORKING, LAWYER AND HUMAN RIGHTS ACTIVist Shirin Ebadi certainly had not anticipated winning the Nobel Peace Prize in 2003. A mere few months before the announcement, she was buried in her everyday life and work in Iran, taking on pro bono cases at her

Defenders of Human Rights Center and working with some of the women MPs in Iran's Sixth Parliament to draft a bill on women's rights within an Islamic framework. The Sixth Parliament, elected in 2000, was one of Iran's most progressive parliaments to date. Reformers backing then President Mohammad Khatami won a majority of the seats and fourteen women were elected, including Elaheh Koolaee, an outspoken proponent of US-Iran diplomacy and women's rights. Capitalizing on a reform parliament and a reform president in power, Ebadi, Koolaee, and others sought to make inroads in overturning legal discrimination against women.

Women's legal reform efforts were primarily focused on family law, embedded in Iran's Civil Code. To prepare this particular bill, Ebadi scoured the annals of classical Islamic law, holding firm to her belief that, as a set of principles, sharia could accommodate women's needs and desires in the family around such things as marriage, child custody, and divorce. Islamic law was not the problem; the stale interpretations of Islamic principles needed refreshing. Iranian family law gives men unilateral rights to divorce, whereas women must prove their cases in the family courts and get their husbands' consent. But Ebadi and her fellow reformers knew that even centuries ago Islamic legal scholars assumed a woman might seek out divorce from her husband simply because, as Ebadi says, "she did not like him" (Ebadi 2007, 187). In the Islamic legal texts Ebadi found justification for a woman to divorce without her husband's consent, and she drafted a bill moored in sharia precepts. The bill ultimately failed, getting conveniently tangled up in bureaucratic procedures by conservative forces in the parliament. The tides were shifting away from reform, and in 2004 the Guardian Council disqualified reformists from running for parliament. When conservative candidate Mahmoud Ahmadinejad won the 2005 presidential election, hardliners secured their control of state power. The era of reform had come to an end, at least on the grand stage of electoral politics. But women's rights activists and other reformers refused to exit stage left. Instead, they shifted gears, turning to new sites, strategies, and organizational structures.

On June 12, 2005, just days before the presidential election, more than two thousand women staged a sit-in in front of the University of Tehran. As Iranian women's rights activist Mahsa Shekarloo reported for the Middle East Research and Information Project (MERIP), the peaceful sit-in was designed to put forward a "gendered critique of the constitution." The constitution of the Islamic Republic of Iran (IRI) guarantees "equal protection" for all and "the rights of women in all respects," but with the proviso that rights and equality are determined by "Islamic criteria." The vagueness of this clause provided the very condition for debate about exactly what those criteria might be, enabling reformers to articulate a women's rights and equality platform within the parameters of sharia. But as the reform period drew to a close, official interpretations of the law, adjudicated by the Guardian Council, remained on the books (Shekarloo 2005).

Shekarloo attended the sit-in, reporting on the coalition of organizers and attendees that represented the "diverse base" of the women's movement—from religious and secular feminist activists to student groups to environmental and educational NGOs. The sit-in and declaration to deliver women's full equality with men under the law received widespread endorsement from Ebadi, who was traveling abroad at the time, and other Nobel Peace Prize winners, including South African archbishop Desmond Tutu. Simin Behbahani, Iran's most famous living female poet at the time, joined the protest, sending "ripples of excitement through the crowd." Although police cordoned off the women, preventing male supporters from joining them, the protest was relatively peaceful due to a general relaxation of security right before the 2005 presidential elections (Shekarloo 2005).

Behbahani, who died at age eighty-seven in 2014, was nationally beloved in a country rooted in and defined by poetry. She reformulated classical Persian poetry, incorporating political themes of nonviolence and women's rights. Children learn poetry in school and in families, and recitation after an evening meal is not unheard of. The famous Persian poet, Hafez, is buried in Iran, and ordinary people visit his tomb in the beautiful gardens in the southern city of Shiraz. Families sit around or drape themselves over Hafez's marble tomb, leafing through books of his poetry, sharing turns at reading. When I visited my extended family in Shiraz in 2009, we encircled the tomb with our big group, kissing and leaning on it and each other, while we sought out our fortunes in Hafez's words. These kinds of everyday outings to Hafez's tomb are spirited in nature, reflecting the timbre of Persian poetry and the commonplace uses by Iranian citizens to read their own trials and tribulations, destinies and fortunes in the words of their poets. That Behbahani was recognized by the crowd, and although banned from leaving Iran, had remained relatively free in Iran despite her outspoken critique of state repression, speaks to the collectively held value and power of poetry and poets in defining Iran's national identity.

One year after this historic sit-in, on the same date, women's rights activists staged another rally to commemorate the 2005 event, this time in front of one of Tehran's busiest squares, Haft-e Tir Square. As Ziba Mir-Hosseini

(2006a) reported, activists raised specific reforms in Islamic law: "a ban on polygamy, equal rights to divorce for women and men, joint custody of children after divorce, equal rights in marriage, an increase in the minimum legal age of marriage for girls to 18, and equal rights for women as witnesses." A year into Ahmadinejad's presidency, security had tightened, and before it even began, police broke up the rally; some protesters were chased off, beaten, and arrested (Mir-Hosseini 2006a). Two months after the rally was broken up, in August 2006, women's rights activists launched the One Million Signatures Campaign (OMSC) as a "follow-up effort to the peaceful protest of the same aim" (Change for Equality 2006e).

This chapter brings a discursive analysis to the campaign website, considering it as the activists' collective voice. Campaign activists framed women's rights within an "Islamic human rights" framework and argued that women's legal status should align with the relatively high status they have achieved through massive gains in education, literacy, health and well-being, and civic participation. I also attend to the organizational culture and methodology of the campaign by analyzing the website, interviews with activists in the Southern California diaspora, and a published account of the campaign by one of its founders, Noushin Ahmadi Khorasani. By committing to a grassroots, consensus-building, and nonviolent method, the campaign activists emphasized the indigenous or local character of their struggle, pushed the IRI to honor its commitments to rights, equality, and justice, and challenged the many violences carried out in the name of postcolonial, anti-imperialist statehood. While conservatives within the state used the notion of "Islamic criteria" to define women's rights and equality along a "separate but equal" axis, the campaign encouraged the state to evolve its understanding of equality in line with explicitly feminist demands for undifferentiated equality under Islamic law.

In addition, the campaign created a transnational network and political culture that remapped the Iranian women's rights community, both spatially and affectively. Campaign activists in Iran and the diaspora negotiated the significance, meanings, and boundaries of identity, nation, and community as they attempted to create relations of solidarity and mutuality from their different locations. In these different geographical and social locations, activists reimagined themselves as a borderless and shared community. As the activist Pardis told me about initial forays into the Southern California community to collect signatures: "The first thing that comes to peoples' minds is that you started something in California and you're trying to change something in Iran. But we wanted to emphasize that this is something going on in Iran and we're adopting it. You can be a part of something that's going on in Iran!"[1]

Activists in the diaspora prioritized their sisters inside Iran, keenly aware that "outside" support for the campaign would be framed by the Iranian government as foreign (Western) interference. Simultaneously, the campaign's online and on-the-ground network structure positioned the OMSC as both local and transnational, as activists inside Iran depended on their diasporic members for wider broadcast and publicity. The campaign's organizational structure and political culture allowed for both a (local) practice of self-determination for campaigners inside Iran and a (transnational) practice of solidarity and affiliation for those in the diaspora. These activists cultivated a decolonial feminist politics in that they took seriously the history of US and other Western interference in Iran, yet they also challenged the binary logics of state-mandated anti-imperialist nationalism that would negate cross-border solidarities. The campaign's feminist practices and strategies originated in Iran, determined by local actors facing a particular set of restrictions on their national legal rights. At the same time, women's rights activists inside and outside Iran constituted themselves and their fellow Iranian women as a shared global community, geographically and affectively bound together.

As the third epigraph that opens this chapter suggests, the campaign activists profiled in this book, including Shirin Ebadi, repeatedly expressed the power that comes through thinking of and being with each other. I theorize this "thinking of" and "being with" as decolonial feminist praxis along the lines of what Catherine E. Walsh has called the "decolonial *for*," or "the creation, and cultivation of modes of life, existence, being, and thought *otherwise*; that is, modes that confront, transgress and undo modernity/coloniality's hold." Key to this decolonial *for*, argues Walsh (2018a, 18), is that it "takes us beyond an *anti* stance." The captivating stories, testimonials, voices, and narratives gathered here take us beyond an *anti* stance, to a world-making project in search of a decolonial feminist otherwise.

ALLEYWAY TO ALLEYWAY

The campaign represented a new stage of the Iranian women's movement, while its discourses, strategies, and methods reflected some of the political possibilities and restraints of the postrevolutionary period. For nearly three decades before the campaign emerged, religious and secular women had been challenging discrimination by the state. Before the 2005 sit-in, as Shekarloo (2005) wrote in her MERIP report, the women's movement was more dispersed, as "political and religious differences and regime pressures . . . prevented the establishment of a disciplined and organized front." Shekarloo, like many Iranians of her generation, was particularly attentive to the problems of sectarianism in the Iranian opposition, as Kaveh Ehsani and Norma Claire Moruzzi wrote in a tribute to Shekarloo, who died in 2014 after a two-year battle with lymphoma. Born in Iran in 1970, Shekarloo grew up in the United States after her parents moved there to pursue higher education. Leftist critics of the Shah, her parents moved the family back to Iran after the revolution, until they were forced to leave in 1982 because of Khomeini's repression of all opposition. Shekarloo moved back to Iran in 1999 and became active in the reform and feminist movements; she founded the online feminist journal *Bad Jens* in 2000, worked as an assistant on international affairs to Shirin Ebadi, and joined the OMSC (Ehsani and Moruzzi 2014).

Key actors in both the 1979 revolution and the vibrant civil society that emerged in response to the revolution's failures, women's rights activists who launched the campaign capitalized on the previous three decades of struggle that had politicized them and brought them into the public sphere in unprecedented numbers. The women who launched the campaign were primarily secular-identified feminists, although campaign members included a variety of social and political identifications—secular, Muslim, Muslim secular, and Islamic feminist, signaling the new coalitional approach that inspired Shekarloo and others. Islamist women in favor of reforms were not key players in the campaign, and this created some tensions among feminists in Iran. But the campaign retained a pragmatic approach of reforming, not eliminating, Islamic law, a tactic used by Islamist reform women, who fall under the broad swath of Islamicate feminisms.

The goals of the campaign were to collect one million signatures through door-to-door contact, meetings, and the Internet "in support of changes to discriminatory laws against women," and to promote dialogue and discussion among women and men in meetings and public seminars and conferences (Change for Equality 2006e). The signatures collection was seen as the first phase of the campaign; in the second phase, campaign activists hoped to work with supportive legal experts to draft new laws to replace unjust laws in the form of a legislative bill. The laws they sought to challenge were mostly family laws pertaining to custody, marriage, inheritance, and divorce—in total forty-six articles embedded in Iran's Civil Code, twenty-two in the Penal Code, and one Constitutional article used to ban women from seeking the office of the president.[2]

As codified, Muslim family law derives from conservative interpretations of the sharia. In Iran and elsewhere many Muslim reformers and feminists, through exegetical strategies of dynamic jurisprudence, argued that in its essence, sharia (as the will of God revealed to the Prophet) has a social and gender justice message. They asserted that it is the ways sharia was interpreted, practiced, and codified—by its patriarchal interlocutors—that produced a discriminatory legal structure. As a response, activists in many different Muslim contexts have developed innovative strategies to challenge patriarchal interpretations of family law, pushing their societies' legal structures to reflect the gender justice and equality messages within Islam. The OMSC in Morocco, Sisters in Islam in Malaysia, the OMSC in Iran, and the transnational organization Musawah are but a few examples of these innovations. The OMSC had "chapters" throughout Iran and a "chapter" in Southern California, as well as clusters and individuals working on the campaign in Europe. Yet calling these groupings of activists in different parts of Iran and Southern California "chapters" betrays the sense in which the campaign was a loose, informal transnational network of activists inside and outside Iran. Activists stressed that the campaign was not an organization but a network or movement of individuals, open to anyone who agreed with its basic tenets. The campaign network tried to be rigorously horizontal and grassroots, rather than hierarchical and bureaucratic (extensively explored in chapter 2).

In its most active period, before the 2009 Green Movement emerged, the campaign's dynamic website Change for Equality publicized the petition, articles, news stories, interviews, photos, and links to human rights groups in Arabic, English, Farsi, French, German, Italian, and Spanish. The collective narrative voice of the campaign articulated women's equality within an Islamic human rights framework that attempted to reconcile Iranian law with Iranian culture. The campaign reconfigured women's rights discourses and decentralized Islamic authority. With its multilingual Internet presence and its network of activists outside Iran, the campaign positioned itself as both local and transnational. As such, the campaign challenged Orientalist discourses that posit religion and secularism as counterpoised and antagonistic, pitting putative traditional and repressive states (Iran) against "democratic" and "liberatory" societies (the United States). By grounding ideas about human rights within Iranian feminist and Islamic reform discourses, the campaign sought to challenge but not undermine the state by illustrating the compatibility and reciprocity of Islam, gender equality, and human rights. In this sense the campaigners' political orientation was pragmatic and reformist. It made particular "achievable" demands by working within the parameters established by the state.

Although the campaign website is now basically defunct, my printed archive of more than two hundred pages of campaign stories serves as a living testimonial of activist labor and love that simply cannot be "disappeared" into the virtual past. As Southern California campaign activists Sahar and Zahra told me, the *kuche be kuche* (alleyway-to-alleyway) strategy of gathering stories and documenting them on the website created an "oral history of Iranian women." They argued that this approach stood in stark contrast to the methods of other activist organizations with their "elitist management and [publication of] pamphlets that are accessible to very few."[3] In a personal account of the campaign, founding member Noushin Ahmadi Khorasani (2009, 44) claims that the "work of recording [stories] was and remains important because the project of social reimagining naturally is impelled by and draws upon experiences that include the witnessing of injustices." In preserving and attending to this documented oral history, I extend the campaign's focus on nonelite and everyday spaces to narrate a recent history that speaks less to success and failure than it does to the power and desire of activists to reimagine and create community and collectivity beyond a number of borders and boundaries.

ISLAMIC HUMAN RIGHTS

In one of the first articles posted on its website, the campaign clearly stated that its goals were compatible with Islam and that Iran has an obligation to abide by international human rights treaties: "The demand to reform and change discriminatory laws is not in contradiction to Islamic principles and is in line with Iran's international commitments. Iran is a signatory to the UN Convention on Civil and Political Rights and as such, is required to eliminate all forms of discrimination" (Change for Equality 2006a). The article embodies a discursive strategy that asserts reform clerics such as Ayatollah Sanei'i and Ayatollah Bojnourdi support "a revision and reform of laws which are discriminatory against women" (Change for Equality 2006a). Campaigners regularly drew on a less formal and more lay method of *ijtehad*—the interpretive practice used by trained Islamic scholars of engaging sacred texts in light of contemporary realities—as a legitimate strategy, reflecting Iran's rich and positive culture of religious debate. The campaign brought these debates (mostly in the domain of clerics, scholars, and the press) to the grassroots through its outreach to ordinary Iranian citizens. By "reminding" the state of its international commitments to uphold civil and political rights in the context of a discussion of Islam's basic principles, the campaign pressured the state to fulfill its duties as a modern Islamic state. If equal rights for women are contained within Islam, and if an Islamic state has already committed to international conventions against discrimination, women's equal rights in Iranian Islamic law must follow.

Building on a strategy from the Islamicate feminist press that engaged with debates about Islam and women's rights, the campaign website had several interviews with reform clerics and religious scholars who support their goals. In this passage Somaiyeh Farid interviews Taghi Rahmani, an independent journalist, human rights activist, and religious activist. Rahmani looks back to the Prophet Muhammad's time, underscoring the ethical precepts inherent in Islam:

> I believe the overall spirit of the Quran is important. . . . In the Al-Omran sura in the Quran, God tells Mary's mother: "I give you a child who is a child close to God." The child turns out to be a girl and Mary's mother asks: "How can a daughter ever be as good as a son?!" But in God's view, there is equality. God says: "Each according to the level of their dedication." At that time, by giving women the right to testify, God gave them a position which stemmed from their gender, not their high esteem in society or family. Or in the case of inheritance, a woman who had no role in the process of production was given a right she did not have before. (Change for Equality 2007a)

Here Rahmani engages *ijtehad* to make a distinction between the patriarchal society that Islam inherited at the time of the Prophet and the egalitarian vision contained in the Qur'an. He argues that the Qur'an gives women moral and ontological equality, but that the patriarchal context in which it was revealed influenced its dominant interpretation. Reformers and feminists argue that from the Qur'an's ethical perspective, women have rights in Islam through the mere fact of their humanity and moral capacity.

But this view did not prevail beyond the early Muslim society of Muhammad. Instead, by the Medieval period, patriarchal ideas about women as the inferior and subordinate gender became codified, and women acquired status through their association with men. While key figures in the revolution such as Khomeini (who mobilized ideas about women's high status as religious beings and within the family—that is, as differently gendered beings who acquire status in relation and service to others) and Shariati (who saw women as equal to men but different vis-à-vis their gender), Rahmani and the campaign challenged this discourse in favor of women's equality as full citizens and moral equivalents of men, undifferentiated by their gender.

Highlighting how the first Muslim society at the time of Muhammad granted new rights to women, Rahmani stated: "The verses which pertain to the rights of women came down to the Prophet after women demanded those rights from him" (Change for Equality 2007a). Using the verses on inheritance as an example, Rahmani distinguishes between the egalitarian vision of the Qur'an and the ways in which it was interpreted and codified into law by the patriarchal societies that flourished at this time, when men, threatening to "resign from our religion," questioned the Prophet's proclamation of egalitarian inheritance. He asks, "If the Prophet's tradition had continued, and the door of exertion (Ijtehad) had remained open, wouldn't some social laws have changed in favor of women in the first few centuries of Islam?" (Change for Equality 2007a). These types of contradictions were openings for women's rights activists and reformers to call on the Iranian state to rethink and revise its own patriarchal laws in favor of the Qur'an's ethical and egalitarian precepts.

The campaign's Islamic human rights discourse was integral to its bottom-up, consensus-building strategy. By working within local frameworks and reaching out to a broad base, the campaign sought to legitimize itself to both the state and Iranian citizens. In a conversation between activists Nahid and Jelve, Jelve argued: "I'm the kind of feminist that lives and tries to work in the specific cultural and religious context of Iran. . . . [T]he Campaign has been able to integrate the discourse of equality into people's religious discourse. Many people have written about the relationship of the two discourses in a positive manner and there have been lots of discussions. I think the Campaign is the first social action that has been able to articulate the issue of women's rights and Islam so broadly among people" (Change for Equality 2007b). While Jelve most likely overstated the campaign's role in the Iranian feminist movement as the *first* to frame women's rights within Islam, she points to the perceived effectiveness of such a strategy and the importance of respecting local contexts. Given the state's promises of women's equality within Islam, its critique of Western feminism as an undesired foreign import, and a majority Muslim citizenry, the campaign's Islamic human rights framework was a part of an effective and culturally resonant discourse.[4]

This culturally resonant discourse lines up with Arzoo Osanloo's (2006, 2009) notion of Islamico-civil rights talk—a discourse resulting not only from the global hegemony of secular-liberal frameworks but also the hybridized Republican and Islamic legal system of Iran that interpellates individual rights-bearing citizens within an ideal Islamic collective. Osanloo (2006, 12–14) argues that Iranian women made rights claims in the postrevolutionary period through "dialogical sites," including Qur'anic meetings, family courts, and state and local organizations. Extending Osanloo's discussion of these sites to the realm of activist projects like the One Million Signatures Campaign, which are both local and transnational, I argue that the campaign enriched the terrain of human rights discourses and practices by drawing on and making accessible key debates within Iranian society. As the campaign circulated and gathered more members and participants, Islamic discourses were "reintellectualized" by ordinary citizens (Eickelman and Anderson 2003) and the doors of interpretation pushed open even wider, decentralizing the discussion of Islam and drawing in additional constituencies.

Whereas Osanloo emphasizes the agency of the state and its legal apparatus in shaping rights discourses, I invite attention to the activist efforts that served as a constant pressure point on authorities. These projects and their discourses could not be contained in only the elite spaces of literary and parliamentary debates; instead, they necessarily leaked into to the everyday understandings and negotiations of ordinary women and men. For instance, in their excellent 1998 documentary film *Divorce Iranian Style*, Ziba Mir-Hosseini and Kim Longino followed women through the Islamic family courts in Iran, finding that they made strong and often successful cases for divorce using specific and general tenets of Islamic law.

In reframing Islam as compatible with women's equality, the campaign enlarged and decolonized feminist conceptions of women's agency by suturing religious discourses and rights language together. In this sense, notions of women's rights shift from strictly secular-liberal frameworks into a more expansive lexicon, breaking down the borders between Western and non-Western and secular and religious discourses. Most feminist notions of agency continue to privilege secularism over religiosity, assuming secularism to implicitly produce agency and Islam to a priori constrain the capacities of Muslim women. Some scholars have responded to such theoretical lacunae by arguing that agency must be considered within the particular historical, national, cultural, and religious contexts defined by the subjects of one's analysis.[5]

Saba Mahmood (2001; 2005) has been particularly helpful in rethinking women's agency within Muslim contexts. She argues that we must read the practices of pious women within the appropriate "grammar of concepts" that give meaning to those acts. Mahmood builds on the work of Talal Asad (2003, 78) who argues that "'agency' is a complex term whose senses emerge within semantic and institutional networks that define and make possible particular ways of relating to people, things and oneself." Considering the agentic discourses and practices of pious women of the Egyptian mosque movement, who conformed to (rather than struggled against) patriarchal norms, Mahmood points to the limits of liberation and resistance as the most privileged, indeed the *only* markers of feminist agency.

Thinking through the discursive strategy of the campaign through the "grammar of concepts" that it mobilizes makes it possible to understand discourses of Islam (religion) and discourses of rights (feminism) as culturally compatible rather than antagonistic. The demands of the campaign "are in no way contradictory to the foundations of Islam," argued activists on the website (Change for Equality 2006a), pointing to Islam's message of justice and equality between all humans in relation to God. Indeed, modifying discriminatory laws to reflect this ethical precept within Islam was framed by the campaign as a holistic or restorative project. Islam could be recuperated to its foundational elements of justice, including justice for women. As Samira Haj (2008) has argued, Muslims in different periods have contended with questions of what a good society is within a flexible and capacious discursive tradition.

Lila Abu-Lughod's (2011, 101–102) notion of the "social life" of Muslim women's rights is also helpful, enabling us to move from asking *if* Muslim women have rights to tracing how the concept is "mediat[ed] through various social networks and technical instruments." As campaigners ground ideas about women's equality and women as individual rights-bearing citizens within an Iranian, Islamic, and feminist framework, they located the notion of rights as inherent in Islam and as a component of what an Islamic government must provide its citizens. Articulating an Islamic human rights framework through its website articles and face-to-face conversations, the campaign produced a particular "social life" of Islamic human rights discourses that both reflected and pointed to what campaigners framed as the "inevitability" of women's equality within Islam.

HARMONIZING LAW WITH CULTURE

A second discourse emanating from the campaign was the notion that Iranian culture—articulated in the campaign as economic and social conditions as well as the everyday practices, ideas, and ideals of the majority of Iranian people—enjoys women's mass participation and reinforces their relatively high social status.[6] As a result of Islamization, the opening of Islamic universities in almost every corner of Iran and the postrevolutionary state's commitment to girls' education and literacy, women entered higher education institutions in unprecedented numbers, comprising "over 60% of those being admitted to university" (Change for Equality 2006d). In this case, the campaign used a strategic discourse in framing the implementation of women's legal rights as a necessary outcome of a society that has normalized ideas about women's equality. The campaign thus sought to bring culture to bear on law and challenge the Orientalist trope of Iranian culture as inherently backward, patriarchal, and antimodern.

The campaign emphasized support among different sectors of the Iranian population for women's equality. As Jelve claimed: "The younger men who are joining the women's movement are different from the young men I knew several years back. They have internalized the discourse of equality more seriously" (Change for Equality 2007b). In a similar vein, Shahla reflected:

> I think that this effort is the most civil of efforts designed to bring about change in line with social demands. . . . Traditional families, with strong religious beliefs, who understand the fact that they are living in a modern world, recognize that a modern existence requires new rules. This is because traditional social relations, for which these laws were established, no longer exist. The legal status of women, even those living in the most traditional of families, who are employed, have an income and are full partners in carrying and handing the economic burdens of the family, must be re-examined with a new perspective. (Change for Equality 2006f)

This discourse sought to reconcile Iranian law with Iranian culture—the changing desires, aspirations, and social and material relationships of all Iranians.

Shahla's discourse resonates with other Islamic reform discourses, which distinguish between "changeable" and "unchangeable" precepts within Islam in an effort to reconcile contemporary law with contemporary social conditions. As Rahmani asserts: "Social laws are laws that describe the relationships of individuals to each other and to society and they also include politics, power, government, etc. Unlike prayers (*namaz*) and fasting (*roozeh*), these laws are not static" (Change for Equality 2007a). While some precepts in Islam are eternal, others are temporal—that is, open to be adjusted to contemporary conditions. Iranian clerics and religious thinkers have long drawn on this distinction in their efforts to modify Islamic law.

For instance, Iranian religious philosopher Abdolkarim Soroush has argued that religion and religious knowledge are two different things. Religious knowledge, the human understanding one brings to religion's eternal message, is temporally bound and therefore open to reform. Consequently, religious laws are and should be susceptible to contemporary human understandings (Soroush 2000). Feminists working within an Islamic framework make similar claims (Abugideiri 2002; Wadud 1992). The campaign drew out this reformist understanding by arguing for laws to be culturally—that is, temporally and socially—bound. "[Religious scholars] believe that considering the circumstances of time and place, laws must change to be in harmony with the level of culture and with the role and presence of Iranian women" (Change for Equality 2006b).

As a distinctly Islamic reformist and feminist discourse, the campaign's demand to harmonize law with culture foregrounded cultural conditions already in place to make legal rights for women meaningful. In other words, in its legal rights–seeking effort, the campaign stressed the importance of socially mandated laws to logically extend the changes in women's status already under way. By pointing to traditions within Islam that legitimize the revision of laws and underscoring the support of the majority of Iranian people for women's equality, the campaign pushed the state to reflect in law what it has, in part, produced: a literate, educated, and socially powerful citizenry whose equality is supported by a majority of Iranian people.

HUMBLE PRACTICES IN EVERYDAY SPACES

While the website drew attention to the campaign, soliciting support both locally and transnationally, activists emphasized the importance of the door-to-door, face-to-face method of gathering signatures. Khorasani (2009, 44) described the transformation of kitchens and living rooms from familial spaces to "cultural salons" of lively political discussion. In her account the campaigners come vividly to life on street corners, and in houses, cafes, tailor shops, doctors' offices, alleys, and parks as they approach neighbors and strangers alike. They fuse customary Iranian hospitality—the "humble practices" of offering sweets and nuts—with new political methods—handing out pamphlets, engaging in discussion, and asking for signatures (Khorasani 2009, 48–49).

The campaigners became modest street lobbyists, appealing to neighbors, friends, family, and coworkers to sign the petition but respecting those who refused. They emphasized consciousness-raising over number-crunching and encouraged those who signed on to become members. In addition to branches in multiple provinces in Iran, network members outside of Iran, and a strong Internet presence, the campaign established multiple committees in each region that gave volunteers experience in grassroots organizing. Among the committees in Tehran were those dealing with the media, volunteers, education, finance, a mothers committee, public relations, publications, and documentation. As new branches of the campaign were established, committees were set up as needed. Communications between branches happened through the volunteer committees and the website, where activists coded the street presence and conversational approach as antielitism:

> Our plan was to launch the campaign at the Ra'ad Residential Complex in Shahrak-e Gharb in Tehran with a large number of supporters participating in the event. Unfortunately, a few hours before the start of the rally, the permit for holding this event was withdrawn. However, the supporters were not willing to leave. Therefore, the program took place in the street. Perhaps the fact that the campaign started in the street and announced its identity and goals right there in the street was a sign of its nature and identity: that it belongs to everyone. (Change for Equality 2007c)

Despite this assertion, the campaign did have some elitist roots. Shahrak-e Gharb is an exclusive, upper-middle-class residential development in Tehran with a reputation for housing Western-identified residents. The choice to launch the campaign from here points to the secular and upper-middle-class roots of some of its founders.

Still, the campaign tried to generate broad-base support from all sectors of Iranian society and strived to work against elitism in its discourses and strategies. Articulating the campaign as the province of ordinary citizens and not an elite group of feminist activists worked to reinforce the idea that women's equality in the law is a desire of the Iranian majority and to challenge the state's frequent framing of the campaign as a "national security threat."[7] This framing relied on a notion of women's rights as imposed from the outside (the West, or more specifically, the United States) and tried to manipulate legitimate concerns about US political and military interventions. But the campaign countered with a consistent antielitist, consensus-building discourse that aspired to disarm the state. Often that discourse asserted women's legal rights as so "tangible" or "elementary" that "no one can be seriously opposed to them" (Change for Equality 2007c).

Activists regularly reported that signature-gathering volunteers had "friendly and sympathetic encounter[s] with the women and men that they approached" (Change for Equality 2007c). In an early article the campaign interviewed poet Simin Behbahani, who urged campaigners to "be generous and kind. When they approach people, they should be patient and open. Women are mothers, sisters, wives, lovers, and friends, and they must continue the long struggle with solicitude and kindness" (Change for Equality 2006c). This strategy of nonopposition, sympathy, and kindness worked to situate women as valued members of larger family, kin, and social networks, who are not only working on their own behalf but for the good of all Iranians. Campaigners wanted to build consensus and dialogue among a broad base of Iranians. Through family and social networks, they argued that women can access far-reaching layers with whom they can exchange ideas in familiar settings, occasionally even collecting signatures.

Jelve recalled: "I gave my mother some Campaign booklets to distribute among the women in her religious gatherings. They were very positive and signed the Campaign petition. They are discussing women's issues and are supportive of such social actions. My mother recently went to another religious gathering and challenged the government's new family bill that is being reviewed in Parliament for passage. She is very involved and discusses the issues with her friends and social circle. Sometimes she manages to collect signatures" (Change for Equality 2007b).[8] Women's social and kin networks thus provided a "safe" place through which to build consensus about women's equality.

Drawing on a collective discourse that urged harmony between state and society, sometimes the campaign shamed the state. In an interview with the campaign, Shirin Ebadi stated: "I hope that judiciary officials realize that after 30 years, the Islamic Republic is strong enough as to not have its national security threatened by the mere act of signature collections. . . . This argument . . . is not valid and it is somewhat of an insult to the Islamic Republic" (Change for Equality 2008b). This strategy was obviously used at a time when Iranians could assume the state would engage in a reasonable amount of political debate, before the heavy repression of 2009. The campaign used discourses of nonopposition and kindness to put an onus on the state to reconcile with the desires and practices of its peaceful, modern, religious, and rights-seeking citizenry. The surprise and outrage that greeted the violent punishment meted out to one campaigner worked to remind the state of its interests in harmonizing its laws with the desires of the majority of Iranians. Sussan said:

> I believe that lashing sentences are a source of shame and constitute disparagement for all Iranians who believe in justice and equality.[9] . . . Again I want to stress that I am shocked and disappointed about the implementation of such a sentence and I can't believe that our officials insist on portraying themselves in such a harsh manner. The recent violent response to women's rights activists takes place at a time when all sectors of society, including the grassroots and lawmakers alike are engaged in a discussion on women's rights and the need to reexamine the laws which govern the lives of women. (Campaign for Equality 2009)

This articulation of shock and disappointment assumed the state would want, as a "strong" and just state, to reflect the desires of its people. Again, this assumption was easier to make before the extreme crackdowns following the 2009 presidential elections. By pressuring the state to respond to this peaceful, bottom-up initiative, the campaign strengthened its consensus-building discourse and further legitimized its demands as nonelitist, indigenous, and broadly supported.

All of the activists I interviewed in Southern California echoed this antielitist and nonviolent ethos. For example, Pardis said: "We weren't after doing something flashy. We were just after doing something small, in our own scale. I mean, I don't want to say we did something small. We did something great. But starting with small steps, talking to people and not forcing anyone to do anything they're not comfortable with."[10] Reflecting a similar sentiment, Sahar claimed: "We don't want one person or group to become a committee that leads other people. Everybody can be involved. We don't eliminate anyone. We don't become top-down, ordering other people what to do."[11] In Khorasani's (2009, 43) account this bottom-up method represents a "feminine imagination" that is "unlike the heroic glorification of will that is a staple of revolutionary regimes. Instead, it is modest, and takes the reality of everyday life as its source of inspiration." These desires for humility, modesty, and convivial encounters with ordinary women and men along the everyday pathways of life were not simply aspirational but structured the collective ethos and organizational culture of campaign activists.

In foregrounding nonviolence in everyday life and politics, Khorasani and her fellow campaign activists made links to social movements that had imagined and birthed a new world. She wrote:

> It is clear that a long road lies ahead of us. . . . We should recall . . . how Reverend King applied [a nonviolent method] against deep-seated racial discrimination in the United States; and how Nelson Mandela oversaw the peaceful end of apartheid in South Africa. None of these triumphs came without years and years of face-to-face training and the publication of hundreds of books and thousands of articles. . . .
>
> If the civil and democratic movement of the Iranian people is also to remain peaceful and nonviolent, its power must come not from blood, clenched fists, bulging veins, and zealous revenge-seeking, but rather from *life-affirming endurance, persistence, and thoughtfulness.* (Khorasani 2009, 96–97, emphasis added)

Here, I invite attention to "life-affirming endurance" as a decolonial feminist insistence on rejecting the multiple forms of violence produced by coloniality. If imperial and state-sanctioned violence, the hierarchical ordering of gendered, racialized, and sexed subjects, and militarized patriarchal nationalisms are some of the defining features of modernity and coloniality, those who have challenged, even thrown off colonial oppression, have often reproduced such modes of power. The postrevolutionary, postcolonial Iranian state is emblematic. Echoing Khorasani, Mitra argued that the campaign tried "to include everybody, regardless of their religion, political views, gender, whatever," with the aspirations of "networking between activists and the mainstream."[12] In "life-affirming endurance, persistence, and thoughtfulness," in aspirations for inclusivity, horizontalism, for thinking of and being with each other, campaign activists reimagined and struggled for a new, nonviolent, and deeply feminist world.

REDEFINING SUCCESS

By 2009, three years into the campaign, that millionth signature remained a long way off. At that time campaign members estimated that just over one hundred thousand signatures had been collected, which may be the result of a few factors. First, campaign members suffered constant harassment and arrest. One can assume this was a tremendous drain on the campaign, as energy and resources were spent trying to support and free imprisoned women. Second, the 2009 election debacle funneled most political activists into the Green Movement while shutting down spaces for previously tolerated efforts such as the campaign. This reality presented new coalitional possibilities for activists but also forced activists, including those in the campaign, to reevaluate their goals. The extreme repression in the wake of the Green Movement forced many activists to go underground or exile themselves. Let us also remember that inside kitchens and living rooms, in doctors' offices and workplaces, Iranian citizens were also talking to each other about many decades of US sanctions that have choked the Iranian economy and made life exceedingly difficult for so many people. High inflation and unemployment, shortages of food and medicine, increased air pollution from unrefined gasoline—these factors most likely limited the capacities of campaign activists and their interlocutors, real people after all.

Finally, political divisions among feminist groups in Iran might have worked against the campaign's effectiveness. Shekarloo (2005) and Mir-Hosseini (2006a) cautioned that the women's rights activists who organized protests in June 2005 and 2006 were secular-identified and may have alienated some key Islamicate feminists who were part of the reform movement. It is these secular-oriented women's rights activists who went on to launch the campaign. Indeed, when I interviewed Maryam, she intimated that the campaign failed to pull in these key Islamicate feminists from the beginning, which caused some initial tensions and divisions in the campaign. Many years later, Sahar reflected on some of the shortcomings of the campaign.

> The campaign was not successful in increasing participation from all women with different socioeconomic statuses, nor successful in creating unity between [all] Iranian women. Another issue was that after a few years, women activists wanted to know if we achieved anything? . . . Could we influence law and legislation? Some criticized us that collecting signatures for the campaign caused some attacks and arrests, which was true; however, each movement has its expenses. The failure mostly was that the aim of the campaign was not creating a hierarchy but somehow it became a hierarchy. I experienced some discrimination among us as a Kurdish woman. Some of [the activists] did not want to get labeled and they had fear of any affiliation with Kurds. Smaller cities were more

> marginalized. I remember how hard I tried, writing letters about women who were arrested in Kurdistan, in affiliation with the campaign and I was not able to get support. It was a very frustrating time.[13]

However, when I followed up with OMSC activists in 2018, Fakhri reflected: "I do not think failure means anything in this context. All was a gain and positive. I think it's greatest achievement was connecting individuals and creating a body of feminists throughout the country that became the backbone of further gender-based struggles."[14] Feminist scholar and activist Janet Afary (2009, 372–73) has argued that campaign activists "moved beyond the sectarian and ideological divides that hampered the women's movement for much of the twentieth century." Most likely both things are true: that the campaign alienated some activists and that it tried to work against sectarianism and divisiveness by having a horizontal structure and using discourses that resonated with ordinary Iranians.

Nonetheless, the campaign received more international attention from Western feminist groups than most other feminist groups inside Iran, perhaps disproportionate to the campaign's actual effectiveness within Iran. The campaign received several awards from groups like the Feminist Majority Foundation, raising dilemmas for the campaign (detailed in chapter 2). And while the campaign refused award money from Western groups and worked hard to articulate itself as nonelite and horizontally organized, it may be that this Western attention and recognition exacerbated any tensions or divisions among feminist groups within Iran.

Despite the high number of signatures that were never gathered, and new political conditions that would raise questions among the campaign activists themselves about their direction after 2009, the campaign contributed to what Jean-Pierre Reed and John Foran (2002), in describing Nicaraguan citizens' relationships to the Sandinistas, have called "political cultures of opposition." These cultures of "individuals, groups, and organizations" articulate "plurivocal and potentially radical ways of understanding" (Reed and Foran 2002, 338–39) the period they are living through. Indeed, using human rights within an Islamic framework and women's equality discourses, the OMSC and its network of supporters were successful at capitalizing on the shifting social practices, beliefs, and desires of millions of Iranian women and men who have internalized a radically different version of Islam than that codified by the hardliners.

The June 2009 presidential campaigns reflected the strength of the OMSC and other feminist projects in putting women's legal rights on the national agenda. A loose network of secular and Islamicate feminist activists, including those in the OMSC, called the Women's Convergence pushed for reforms in the law before the elections and engaged both reform candidates, Mehdi Karroubi and Mir-Hossein Mousavi, around women's issues.[15] As the campaign website reported, Karroubi "promised to submit bills to parliament intent on reforming laws which discriminate against women" (Farhang 2009). Following Karroubi's promise, Mousavi "issued a comprehensive programme on women as part of his election platform, in which he also committed to reforming discriminatory laws against women" (Farhang 2009). Mousavi and his wife, Zahra Rahnavard, emblematized a modern, Islamic couple by holding hands in public and using every opportunity to put forward Rahnavard to speak about women's legal rights and equality.

Rahnavard, like many Islamicate feminists in Iran both inside and outside of the campaign, has a long and compelling history of political activism. As Afary (2009) has written, the young Rahnavard was influenced by Marxism and participated in the broad anti-Shah left. Ultimately, she wanted to integrate her religious beliefs into her politics. Rahnavard became a follower of Shariati, then Khomeini, and was part of the Islamist intellectual and political forces that supported the revolution. Highly educated—she has a master's degree in art and a doctorate in politics—Rahnavard has "lived a life that seemed to offer many new choices," more than those available to previous generations (Afary 2009, 256). "By becoming a political activist in the Islamist movement, [Rahnavard] found a compromise solution. She returned to many of her familial ethical principles without abandoning her desire for new ones, such as an advanced education, professional and economic progress for women, and companionate marriage, albeit within the bounds of Islam" (Afary 2009, 256). I would modify Afary to argue that it is precisely Islam, and the particular Iranian Islam of the revolutionary and postrevolutionary state, that made Rahnavard's and other Muslim women's reconciliations of Islam and feminism possible. In other words, instead of a boundary, Islam became the very condition of possibility for Rahnavard's and many other activists' and citizens' struggles for democratization in Iran. Like the OMSC, Rahnavard represented a pragmatic and nonviolent approach to reforming law. As Mitra argued: "We [were] doing everything peaceful and within the frame of law, but we [were] trying to change the law."[16]

The face-to-face, consensus-building discourses and nonviolent strategies worked alongside and encompassed other campaign discourses of Islamic human rights and reconciling law to culture. Together they produced broad support for the campaign and highlighted the campaign's locally driven and locally desired goals by building on feminist and reform discourses internal to Iran, foregrounding the mass support of the "presence of Iranian women" within Iranian culture and demanding the reflection of this cultural reality in law, and bringing bottom-up, conciliatory methods and discourses to bear on the state's formation of itself as a modern, Islamic, rights-securing entity.

The failure of the Family Protection Bill to be ratified in the full Parliament in 2008 signaled the effectiveness of the coalition of feminists, including those in the campaign, in mobilizing opposition to further discriminatory laws, despite the increased harassment, repression, and imprisonment of activists. A similar Family Protection Bill submitted to Parliament in 2010, in the more repressive political atmosphere, had a better chance of being voted into law. However, it too faced massive opposition, including quite public opposition from Zahra Rahnavard, and was tabled then and in 2012. If hardliners continue to introduce these kinds of bills, they are likely to be highly contested by women's rights activists.

Despite failures to completely overturn Iran's discriminatory laws, the signatures campaign succeeded in putting a feminist version of women's undifferentiated legal equality on the national agenda and squashing any new discriminatory laws. Women's presence and involvement in the public sphere and their desires for equality in all spheres of life legitimated these activists' struggles for legal reform. The campaign activists and those that came before them reconfigured and enriched notions of women's rights and contributed to the decentralization of Islamic authority. If the campaign failed to gather one million signatures, it succeeded at influencing the national conversation in Iran around women's rights and equality and grounding it in local debates, ideas, and concepts. It rejected past patriarchal nationalisms that neglect women's issues and valorize a kind of masculinized, often violent resistance. In addition, the campaign refused modes of erasure and silencing within transnational feminism that would revictimize women of the Global South, and created an affective organizational culture of friendship, support, and shared stake-holding among Iranian women's rights activists inside and outside Iran.

Thinking beyond the "failure" of the campaign to scale up the aspirations and sensibilities of Iranian citizens to force the Islamic Republic of Iran to overturn discriminatory law, I return to Walsh's decolonial *for* as a way of holding onto the afterlife of this particular moment of women's rights activism. As Walsh (2018a, 17) has explicated, decoloniality "is indicative of the ongoing nature of struggles, constructions, and creations that continue to work within coloniality's margins and fissures to affirm that which coloniality has attempted to negate." Coloniality, and indeed the particular violences practiced by a postcolonial state like Iran, rests on a set of binarisms that mark the borders and boundaries of home, nation, and identity. "Decoloniality, without a doubt," Walsh continues, "is . . . contextual, relational, practice based, and lived." It is "the ongoing processes and practices, pedagogies and paths, projects and propositions that build, cultivate enable, and engender decoloniality." This "praxis," she argues, is a "walking, asking, reflecting, analyzing, theorizing, and actioning—in continuous movement, contention, relation, and formation" (Walsh 2018a, 19).

In building a local and transnational project—and creating and sustaining a network along the axis of feminist solidarity, friendship, hope, love, and shared community and commitment—campaign activists cultivated ways of *thinking of* and *being with* each other. Chapter 2 further explores these modes through the narratives of diasporic campaign members. By mapping the different locations and negotiations of these activists inside a network of social, political, geographical, and affective ties, I theorize the ways in which Iranian women's rights activism reflects a decolonial feminist politics and epistemology of border-crossing.

CHAPTER 2

WITHOUT THOSE BRANCHES, THIS CANNOT BE A TREE

> Where is homeland? It is the epicenter of any and all emerging worlds that recasts the current geography of domination of one people over others.
>
> —HAMID DABASHI

> From the vantage point of national crossroads I have gained glimpses into the different iterations of the self and the accompanying changing boundaries of the self and the world.
>
> —NASRIN RAHIMIEH

IN THE SUMMER OF 2007, ESHA, A CAMPAIGN ACTIVIST LIVING IN the United States, traveled to Iran to spend time with her family and work on the One Million Signatures Campaign (OMSC). Elated and hopeful, she wrote on the campaign website: "Iran and all that makes it unique—steep streets, narrow alleys and unmarked homes—is still the land of promise that we hold dear to our hearts." Documenting her experiences of gathering signatures in Iran, Esha reflected on and contributed to the campaign as a project of reimagining the present and future. "The women of this land are peacefully writing a glorious end to the bitter long story of inequality and injustice. . . . My grandmother everyday practices her signature, as evidence of her existence and her uniqueness." Esha's pride sings as she poetically writes herself, her grandmother, and Iranian women into history. "Here in Iran, I, you, and our mothers . . . with our peaceful approach we dance in the alleys from house to house so that our promise of equality and unity transforms the sounds of the chains on our feet to the melodies of an anklet" (Change for Equality 2008a).

Back in California, the elation Esha felt in Iran turned to deflation as she attended a Mehregan Festival (Iranian festival of autumn) in Orange County. With other campaign activists, she was there to gather signatures among festival goers who had come to celebrate the fall with food and music, and browse the business booths, many of them offering services geared to brides and weddings—limousine rentals, hair stylists, bridal dresses. Esha and her fellow activists had rented a booth next to a nonprofit organization soliciting financial sponsorships for orphans. She noticed an album of children available for sponsorship, and wryly commented on their images, slickly packaged like "a catalogue for furniture." She recalled: "I pick up a few petition forms . . . and scan the people to see who would be most receptive to what I have to say." Approaching a young woman, Esha asks, "'Excuse me, but may I have a few minutes of your time?' There is no reaction so I continue. 'Have you heard of the One Million Signatures Campaign?'" The young woman shakes her head "no," and Esha asks her if she'd like to learn about it. The woman interrupts Esha, blurting, "I don't travel to Iran." While Esha managed to gather some signatures, overall she left the festival feeling alienated and deflated, wondering if she, her mother, and her sisters "were all just images, just like pictures that one quickly browses through in a furniture catalogue" (Change for Equality 2008a).

Esha's reflections were resonant in the interviews I conducted with Leyla, Maryam, Vashti, Pardis, Fakhri, Mitra, Sahar, and Zahra, campaign activists living in different parts of Southern California. Each spoke of feeling inspired by and hopeful for the activists inside Iran who were traveling *kuche be kuche* (alleyway to alleyway) to talk with families, friends, and neighbors about women's rights. They highlighted the many innovations of the campaign, theorizing the methods, strategies, and scales of this new movement, several years before other globally networked movements like the Arab Spring uprisings and Occupy Wall Street entered the scene. These activists echoed Esha's feelings of alienation from many of their fellow Iranians living in the larger Southern California diaspora, particularly those who were disconnected from the everyday lived experiences in Iran, and out of this disconnection, reified images of Iranian women as without dimension or nuance, a catalog of captive prisoners to a hostile regime.

This chapter considers the vibrant political affiliations and modes of solidarity produced through the campaign's transnational network. Through the narratives of this small but determined group of Iranian feminists, I explore what it meant for Iranian activists living outside Iran to have participated in the campaign, particularly as they negotiated several distinct phenomena: their location in the United States vis-à-vis their counterparts in Iran, attention from Western feminists, ongoing anti-Iran prejudice in the United States (including but not limited to Islamophobia), and the persistent elision of Iranian women's agency within human rights frameworks as well as among Western feminists and Iranians themselves. I investigate the dilemmas and opportunities that emerge in feminist solidarity work, showing the important ways in which Iranian women's rights activists have practiced and sustained decolonizing notions of solidarity and feminism through their ideas and organizational practices as well as remapped notions of home and belonging. By detailing the ways in which these activists critically engaged Western feminism, I point to the possibilities of "downsizing" Western feminism from universal signifier to particular site. I place the campaign in proximity to other innovative social movements that have mobilized new media and organized themselves in similarly decentralized and horizontal networks. I hope to give the campaign—whose novel organizational structures and use of new media technologies challenged geographical, political, and epistemic borders—its rightful place in the narrative of recent global social movements.

WE DIDN'T FORGET ABOUT YOU: COLLECTIVE STANDPOINTS

Four months after the June 2009 elections in Iran, I flew from New York to the greater Los Angeles area to interview activists involved in the One Million Signatures Campaign. The elections led to Mahmoud Ahmadinejad securing a second presidential term, much to the surprise of those inside Iran and around the world, who had predicted a landslide win from reform candidate Mir-Hossein Mousavi. Mousavi declared himself the real winner, accusing Ahmadinejad of election fraud and sparking a massive opposition movement in Iran and the diaspora. Coined the Green Movement, protesters marched in the streets of Iranian towns and cities, and Iranians in the diaspora mobilized solidarity rallies. The slogan "Where Is My Vote?" went viral.

I was active in the New York Iranian feminist activist diaspora and at the time heavily involved in solidarity work with the postelection uprising in Iran. As an Iranian national, I had cast my vote in the Iranian elections for the first time, in the lobby of a New York hotel on June 12. Six months earlier,

I had been in Iran, riding the wave of excitement among my family members about the upcoming elections and their certainty that Mousavi would win. I carried that excitement into the hotel lobby, surrounded by fellow Iranians and my activist friends, and proudly marked the box by Mousavi's name. As news of the stolen election spread, we watched and listened in disbelief, our shock, anger, and sadness tempered only by the vigorous protests inside and outside Iran.

Touching down at LAX in October, four months after the elections, I was eager to spend time with campaign members, to talk with them about their activism, and to learn about the campaign and the Green Movement as these movements were happening. The first contact I had reached out to referred me to another, who then referred me to several more, and so on. After renting a car and getting my bearings, I traversed greater Los Angeles County over several days to talk with Leyla, Maryam, Vashti, Pardis, Fakhri, Mitra, Sahar, and Zahra in their homes, in cafes, in parks along the Pacific Ocean—any place they were able to meet given their busy work and activist schedules to speak with me. I was not surprised to learn that this "chapter" of the One Million Signatures Campaign was quite bare-bones and grassroots. They had no office or budget, and like grassroots activists everywhere, they carved out time before or after the demands of work or school or family, in between weekend chores and leisure time, to meet in person, by phone, or online. The eight activists I spent time with were more than half of the small cluster working together in Southern California. They ranged in age from twenty-two to the mid-fifties. Seven of them were first-generation Iranians, and seven of them had been in the United States for fewer than ten years at the time of my interviews. They varied in class and social location, from students to cultural workers to professionals, although all of them had at least an undergraduate university education. Five of the eight activists traveled regularly to and from Iran and attended campaign meetings in Iran when there. Unlike many Iranians in the Southern California diaspora, the campaign activists were not those who fled Iran after the 1979 revolution, but they were deeply connected to activist networks inside Iran and strongly committed to the possibilities for change from within.

The campaign network, with its website, email lists, and connections among activists inside and outside Iran, created new transnational political spaces and cultures that challenged national and regional boundaries. Nayereh Tohidi (2002, 878) has argued that the Iranian feminist diaspora has strengthened transnational feminist networks: "Diaspora women activists have contributed to the women's movement inside Iran at different levels, including the political, informational, theoretical, technical, and organizational. They have made these contributions through teaching, research, women's activist groups, and, more recently, Internet sites." This is not to say, however, that national boundaries and the authority and power of nation-states are irrelevant. What was striking in my interviews was the ways in which the campaign activists sometimes spoke as Iranians having relocated to the United States, enmeshed in some ways in American culture and society, while at other times they spoke as Iranians deeply tied to Iran, as Iranian observers of American life. These different senses of location and identity signaled activists' understandings of how their work in the United States enabled particular kinds of privileges and restraints as well as how their experiences as Iranians now living inside the United States afforded them specific insights about both Iranian and American society. This sense of multiple or fluid locations illustrated how different diasporic populations can trouble the rigid binaries established around center/periphery, national/transnational, local/global, and West/rest.

As part of a larger Iranian diaspora in Southern California, the campaigners often faced opposition from Iranians whose political affiliations are much different from theirs.[1] Nilou Mostofi (2003, 683) has described Southern California Iranians in the following way:

> These immigrants are, for the most part, products of the Pahlavi [Shah] era, in that they were economically prosperous, inclined to Western influence, and belonged to Iran's newly formed, predominantly secular middle class. . . . They were the majority class in Iran who not only immigrated with the principles of Westernization, secularization, urbanization, and modernization but also with traditional "Persian" and anti-Islamic, therefore anti-Muslim, ideals. They immigrated to Southern California prior to or soon after the Islamic Revolution. They came to the United States as professional or entrepreneurial immigrants living in exile while creating an identity in diaspora based on these notions.

In their work in Southern California, campaigners often had to field hostile reactions from this diaspora majority, staunch secularists who had been away from Iran for a long time, did not support reform efforts in Iran, and had deep anti-Muslim biases. When I asked these activists what some of their challenges were, most identified the hostility from some of the Southern California diaspora as a major obstacle to their work. The following dialogue contains an exchange between myself and two campaigners,

Vashti and Fakhri, that illustrates the ways in which some of the diaspora is still steeped in ideological battle:

> VASHTI: They don't believe in the whole system. They don't believe in reform. And it's a challenge talking to them.
>
> FAKHRI: Actually once, in Berkeley, there was a human rights panel, it was three days, and the campaign had a panel from the program. So people start cursing us, like "I want to spit on you. You are the ones who are helping this government to survive." So this is how they look at it. They don't like to hear anything good out of Iran. I've seen them, like when they talk about all the executions, stoning, everything.
>
> ME: What can they say now? The reform movement just got even bigger.[2]
>
> FAKHRI: Now I think they just don't say anything. They better not say anything. But they really don't like to hear about any changes, because I think they think, you're here because of all these bad things and we can't go back to Iran, because they're going to kill us. But 80 percent, 90 percent of them, if they go back, nothing is going to happen. Nobody is going to touch them. But they have to keep that imagination for themselves, in order to survive and be nationalists.[3]

In this exchange "nationalism" is referenced as secular nationalism of the Shah era. In this nostalgic framing, many diasporic Iranians erase the massive repression of secular and religious critics of the Shah and consolidate the Orientalist rendering of the Islamic Republic as a static and immutable space, incapable of accommodating demands for social and political change.

As Nima Naghibi (2016, 15) has argued, trauma and nostalgia are the dominant affective modes transmitted through "diasporic Iranian women's life narratives in English in the late twentieth and early twenty-first centuries," who narrate "the 1979 revolution as a traumatic event" and express a "powerful nostalgia for an idealized past." Her analysis of these popular and well-circulated memoirs can be extended to the affective responses of many diasporic Iranians when discussing contemporary Iran. To clarify, I have no intention of minimizing the experiences of those who experienced political repression during the revolution, including those who are or who feel exiled. My aim instead is to bring focus to an alternative set of discourses, feelings, and modes of the Iranian story narrated by those whose experiences, relations, and activist commitments challenge a rather normative and unyielding Iranian exile identity.

Hamid Dabashi, quoted in the chapter epigraph, complicates the idea of homeland as fixed, and therefore diaspora and exile as affectively and structurally bounded categories that emerge in binary opposition to home: "If one's home and habitat, where one was born and raised, is to have invested a person with an emotive universe of principled loyalty to some abiding ideas, then that homeland drives across borders and dismantles any disabling notion of exile. Once we expand the inviting horizons of any homeland towards its neighboring climes, *alterity* replaces *identity* as the site of consciousness—and upon that site a different mode of self-knowledge soon announces itself" (Dabashi 2016, 188). He takes issue with how the concepts of diaspora and exile have become normalized, particularly by Iranian intellectuals outside of Iran, who, Dabashi (2016, 25) argues, reify the "fetishized borders and frontier fictions" of postcolonial Iran by fixing a category of home/homeland from which a category of exile can emerge. He mobilizes the notion of alterity as a challenge to rigid identity formations (national, diasporic, and otherwise) produced by forms of political, military, and epistemic authority structured by colonial relations. For Iranians, like other Others of the Global South, this colonial relationship with the West has also structured anticolonial/postcolonial responses that symptomatically reentrench a West-versus-rest or Islam/West binarism.

Iranian American feminist scholars have theorized notions of homeland and diaspora in particularly generative ways, often focusing on second-generation Iranians in the United States, those who, as Persis M. Karim has written, are living in "the aftermath of their parents' migrations" (Karim and Khorrami 1999, 19). Karim and Mohammad Mehdi Khorrami (1999), Karim (2006), Amy Malek (2006), Amy Motlagh (2011), and Nasrin Rahimieh (2007) have drawn much-needed attention to those in the Iranian diaspora who, through cultural production, negotiate their particular identities. Karim and Khorrami and Karim deploy betweenness, neither Iranian nor American, and Malek, drawing on Hamid Naficy (1993), mobilizes the notion of liminality as material-affective spaces that have generated a prolific body of work from Iranian American women who have sought recognition and voice through creative writing.[4] Rahimieh (2007) explores the crossing of national borders as painful yet generative processes for reconfiguring one's relationship to self and society.

The activists I spent time with signaled this material-affective space, a space marked by difficulty, pain, and loss as well as creativity and opportunity. They would often resist my own attempts to categorize them as "diasporic" or "exilic," even "Iranian American." Indeed, what they strove for was to "recast the current geography of domination of" (Dabashi 2016, 188) the United States over Iran, of the Iranian government over citizens and activists, of Western feminism over other feminisms, and of patriarchal Iranian or American nationalisms over feminism. The conceptual frameworks of transnationalism, translocality, and decoloniality provide some legibility for the different political and affective affiliations and interconnections between activists in Iran and the United States. As Inderpal Grewal and Caren Kaplan (1994, 16) have argued, diasporic communities are not homogeneous but "multiply organized" outside essentialist or naturalized ideas of what is home and what is the diaspora. The diasporic network of the campaign can be understood more complexly through what Grewal and Kaplan (1994, 16) point to as a "specific agenda and politics," or the ways in which affiliations are made through political goals and struggles rather than fixed racial, sexual, and national identities, or geographic location.

The sense of alienation from fellow Iranians in Southern California, expressed by Vashti and Fakhri earlier in the chapter, certainly echoed that of Esha at the Mehregan Festival, as campaigners found it difficult to connect to Iranians who had essentially given up on or distanced themselves from Iran. As Kaplan (1994, 139) has argued, a politics of location "is not useful when it is construed to be the reflection of authentic, primordial identities that are to be reestablished and reaffirmed." Indeed, the campaigners in Southern California represented a minority political view within the larger Southern California diaspora. Like their counterparts in Iran, they believed, at least at the time of the campaign, in change from within Iran and the possibility for engagement with the state. They contested the hegemonic narrative emanating from the diaspora majority that "nothing good" can come from within the Islamic Republic. Although this narrative circulates within neoconservative and neoliberal Western discourses alike, when it comes from within the larger Iranian diaspora, it intensifies the "civilizational" discourses that construct Islam as inherently repressive.

On this point, Pardis spoke to the ways in which the diaspora majority in Southern California, often hostile to Islam, forecloses the possibility of change from within. "But most of the conversation, if it comes up about Islam, they are against Islam. They say, 'What are you talking about, this is all Islam, Islam is to blame for this.' And Iranians, because religion has been either shoved down our throat or shoved out of our throat, whatever you want to call it, we're all very passionate for or against it. People blame Islam; they say unless you change that we can't change anything."[5] Pardis illustrated how alliances among Iranians based on "essential" categories of identity cannot be assumed. Many other campaigners I interviewed spoke of similar experiences of hostility from the diaspora majority and how challenging it was for them to reframe the terms of the debate when engaging with those in this majority.

As most campaigners relayed, they constantly worked against the hegemonic narrative coming from parts of the diaspora majority which argues that rights for women inhere in the putative secular cultural and political space of the United States, making it a safe harbor for women, and that an "essential" Islam is to blame for women's oppression. Pardis gave this example: "And then we have to argue with them and say, well, you know, or sometimes they say it's because of the Islamic Republic, and we say, well, you know, even in America, if you think about it, women's rights activists have to fight for their rights here. They don't have Islam here. They don't have an Islamic Republic here. They have somewhat of a democratic system set up and women don't have equal rights. So we have to have that conversation and just kind of get people to think that there's a complex situation."[6] Pardis shifted the narrative from a civilizational discourse about Islam versus secular democracy to one in which women from different contexts might engage in shared political struggles. In this sense she and other campaigners used a transnational feminist politics of location that disrupted the multiple binaries enforced by the diaspora majority.

As I have argued elsewhere (Sameh 2017), transnational feminist theory has generated ways of thinking through the possibilities for and barriers to building bonds of affiliation and solidarity across multiple differences. It offers an alternative to the "global sisterhood" model that assumes a universal category of women and an essential sameness based on national or regional locations. Transnational feminist theory has also helped theorize the complex and power-laden relationships between people, ideas, commodities, and information. As Kaplan has argued, transnational feminism builds ties across geographical and other divides, rendering similarity and difference in historical rather than essentializing terms. Using the idea of coalition and Edward Said's affiliation, Kaplan (1994, 139) has claimed that "a practice of affiliation, a politics of location identifies the grounds for historically specific differences and similarities between women in diverse and asymmetrical relations, creating alternative histories, identities, and possibilities for alliances."

The notion of translocality is also useful for thinking about the dynamics of connection among people and places, particularly the different places and spaces of diasporas. Translocality builds on the insights of transnationalism yet also tries to decenter the nation-state through a consideration of the many forms of "situatedness" among "mobile actors" (Greiner and Sakdapolrak 2013, 375). In their capacity as activists within a larger diasporic community, one might assume a naturalized affiliation among all diasporic Iranians. However, when discussing the possibilities of change and reform inside Iran with other Iranians, campaigners were often met with hostility and cynicism from strict secularists, whose Islamophobic discourses reinforce binaries around religion and secularism, repression and democracy, Iran and the West. The activists I interviewed came up against and critiqued the limits of national identity as a unifying framework, even as they aspired to make connections to other Iranians in Southern California. Subsequently, the Southern California activists aimed to build a coalitional politics around decolonial affiliations that broke down these binaries and built solidarity and a sense of community between feminists in different locations.

While the use of new media did not automatically create connection and solidarity among activists inside and outside of Iran, it did help facilitate the sense of a collectively owned project. As Sahar claimed: "Through this networking and website, the same day that one person gets arrested, *we publish it and they have a voice*. Somebody takes a picture with one cell phone, then we tweet it to each other, send it to Facebook, write about it or put in in the news."[7] New media platforms, certainly ubiquitous today among activists in many locations, campaigns, and movements, solidified the sense of a collective standpoint among campaigners, even if their geographical, social, and political locations were not shared. Sahar continued: "We want to tell our Iranian sisters, 'You're not alone. We care about you. We didn't forget about you. We think about your causes.'"[8] This refusal to forget opened up a space of affective investment rooted in solidarity, friendship, and affiliation around women's similar and different experiences of oppression and struggles for rights. As Iranian women's rights activists stood with their sisters in Iran, they created an organizational culture of connection and collective belonging, a beloved feminist "home" containing their desires to *think of* and *be with* each other. Building such connections was not without difficulty, and aspirations to collectivity and solidarity did not inoculate the campaign against internal struggles or hierarchies. The campaign tried to work against sectarian Iranian politics of the past as well as the self-proclaimed superiority of Western feminism. Negotiating transnational feminist work within the various trappings of coloniality/postcoloniality, Iranian women's rights activists more than gestured toward a decolonial otherwise.

AUTONOMY AND COLLECTIVITY

The activists I spent time with all emphasized the inclusivity of the campaign, and the fact that anyone who agreed with its goals could join. This horizontal, democratic, and inclusive practice came through very clearly in the discourses of the campaign. The heavy emphasis on this practice by the California activists confirms that the discourses of the campaign were not just aspirational but derived largely from its practice. Many stressed that the campaign is not an organization but functions more like a network or a movement. As Zahra asserted: "It's something you can start anywhere, anytime. So it's not like an organization you can found."[9] This organizational structure—defined by no single ownership but a loose collectivity of individuals, each empowered to be part of and amplify the campaign—was part of what many activists attributed to its appeal. Sahar reiterated Zahra's appraisal of the network model when she argued that "the campaign has been one of those success stories, and that has been heartwarming and meant a lot to me. Organized anything have [*sic*] made me really cynical in the recent years especially."[10]

The cynicism about and distrust of centralized political movements and their ideological discourses can be explained in two ways. First, the main theorists of the revolution, Ali Shariati and Ayatollah Ruhollah Khomeini, addressed women's rights and equality only at the level of ideology. Their discourses addressed gender equality within Islam largely at the level of abstraction, avoiding specific promises around political or legal changes. Ervand Abrahamian (1982, 466) argued that Shariati "spoke in allegories, used words with double meanings, and often avoided direct reference to immediate issues." Similarly, Khomeini mobilized women's participation in the revolution by arguing that Islam offered an alternative to women's sexual and commercial exploitation under capitalist relations. During and after the revolution, women came to bear the burdens of shoring up and "protecting" revolutionary ideals. Their prescribed gender roles—which included imposed forms of dress, exclusion from certain professions, and limits to participation in public life—were rationalized under a state-sanctioned discourse of separate but equal.

Second, like many left and progressive movements, Iran's left has seen no shortage of sectarian battles, splits, and intragroup divisions. As Ali Akbar Mahdi (2003) has argued, the decades following the revolution signaled a new nonideological stage in Iranian politics, as activists, particularly women, sought to make social changes without subsuming individual identities or interests. Mahdi asserts that postrevolutionary women's activism in Iran is "suspicious of 'vanguardism' and 'practical rigidity' of leftist and nationalist movements of earlier periods," and "less committed to totalizing ideologies, grand theories, and broad organizations." In addition, "the collectivist identity [forced] on the Iranian woman [has] not only failed to produce the desired outcome," Mahdi asserts, "but [has] actually given rise to a desire to strike a balance between the extremes of Western individualism and Islamic collectivism." Women now care less about revolution and more about "control of their own lives within political, social and economic institutions, whatever the ideological configurations of those institutions" (Mahdi 2003, 67).

The campaign certainly reflected this trend, as all of the activists I talked to repeatedly emphasized decentralization, flexibility, and the focus on individual participation within a collective but a loose and nonhierarchical one. Sahar asserted that the campaign was even part of an epochal trend in the world toward inclusive, democratic, nonideological movements, including the movements for democratization that emerged in Eastern Europe in the 1980s and 1990s. She argued that this trend was "not only the characteristic of the campaign, [but] worldwide, during these last two decades." Connecting the campaign's nonideological ethos to earlier movements, she said: "It started in Eastern Europe, places that started with democratic, peaceful movements through grassroots organizations or grassroots campaigns, with no leader or specific leadership. So it's kind of worldwide."[11]

Although the campaign originated in Iran and was based in several provinces there, the network structure enabled activists as far away as California to participate in ways that often didn't entirely distinguish them from their counterparts in Iran. Maryam likened the spatial and relational interconnections to a tree, "rooted in Iran, but with branches [that] have spread outside. And without those branches, this cannot be a tree."[12] When I asked how the California group began, Sahar answered: "I was part of this social networking website and there was a forum there, and we were chatting with other people on the forum about women's rights. . . . Some of them were in other countries, but then there was one person who was in Southern California." Excited by this connection, Sahar reached out. "We were like, okay, we're going to go meet up. And so I just met up with this stranger, and we decided we should email the campaign in Iran and see if we can start something. We did and they were like, 'Sure, we don't give permissions. If you like it, do it.'"[13]

This synergistic relationship between Iranian campaign activists in California and those in Iran sheds a light on fresh kinds of political cultures enabled by this postideological moment in Iranian politics and also by new media technologies that facilitated connections among activists across the world. According to Zahra, "[Women's rights activists in Iran] developed a culture [of nonhierarchy and cooperation]." She discussed the initiative feminists took in trying to build horizontal connections among different movements. "You know even if they weren't completely successful in linking, for example, the workers rights movement with the women's movement, they tried. They tried to build this [activist] culture through nonhierarchy and the Internet. The women's movement really worked on that and tried it, and saw that it works."[14] The desire for a nonhierarchical organizational culture is not unique to the campaign. Many feminists and other activists in Iran and elsewhere have committed themselves to nonhierarchy within their organizations, and long before the explosion of new media. The Internet does not implicitly produce relations of equality and horizontalism among activists. But the Internet certainly assisted the campaign network in its effort to offer an appealing and flexible way for members to plug in. The campaign's network structure allowed people to work together across differences that might have seemed insurmountable in the past. Zahra was particularly animated about this. "The campaign was defined as anybody can join, anybody can be part of this movement," she said. "There's no centralized group that can tell you yes or no. So nobody asks you what you believe in, nobody asks you what you do, nobody asks, where else are you active?" Having participated in more sectarian groups in Iran in the past, Zahra valued the openness of the campaign. "If you support this campaign, you can be part of it," she recalled. "So that's something I think that is very valuable in the Iranian community, focusing on that one thing and being able to work together on that one thing, even if you completely disagree on some other things."[15]

The campaign's nonideological, democratic practice and the interplay between activists in different locations and their shared political community, enabled in part through the Internet, is an example of what Tohidi

(2002, 856), drawing on Alberto Melucci (1996), has called "fragmented, heterogeneous, and dynamic forms of collective action, continually reconstructed through diffuse, decentralized, and subterranean networks . . . in the 'Information Age.'" Valentine Moghadam (2005, 81) has drawn on Manuel Castells (2000) to argue that networks have become the predominant mode of feminist organizing: "As Manuel Castells argues, the advantages of networks are flexibility and adaptability, which are especially conducive to conditions of rapid change, such as the current era of globalization." Further drawing on Castells, Moghadam (2005, 81) adds that new information technologies like the Internet have strengthened the capacity of networks to perform tasks previously carried out by more centralized organizations and facilitated new transnational connections "among political actors across borders."

These dynamic networks radically destabilize the local and global as always already counterpoised and distinct sites; instead, they point to the ways that such networks produce flows of ideas, information, and relations that open up and make less certain the boundaries of the local and global. In this sense these networks can also undermine the power imbalances between elites who come to staff or represent global feminist organizations and those working on the ground, who receive no personal recognition or remuneration (Alvarez 1999, 2009; Desai 2005). Later in the chapter I discuss some of the tensions within the campaign, tensions that even the campaign's loose network structure and commitment to horizontalism could not completely smooth over. Networked activisms aspire to challenge power and hierarchy but are never completely outside of it.

These networked projects both reflect and produce particular kinds of meanings (Castells 2015) of Iranian democracy—in particular, the ways in which activists have aspired to democratic participation in their society, and democratic relations in social and political life. Activists in the campaign not only made clear the necessity of legal structures to "catch up" to the positive shifts in social and cultural practices around gender equality but also strove to build relationships of equality with each other. The One Million Signatures Campaign was one of several feminist projects that emerged in the postreform period, and it shaped some of the particular forms of feminist organizing that came after it. Mahboubeh Abbasgholizadeh (2014, 833), the longtime feminist activist profiled in chapter 4 and founder of ZananTV, an Internet-based television station broadcasting short videos about Iranian women's issues, has argued the following:

> Each of these sites represents a cohort of social networks and differs greatly from a typical online newspaper or magazine. While these websites do contain various news reports and articles, an editor or an editorial board does not manage them. Their contributions come from citizen journalists, advocates, and theoreticians. The operators of these sites consider them to be alternative media, and any member of their audience can participate. One may contribute to the publication by sending an e-mail to the site's administrator requesting permission to publish on a particular topic, and one may join one of the campaign debates through the same action. Once a member becomes a regular contributor, he or she will be put on a mailing list, which constitutes the social network represented by that site.

This explication of activism and social networking illustrates the ways in which new media technologies have enabled groundbreaking political cultures to coalesce and vice versa. More than simply method or platform, these feminist new media activist sites both reflect and produce a participatory political ethos that aspires to collectivity without sacrificing individual participation and autonomy.

This participatory ethos itself is not novel; it builds on several decades of what Asef Bayat (2013, 288) has identified as "a broader process of *individuation* that Iranian society has been undergoing in the thirty years since the 1979 revolution." Bayat (2007, 2013) is particularly attentive to the ways in which the women's movements of the reform and postreform periods in Iran have been central to the reconfiguration of political life in the Middle East. In particular, he argues that ordinary activists and citizens have become weary and wary of revolutionary politics, opting instead for more pragmatic reforms and engagements with the state. In part, this pragmatism is reflected in his "post-Islamist" thrust of merging religion and rights, collective ideals and needs with individual freedoms and aspirations.

In my conversations with Leyla, Maryam, Vashti, Pardis, Fakhri, Mitra, Sahar, and Zahra, they each variously spoke to this pragmatic, reformist discourse around Islam and a democratic, anti-ideological practice. As Maryam explained:

> To make [Islam] compatible with contemporary, worldly, universal values, it's a radical move from a very ideological Islamist system. So that's why it's hard to really define the campaign in a conventional, you know, division of schools of feminist discourses, political discourses that we are

> usually exposed to. That's why maybe what is more applicable here is that it's a pragmatic approach, and it's a demand oriented movement, which is a kind of translation of *motalebe-mehvar. Motalebe* means demand, *mehvar*, centered. It's around certain demands, which makes it more inclusive, because whoever wants these demands, shares these demands, then are part of this campaign. Make it more inclusive, but also more, therefore more flexible.[16]

This pragmatist approach has been criticized by parts of the Iranian diaspora whose secularism takes the form of rigid anti-Islam politics.

Maryam spoke at length about how the pragmatism of the campaign reflected "the predominant trend now" in Iran. She claimed that "society has moved beyond sectarianism, beyond Islamism," and that the Green Movement reflected a "post-Islamist" trend in politics.[17] This post-Islamist trend is precisely what defined the campaign's discourses, methods, and practices, and explains, in part, the resonance of the campaign in Iran. Maryam explicates this post-Islamism: "It doesn't mean that people have left their religion behind. . . . But there has been now this official Islam and people's Islam, or ordinary Islam. . . . They want to make life easier for themselves, rather than following all these strict rules and prohibitions that the government imposes on them. So society in general has become very pragmatic."[18] The desire for individual freedoms within a larger collective, and the recuperation of religion by everyday citizens, speaks to the slow burn and long haul approach to reform. "They want feasible solutions and they're not revolutionary. They are not after utopia anymore. They want to make life easier. So it is not like 1979," says Maryam. Active in the 1979 revolution, she offered a particular lens on the current moment:

> Our generation were [*sic*] very idealistic. We were of course either Marxists. Some Maoists, some Islamists, some for Shariati, some for Khomeini. But these [Green Movement activists], as you can see, there is no single charismatic leader for the movement that people say, "I'm ready to die for you," like the way that they were ready to die for Khomeini. Which is good, it's promising and extremely hopeful. So I think that the campaign and the women's movement in general is actually a very good example of the exemplary component of the general trend that is out there.[19]

Maryam came to the United States in 1975 to pursue graduate school. During the revolution she returned to Iran and stayed for a year. "I was very excited, like many who lived during those days, to be part of the revolution." Returning to the United States to complete her studies after a year in Iran, Maryam had hoped to go back to Iran to teach. "But then everything started getting really repressive and ideologically exclusionary. . . . When my [Iranian] passport expired, I tried to renew it and they wouldn't renew it, saying, 'You are active in antirevolutionary activism.' So I became kind of self-exiled."[20] As Maryam explained, her self-exile was not because she didn't support the revolution. Active in the student movement against the Shah's dictatorship, she believed in the struggle for greater democracy in Iran, once again under threat from the new postrevolutionary government.

A seasoned activist over many decades, Maryam connected the ideological purity of the postrevolutionary regime to the sidelining of women's issues. She told me: "We have always been told that this is not the right time."[21] Her critique of revolutionary idealisms, male-centered movements, sectarianism, and patriarchal nationalisms resonated with Noushin Khorasani's calls for nonviolence and cemented a bond to other campaign activists as they sought to build a decentralized and demand-centered movement that aspired to include everyone yet center around no one. Zahra explained that in many movements "the direction of the leadership changes, and members no longer agree. And so conflicts often led to the downfall of an organization. The campaign felt like the goals were so much bigger than the people, so much bigger than ideologies of individuals."[22] While feminist movements are not immune to ideological sectarianism, the activists profiled here self-consciously rejected exclusionary and hierarchical political practices and organizational cultures, understanding that women and other marginalized groups were historic losers in such politics as normal.

Castell (2015, 258) has referred to networked social movements, enabled by new media, as sharing "a specific culture, the culture of autonomy." As individuals and collectives, autonomous political actors "creat[e] new forms of conviviality by searching for a new social contract." While Castell (2015, 259) often strikes an overly optimistic tone about the Internet as a "culture of freedom," his theorization of autonomous networks through and alongside of cyberspace is useful in elucidating the strategies and ethos of the signatures campaign. The signatures campaign was more directly in conversation with the state than some of the projects to follow and ultimately hoped to translate their campaign into reformed state policy. However, there was an emphasis on "the values and interests of the social actor" (Castell 2015, 259) as a political subjectivity capable of making and refracting meaning within her society. Such meanings are not set a priori but produced in the cultures and networks of social movement activists as they shape and intersect with their own historical contexts.

The divestment from ideological battles and the move toward individuation or autonomy also resonates with Michael Hardt and Antonio Negri's (2004, 99) conception of plural singularities. "The plural singularities of the multitude . . . stand in contrast to the undifferentiated unity of the people." Foregrounding the ways in which narrow formulations of class exclude a multiplicity of political actors, their multitude reconfigures a social and political ontology of individual/collective or "plural singularities." While "multitude" has a number of limitations for my purposes, the conceptual framework of plural singularities is useful for explicating how Iranian women's rights activists, as individuals within flexible and dynamic networks, "make and remake the common [they] share every day" (Hardt and Negri 2004, 128). Like Castells, Hardt and Negri speak implicitly to the ways in which particular social locations and identity formations—broader than class—are animating and redefining struggles for democracy.

The women's rights discourses and practices considered here and throughout the book reflect a collective autonomy within networked social movements and platforms. They emblematize the "coterminous" nature of politics and culture (Semati 2008), and "life as politics" (Bayat 2007, 2013), or the ways in which everyday life, social practices, and shifting popular sensibilities constitute political life. They cannot be understood simply as failures if they don't scale up to produce larger structural changes in the state but must be examined for the work they do in reflecting and producing transformations in attitudes, practices, and sensibilities around gender, feminism, and equality. The activists I interviewed highly valued the ability to maintain their individual autonomy, while still belonging to a larger networked collectivity. They also negotiated their translocal "situatedness" working inside the heart of empire.

NEGOTIATING LOCATIONS: EMPIRE

In terms of amplifying and supporting the campaign in Iran, the United States–based Iranian activists I interviewed stressed again and again that they would not do anything to jeopardize the safety of those in Iran. The hardliners' control of the state since 2004, the failures of Mohammad Khatami's reform era, and the rhetorical war on Iran waged by the Bush administration bolstered the Iranian state's security apparatus, leaving activists vulnerable to harassment, imprisonment, torture, and even death. These actions were rationalized by the state, as labor, student, and feminist activists, including many from the campaign, were accused of endangering national security. The state's tactics became more intense and violent after the emergence of the Green Movement in the wake of the 2009 presidential elections.

The particular strategic, methodological, and discursive negotiations of Iranian diasporic activists of the campaign network around issues of location and security point to the kinds of effective practices and affective bonds constituted by and through this innovative movement. The campaign network prioritized the safety and security of those most affected by transnational political decisions and actions—those inside Iran. This set of practices stands in stark contrast to some of the modes of "solidarity" activism practiced by activists in the United States and other parts of the West—from international human rights interventions to identifications with putative anti-imperialist leaders from the Global South (the enemy of my enemy is my friend)—which ultimately intensify the vulnerability of the very political actors these interventions claim to be in solidarity with.[23]

Campaign activists had the burden of educating Western feminists about these particular sets of dilemmas and restraints, as the campaign began getting recognition and awards from Western feminists. In 2009 it received the Global Women's Rights Award from the Feminist Majority Foundation and an award from *Glamour* magazine; it was also the recipient of the European Simone de Beauvoir Award for Women's Freedom. Transnational support and recognition drew much-needed attention to the work of the activists in Iran, amplifying their work for a larger audience, something most, if not all, campaigners would certainly desire. But this recognition also created a whole set of new dilemmas and tensions for the campaigners and affected their relationships with one another. On the one hand, the attention garnered more transnational recognition for the campaign, which proudly and publicly displayed the awards on their website. On the other hand, it made it easier for the Iranian state to target activists inside Iran. Many activists I spoke with expressed deep ambivalence about accepting an award from the Feminist Majority Foundation, given their support of the invasion of Afghanistan as a means of "liberating" Afghan women.

To complicate matters further, the awards were not just congratulatory; they came with money, which the campaign ultimately decided to refuse after many days of debate and discussion, in order to protect the activists inside Iran and immunize the campaign against internal divisions. Many of my interviewees reported that the awards and their prize monies created a set of tensions within the campaign around who should be the one to accept the awards on behalf of the campaign, given its horizontal nature, and whether to accept the monies. As a good number of the activists told me, the campaigners in Iran and the diaspora spent many painstaking hours and days in online and offline conversations, discussing and debating the issues that emerged as each award was conferred. Deeply committed to retaining the campaign's horizontal structure, activists were confronted with difficult decisions about who would represent the campaign when receiving awards. Campaigners came up with a strategy to ask those granting awards to bestow them on the campaign as a whole and not individuals, but even this didn't resolve dilemmas that had taken root.[24] Maryam outlined some of these dilemmas:

> That's why we are trying to say, instead of giving the prizes to an individual, give it to the whole campaign. But then when you want to give it to the whole campaign, then the question is, who is going to accept the prize, who's going to be in the forefront, right? That usually happens to be the people who are centered in Tehran, who know some language, who are more or better connected to the Western sources, right? And they're the ones who can travel easily. That also itself creates resentment in the provinces for those who have a harder time, and paying higher prices with their own lives, time, money, getting imprisoned, all that. But [they are not] the ones who are getting the recognition and advantages of it.[25]

While committed to horizontalism and democratic practice, the very real differences in class, education, transnational connections, and mobility among campaigners could not ultimately be transcended, and the awards brought to the surface and even exacerbated these differences.

Perhaps the biggest dilemma campaigners faced was how to handle the prize money that came with the awards. These decisions and dilemmas were indeed terrible, produced by the larger structuring mechanisms of war, imperialism, and the long history of US encroachment on Iran. As the United States engaged and continues to engage war by other means (through containment, isolation, and sanctions), the Iranian state has pushed back through a discourse of anti-imperialism and a practice of internal repression. All activists, including the campaigners, were caught in this fraught triangulation, as any opposition or challenge to the state was labeled as Western-backed. In addition, many NGOs in Iran are indeed funded by US and other Western monies, creating a minefield for activists inside Iran who work against both Western encroachment and state repression. By rejecting outside monies, they tried to protect themselves from the possibility of heightened targeting by the Iranian state as well as fulfill their commitment to bottom-up organizing practices.

Against this geopolitical backdrop, campaigners had to fight for the space to articulate their own anti-imperialist and decolonial feminist politics, which neither apologized for the repression of the Islamic Republic of Iran nor supported US intervention. Their political commitments to democratic practice were constantly tested, as transnational recognition threatened to impose unnecessary divisions among activists. Indeed, the very activist labor—all the affective, strategic, and political work that goes into enacting such solidarity politics and that can never be fully quantified—was intensified, as campaigners worked against internal divisions created by outside pressures. Increased international visibility, especially attention from Western feminists, led to heightened targeting of individual activists by the Iranian state, while exacerbating tensions among the activists themselves, undermining their efforts at resisting internal hierarchies and power differentials. Activists responded with even more internal self-reflection about why the campaign was receiving so much more attention than projects undertaken by other grassroots groups. They pointed out that this was the result of the ignorance of even well-intentioned Western feminists with regard to the local politics within which their current "favorite groups" were embedded. While campaign members certainly wanted international support and recognition, they desired this on their own terms. Khorasani's (2009, 80) account of working transnationally illustrates this problem: "International organizations, unfortunately, tend to focus on sensational cases at the expense of real civic work that addresses the institutional and legal roots of the problems of women's intensely precarious position in Iranian society. These organizations are ill equipped to grasp the intricacies of Third World societies, especially Muslim ones, and consequently encourage a 'victim' mentality while at the same time risking counterproductive confrontations with governments and jeopardizing the work that local women's movements are trying to do."

Khorasani echoes other campaign members' implicit critique of many transnational organizations and relations, which enact "support" and "solidarity" in ways that reproduce the kinds of social differentiation and hierarchies of coloniality. For decades, feminist scholarship has drawn attention to the deep imbrication between some forms of feminism and militarized humanitarianism as well as the proliferation of bureaucratic and top-down feminist organizations, which reproduce the colonial "victimhood" status of Global South and Muslim women. As it circulates globally, feminism often becomes an alibi for military intervention "on behalf" of women's rights, reproducing the colonial racialization of Muslim Others.[26] Given these troubling intersections between war, coloniality, imperialism, and feminism, transnational feminism has necessarily devoted much of its theoretical labor to a critique of these conditions.

However, the possibilities for transnational affiliation and coalition are often obscured by a kind of single-minded critique of what might be called feminist governmentality—the imbrication and intensification of hegemonic forms of feminism within circuits of war, colonialism, and neoliberalism—a mode of politics now globally hegemonic. While this governmentality is deeply troubling, I am concerned that such an intensive focus *only* on the perils of transnational feminist engagement can produce the unintended and quite undesired effect of silencing vibrant local, translocal, and transnational movements as they are unfolding, and the ways in which they are at least trying to decolonize feminist practices.

Given the escalation of all the crises that transnational feminism originally responded to, it is all the more imperative to maintain the possibility for transnational feminist solidarity, as difficult as it is to come by. Understanding transnational feminism only as critique, and silencing its epistemological, political, and affective possibilities, significantly pares down what transnational feminism has to offer in terms of an analysis of and guidepost for solidarity activism. As the campaign activists carved out a space for their political affiliations, strategies, and commitments, they interrupted the dangerous triangulations that constantly threatened to entrap and silence their project. Through the translocal and transnational political affiliations between activists in Iran and an engaged diaspora with active ties to Iran, the campaign offered a deeply powerful alternative to some of the bureaucratized and stratified organizational structures found in many feminist NGOs. In addition, because the network was made up primarily of Iranians in Iran and those in the diaspora with strong connections to Iran, the campaign network avoided at least some of the tensions, hierarchies, and divisions that befall global NGOs. The campaign network challenged the discourses and practices of colonial and imperialist feminism by foregrounding the agency and activism of Iranian women themselves and offered a deep challenge to feminist governmentality, even if it could not completely escape its trappings.

PROVINCIALIZING WESTERN FEMINISM

The campaign activists articulated a desire for a conception of feminist solidarity that acknowledges the cross-cultural construction of ideas and practices, as Mitra asserted: "When activists from different countries sit and talk with each other, it's a huge vote for both sides. Because I've seen a lot of problems for women in Iran. . . . But now I see a lot of problems that are very specific to women in America."[27] Working against the "moral superiority" of American discourse, which authorizes Western feminism as the benefactor of "oppressed" women around the globe (Grewal 2005), the campaigners instead pushed for relations of mutuality that acknowledge shared oppressions. As Mitra suggested, opportunities for new concepts of justice created through relations of solidarity, which might actually address transnational geopolitical power, were foreclosed through this discourse of moral superiority:

> Like this Feminist Majority Fund. We got the award last year [early 2009], so we got to talk to a lot of activists who were primarily working on Afghanistan and that whole mentality was kind of bothering me, like why do you think you know better than them? I wish you knew, because then you would fix it! But the fact that it is ten years and you are doing the same thing and it's not working the way it should be after all of this money and time and this passion you have. I wish there was [*sic*] conversations between you and Afghan women about what is the solution.[28]

Indeed, the Feminist Majority Fund received widespread criticism from many feminist activists and scholars for reproducing Orientalist and colonialist discourses in their campaign to "liberate" Afghan women from the Taliban and aligning themselves with the US invasion of Afghanistan in 2001.

Instead of depending on colonial binaries of oppression and liberation, campaign activists mobilized recognition of shared contexts of struggle that challenged, rather than reproduced, power differentials between activists in different locations. They articulated how Western societies are also patriarchal and argued that through relations of mutuality and dialogue, new practices of feminism might be built by individuals working together. In this formulation Western women are not "helping" Afghan or Iranian women but struggling with them around shared political agendas. Moreover, they claimed, expertise about what is needed in specific local contexts must come from the very actors in those contexts, not imposed or transplanted. Indeed, as Mitra suggested, Western feminism is in fact a local phenomenon (im)posing (itself) as universal/transnational, and the transnational concomitantly becomes the space for reinforcing the particular (masquerading as universal) subjectivity of Western feminists.[29]

Campaign members repeatedly stressed that they wanted support from and alliances with Western feminists, but not at the cost of surrendering their own agency, subjectivity, and specific knowledges. Working against the colonizing nature of Western feminism, the activists laid bare the subtle and overt mechanisms of power inhering in their engagements with feminists from the West. As Chandra Mohanty (1991, 53) has argued, colonization might signal different modes (economic, political, or cultural), but it "almost invariably implies a relation of structural domination, and a suppression—often violent—of the heterogeneity of the subject(s) in question." By crafting their own epistemic authority through the construction of a simplified, universal, and homogeneous woman, Western feminist groups like the Feminist Majority Fund enforce and reproduce the operational dynamics of colonization.

The campaign activists undermined such violent maneuvers by asking Western feminists they encountered—for instance, at activist gatherings in Southern California or when given awards at national gatherings—to reflect on the sexism within their own cultures and to refrain from approaching transnational feminist alliances as if they (the Western feminists) were the feminist heroines rescuing non-Western women (Abu-Lughod 2013). Indeed, as Grewal and Kaplan (1994, 18) have argued, this subject-object relation of power must be replaced by relations of solidarity in which feminists in different locations can form affiliations across shared understandings of power: "Feminist movements must be open to rethinking and self-reflexivity as an ongoing process if we are to avoid creating new orthodoxies that are exclusionary and reifying. The issue of who counts as a feminist is much less important than creating coalitions based on the practices that different women use in various locations to counter the scattered hegemonies that affect their lives."

As many of the campaign activists asserted, they desired coalitions built on the principles of self-reflexivity, mutuality, and cross-cultural notions of justice. They felt they had particular kinds of experience and knowledge that could enrich feminist understandings of power and oppression, as Pardis articulated:

> I think what drove me to call myself a feminist, and I told you, I think I've always been a feminist, but what drove me to call myself a feminist is sexism in America. It's always easier to, I mean I lived in Iran and sexism exists everywhere in society, culture, in our own beliefs. But you get to navigate those things, and you also separate yourself and you say, this is them, and they're stupid and I'm not going to do that. . . . But then when I came to America, I mean America projects this idealized, cool, you know, image outside. So I expected America to be much cooler than it is. I'm not saying it's not cool. I love America, I love the freedoms, and in some aspects, it's very cool. But I didn't expect there to be as much sexism and I didn't expect people to accept it so easily.[30]

Pardis eloquently maps out how "feminism" often appears to travel only in one direction, from the West to "the rest." She and the other activists challenged the binaries of "core/periphery" or "West/rest" that structure hegemonic discourses of colonialism and Western feminism. As Iranians growing up in Iran but with some adult experience in the United States, many interviewees spoke of the sexism of US culture, in particular the exploitative focus on women's bodies and everyday discourses. As Mitra said, "I can see [sexism] in my relationship with my boyfriend. When I moved to the U.S., I felt the whole conversation about my body type, what I wear, how I look, got way more important. . . . I was all of a sudden a beauty object. So I'm not going to say that one culture is better than the other."[31]

As transnational activists with particular experiences and knowledges, and situated in multiple locations, the campaigners created a "comparative, relational feminist praxis" (Alexander and Mohanty 1997, xx) that works to decolonize feminism by decentering Western feminism as pedagogically superior and Western women as inherently liberated. Their observations about American sexism challenged the notion that American women are implicitly rights-bearing, revealing the ways in which American culture *needs* feminism. In addition, they worked to historicize their contexts of struggle, challenging the incredible misinformation about Iranian women, as implied by my conversation with Pardis.

> The first thing I have to do when I speak with Americans, I have to bring them back to what reality is in Iran. Because people usually think that it's worse than it actually is. So I've had a lot of conversations where people think that all women, you know, have circumcision in Iran, or women can't go to school, like education is much worse than it is. So I always have to

> put it in context and say, listen, . . . the first woman who became a surgeon in Iran was from the generation of my grandmother. But then that same woman right now who can be operating on your eye could be an eye surgeon and cutting you up, her testimony is considered half of a man's.[32]

In grounding her discourses in historical nuance and complexity, Pardis, like other campaigners, worked against a static and ahistoric notion of women's lives in Iran. She articulated the complex status of women's lives in Iran—the high levels of education and engagement in social and professional life on the one hand, and persistent legal discrimination on the other. Moreover, she recognized women's contradictory status in the United States as well, making a connection between Iranian and American women along the necessity for each to struggle for change in their societies:

> So there are all these contradictions, and there are contradictions in America as well. You see that here too, but it's just more invisible when you're part of it. You don't see it as so shocking, so weird. But you do see it in other cultures, so I have to say that. . . . I thought always that the best way to talk about women's rights in Iran is to talk about women's rights activists. Because it shows strength and it acknowledges that there are problems, but women aren't just sitting there for you to go save them, for us to go save them.[33]

The campaign's strategy for bringing the relatively high status of women in Iranian culture to bear on the formal legal structure unsettles the prevailing notion that Iranian culture is inherently oppressive to women. The campaigners I interviewed further destabilized this idea and also deepened the principles of decolonial feminist praxis by challenging Western feminism to unpack its own assumptions and workings of power. Still, campaigners' agency and subjectivity, and the particular knowledge they bring to transnational feminist praxis, were often overlooked as they negotiated cross-cultural spaces within circuits of transnational feminist governmentality. "I tremendously [*sic*] learned a lot from [American] culture. I feel I'd like to share the things that are missing here and I had at home, but there is no opportunity for that," said Mitra. "It's like what we have here is the best. It's just unfortunate. I'm not angry, I just feel sorry. Where is this coming from?"[34] Mitra's declaration that she was not angry should not detract from what she experienced—a foreclosure of the particular knowledge she accumulated through different locations of struggle. This mode of epistemic silencing works to incorporate non-Western feminists only insofar as they are objects of Western feminist projects. What the campaigners spoke to was the sense in which their own feminist subjectivities were erased through collaborations with Western feminists.

Pardis echoed this frustration, pointing to alternative practices of connection and solidarity:

> You know when you speak to American feminists, and I know they've been trying very hard to get over that, some of the attitudes, but *you always have to remind them that we're working on something together.* You're giving us an award, and *we're giving you the opportunity to look at this amazing thing, ingenious thing, that they did in Iran and learn from it and try and do it in your own country.* You know, I think, I've genuinely felt like some of the things that the campaign has done are things that people should adopt in other parts of the world, and not just the Middle East. I'm talking about America and European countries.[35]

Challenging the "originary status of Western feminism" (Alexander and Mohanty 1997, xx), the campaign activists sought to have their particular experiences and knowledges inform and shape feminist politics writ large. By enacting their own agency and subjectivity through discourses of decolonization and solidarity, the campaigners downsized Western feminism from its universal status to its situated particulars. By positioning themselves in relations of mutuality and exchange *with*, instead of as objects *of*, Western feminism, the campaigners articulated their own histories of struggle and the particular methods that emerge in their contexts as the basis for solidarity with other feminists.

In their work to build support for the campaign, the activists in Southern California constructed notions of feminist solidarity around women's shared experiences of sexism, recognizing that sexism operates differently in different contexts. Radically interrupting the colonial discourses of rescue and saving, the campaign activists pointed to the ways that the campaign's network, like other transnational networks originating in the Global South, had much to offer the global women's movement. While US and other Western feminists weren't always listening, campaign activists continued to push back against epistemic and political silencing. The long, laborious project of decolonial feminist solidarity is indeed difficult to realize. OMSC activists insisted on its potential and possibility, nonetheless.

SANCTIONS, SCREENS, AND FURTHER SOLIDARITIES

In further explicating the complex local, transnational, and translocal contexts that confronted activists, I offer two vignettes. First, Fakhri elatedly described the scene on the ground during the summer of protests that followed the June 2009 presidential elections:

> I was talking to one of the guys in Iran and he said one of the beautiful things he saw was a middle-aged woman talking to a *basiji* [paramilitary civilian police member]. She would say, "*Pesaram* [my son], why would you do this? I know you have to do your job, but don't beat [the protesters] so hard." He said he didn't know what the woman then said to the *basiji*, but the *basiji* kissed her hand. All the time I see these women standing and talking to the military people, talking to the *basijis*, trying in a very sophisticated, peaceful way to say, We're the ones who are going to live together. You are like my son.[36]

In the second snapshot, in January 2012, Asghar Farhadi, director of the critically acclaimed Iranian film *A Separation*, comes to the stage to accept the Golden Globe for Best Foreign Film. In a hushed tone, Farhadi (2012) says: "When I was coming up on the stage, I was thinking what should I say here. Should I say something about my mother, father, my kind wife, my daughters, my dear friends, my great and lovely crew. But now I just prefer to say something about my people. I think they are a truly peace-loving people. Thank you very much." As Iranian family, friends, and fellow activists madly posted to Facebook in the next hours and days, we all felt an overwhelming sense of hope that just maybe that the US government would lift the sanctions and cease its war talk. Farhadi also won the Oscar that year and made a similar speech, dedicating his award to the people of Iran, who "respect all cultures and civilisations and despise hostility and resentment."

In 2017, Farhadi won another Oscar, this time for his film *The Salesman*.[37] He boycotted the awards ceremony in response to Donald Trump's Muslim ban. Anousheh Ansar, an Iranian American businesswoman, delivered his speech:

> I'm sorry I'm not with you tonight. My absence is out of respect for the people in my country and those of [the] other six nations whom have been disrespected by the inhumane law that bans entry of immigrants

> to the U.S. Dividing the world into the "us" and "our enemies" categories creates fear, a deceitful justification for aggression and war. These wars prevent democracy and human rights in countries which have themselves been victims of aggression. Filmmakers can turn their cameras to capture shared human qualities and break stereotypes of various nationalities and religions. They create empathy between "us" and "others," an empathy which we need today more than ever. (Farhadi 2017)

In presenting these two snapshots, I do not mean to instantiate a simple opposition between Iranian rulers and the Iranian people, a move often made by the neo-Orientalists to legitimize Western intervention in Iran. As the last three presidential elections in Iran have revealed, there are and have always been different fissures and factions within the postrevolutionary state, and not just along conservative and reformist lines but differences within both camps. The last three presidential elections in the United States have shown US policies toward Iran of isolation, war talk, and sanctions cut across party lines. Sanctions against Iran are not new. Since 1979, Iran has suffered from some type of economic sanctions. When Barack Obama took office, "the sanctions [were] amped up to new heights," according to the Raha Iranian Feminist Collective (2011).[38] "In June of 2010," a report from the collective asserted, "a US-led United Nations coalition passed the fourth round of economic and trade sanctions against the Islamic Republic since 2006. The stated goal: limiting Iran's nuclear program. Soon after, the European Union imposed its own set of economic sanctions. A month later, President Obama signed into law the most extensive sanctions regime Iran has ever seen with the Comprehensive Iran Sanctions Accountability and Divestment Act of 2010 (CISADA)."

As David E. Sanger and William J. Broad reported in the *New York Times*, a November 2011 report by the International Atomic Energy Agency represented "the strongest judgment the agency has issued in their decade-long struggle to pierce the secrecy surrounding the Iranian program" (Sanger and Broad 2011.) Mark Landler, also reporting for the *New York Times*, wrote that the IAEA report set off a new round of sanctions from the United States and the EU. These sanctions targeted Iran's central bank and its commercial banks. The United States "also imposed sanctions on companies involved in Iran's nuclear industry, as well as on its petrochemical and oil industries," as a way of strengthening "existing measures that seek to weaken the Iranian government by depriving it of its ability to refine gasoline or invest in its petroleum industry" (Landler 2011). In response,

Iran threatened to block the Straight of Hormuz and stop oil exports to Britain and France. In January 2012 an Iranian nuclear scientist was killed by an explosive device attached to his car. Iran blamed Israel and the United States. When bombs exploded in February in the country of Georgia, and in India and Thailand, Israel blamed Iran and intimated at a military strike.

If Iranians had hoped in 2009 that Obama was with them, they experienced instead something they had not anticipated. Taking US-Iran tensions to an intensified level, Obama and his hawkish secretary of state, Hillary Clinton, pursued war by other means. New sanctions from the Trump administration are aimed at choking Iran's economy and toppling the regime. Sanctions are not a diplomatic alternative to war; they are part and parcel of the colonial and imperialist drives toward hegemony and war. Some parts of the US and transnational activist community still believe that targeted sanctions are a humane substitute for war, that they are a component of human rights discourses that target the Iranian state for its human rights abuses. In calling for and supporting sanctions, these human rights activists believe they are enacting solidarity with the Iranian people. Some of these activists will align with conservative and far-right bedfellows and ultimately come to rationalize or outright support military intervention in Iran, arguing that it is the only means for shifting or ending the power of the current regime.

In response to Obama's sanctions program and increasing calls for military intervention during his first term, other solidarity activists defended Ahmadinejad and the Iranian regime, arguing that they represent the Iranian people's desire for peace and self-determination. Framing their argument as anti-imperialist, these activists believe that any opposition to the Iranian government inside Iran is backed by the US government, imposing regime change by orchestrating protest movements against the Islamic Republic. They didn't support the Green Movement, believing Ahmadinejad won the 2009 presidential elections fair and square, and generally look with suspicion on pro-democracy activities and discourses emerging from within Iran. They believed that by supporting Ahmadinejad and the regime, that the enemy of their enemy was their friend. As this book makes clear, these two positions represent an utter poverty of choices about how to build ethical and effective modes of solidarity.

From its most active period of 2006 to the post-2009 presidential elections, the One Million Signatures Campaign provided significant insight into how the new organizing modes emerging from Iranians and their diasporic counterparts connected through cyberculture enabled the creation of transnational and translocal political networks, thereby affecting how local political cultures coalesced—and vice versa. The various burdens and possibilities placed on diasporic Iranian feminist activists as they grappled with the importance of their location point to the immense difficulties of solidarity work. In considering how they navigated certain iterations of global feminism that left them vulnerable to accusations of being either "puppets" or "darlings" of the West, I have pointed to the very real triangulations that so often ensnare solidarity activists. However, the campaign successfully negotiated many of the dilemmas of working transnationally and translocally in an age of war, feminist governmentality, neocolonialism, and Islamophobia, indicating new possibilities for feminist solidarity. The campaign neither subsumed local politics to the demands of global paradigms nor reinscribed ideas about innate "cultural" differences.

The work of the campaign network also built a sense of collectivity organized around relations of decoloniality. Although the perils of transnational feminist solidarity have been well documented, not enough has been written about the ways in which activist work against tremendous odds can be, among other things, a deep engagement with and effort to build new kinds of social and political relationships. All too often, Iran has been framed as the space where change is impossible, both by parts of the Iranian diaspora, cynically removed from the complex everyday life of Iranians inside Iran (as pointed out by Leyla, Maryam, Fakhri, Pardis, Fakhri, Mitra, Sahar, and Zahra) and by members of both conservative and progressive sectors of the West who seek different kinds of dangerous interventions "on behalf of" the Iranian people.

In part, the successes of the campaign can be measured by how it animated those who joined with a sense of connection and possibility, built a transnational and translocal network that offered activists autonomy and collectivity, produced innovations in organizational structure and method, and generated world-making practices that weakened various kinds of borders and boundaries. With the Green Movement erupting in 2009, then the Arab Spring uprisings in 2010 and 2011, Occupy Wall Street in 2011, and the many global eruptions that have followed, there is no question that the One Million Signatures Campaign in a sense prefigured the networked structure and horizontal ethos of these movements. Perhaps these activist uprisings had followed and learned from Iranian women's rights activists. Perhaps they hadn't. Whether they had or hadn't, the project of Iranian women's rights activism in the twenty-first century unfolded in dynamic, complex, and ongoing ways, and contributed to the archive of knowledge about social justice movements in a highly mediated age. Iranian women's rights activists generated important discourses, strategies, ideas, spaces, practices, and organizational cultures that pointed toward a decolonial *for.* Among those activists is Shirin Ebadi, most widely known for her Nobel Peace Prize in 2003. In chapter 3, I return Ebadi from the individual Nobel Prize–winner frame back to the social contexts that produced and continue to shape her intellectual and activist frameworks, exploring the possible meanings of her life narratives for a decolonial feminist episteme.

CHAPTER 3

HUMAN RIGHTS WORK IS AN ACT OF WORSHIP

> Islam is a religion whose first sermon to the Prophet begins with the word "Recite!" The Koran swears by the pen and what it writes. Such a sermon and message cannot be in conflict with awareness, knowledge, wisdom, freedom of opinion and expression and cultural pluralism.
>
> —SHIRIN EBADI

> I have lost more than I ever thought possible, but I nevertheless thank God that even from exile I can still work to build my country. It is for the sake of Iran and its people, its potential and its greatness, that I have taken each and every step along this journey. And I know that one day Iranians will find their own path to the freedom and justice they deserve.
>
> —SHIRIN EBADI

IN 2003, THREE YEARS BEFORE THE ONE MILLION SIGNATURES Campaign (OMSC) began, Shirin Ebadi won the Nobel Prize for Peace. The day after delivering her Nobel lecture in Switzerland, Ebadi and her daughter boarded an Iran Air flight and returned to Tehran. As she recounts in her first memoir, the excitement on the plane was palpable. Flight attendants delivered Ebadi notes of congratulations from passengers, so many notes that Ebadi was finally compelled to walk through the plane and shake her admirers' hands. The captain announced over the loudspeaker that he was naming the trip Flight of Peace, and invited Ebadi and her daughter into the cockpit. As the plane landed, Ebadi looked out in amazement. "I could tell the crowd must number in the hundred of thousands. . . . The last time such a great human mass had descended on Tehran airport, the year was 1979 and the figure on board the flight from Paris was Ayatollah Khomeini."

Drawing this comparison, Ebadi marked a particular contrast. "Only this time, you could see from the mass of head scarves that women composed the majority of the crowd." A stunned Ebadi greeted her family. "'They walked here,' my brother whispered in my ear. 'They drove until the roads were jammed, left their cars, and walked. The flights have all been canceled because all the roads to the airport are blocked with people.'" Ayatollah Khomeini's granddaughter greeted Ebadi (2007, 205–207) as she descended from the plane, placing flowers around her neck. In connecting her own return to that of Khomeini's, Ebadi sketched two national heroes, two historic returns, and two figures inspiring national pride and international recognition. She did not disavow her past or the revolution. Rather, Ebadi implicitly called out its patriarchal biases and exclusions, narrating a present marked by women's determination to shape a nonviolent, antiwar, and feminist politics of the present.

The contrast between Khomeini's return to Iran and Ebadi's own—the striking image she drew of masses of people filing down the roads to the airport, the majority of them women, to greet their national hero—powerfully underscores the impetus for this book. The presence of women, not as a static and essentialized representation but as a political and epistemic force, must be considered through the discourses and practices of the social actors that make up this very presence. Like the OMSC activists, Ebadi is uncompromising in her insistence that achieving the undifferentiated legal equality of women is a thoroughly Iranian project, and that the fate of Iran lies in the hands of its people, a sovereign people with ties to the world at large. This chapter focuses on Ebadi as a Nobel Prize winner but also as an everyday activist, citizen, and political thinker to investigate how Iranian women's rights activists foreground the viability of democratization from within Iran, even under periods of intense state repression against activists. I examine Ebadi's autobiographical works and other writings, locating them within a decolonial feminist episteme that has been largely neglected in the theoretical examinations of Iranian resistance. I contend that although she is widely known, Ebadi has been undertheorized, in part because she has consistently articulated a nuanced critique of the coloniality of the United States and other Western powers alongside an engagement with and critique of the Iranian state. Her narratives do not fit with many other Iranian women's memoirs that cast Iran in more narrow and caricatured terms—that is, as an essentially permanent cage—and the United States as a site of unmitigated freedom, especially for Muslim and/or Global South women.

Instead, Ebadi attempts to make sense of Iranian politics and social life within a larger and more complex geopolitical frame and historical context. Her political analysis and her life work underscore a decolonial feminism marked by a politics and practice of nonviolence as well as a belief in an indigenously determined feminism that can stake out its own terms within transnational engagement. Ebadi, much like the OMSC activists, presents an alternative to the hegemonic framings of Islam and women's rights as mutually exclusive and irreconcilable frameworks, and she articulates a feminist politics that challenges the militarized and patriarchal nationalisms of both Iran and the United States. As a political thinker and activist, Ebadi draws her readers to the intertwined fates of the United States and Iran, developing an analysis of Iranian sovereignty that is not antagonistic to a peaceful relationship between Iran and the United States. She consistently gives voice to women's human rights as they emerge from within Iran, and Iranian feminism as part of a nonviolent and decolonial movement for democracy and self-determination.

I examine the meanings and circulations of Ebadi's Nobel Peace Prize win and provide a close reading of her two memoirs as well as a number of articles written by and about her. Ebadi's 2007 memoir, *Iran Awakening: One Woman's Journey to Reclaim Her Life and Country*, focuses primarily on her life as a human rights and feminist activist in the decades that follow the 1979 revolution. In paying considerable attention to Ebadi's insistence on staying in Iran and her critique of chosen exile, I bring into focus an indigenous women's rights effort that unsettled a number of troubling discourses. She challenges patriarchal Islam's claim to authenticity over and against the encroachment of a foreign (Western) feminism. She upends the logics of the "freedom flight" narrative so often central to the Iranian women's memoir genre, which constructs Iran as an ultimate space of capture and imprisonment, and the United States or other Western countries as naturalized sites of freedom. Ebadi was forcibly exiled after her human rights activism in the aftermath of the 2009 presidential elections. Yet her departure was coerced, and her 2007 memoir represents a significant alternative to those that focus on exile as the only chosen possibility for Iranian feminists.

Ebadi's 2015 memoir, *Until We Are Free: My Fight for Human Rights in Iran*, was written after her forced exile. Expending tremendous effort to stay in Iran after years of intense harassment, Ebadi strikes an understandably more critical tone toward the Iranian government, explicitly naming it a police state. Detailing the intimate conversations with and maneuvers by the security operatives who unrelentingly threatened and violated her, her family, and her colleagues, Ebadi poignantly reminds readers in this new memoir of the immense suffering and often tragic fate of countless numbers of Iranian citizens and activists during different prerevolutionary and postrevolutionary political periods. Whereas her first memoir is a testament to the possibilities of engaging the state along pragmatic possibilities for reform, Ebadi's second memoir is a testimonial of profound struggle and a harrowing tale of the cost of such struggle. It is a powerful indictment of the very government she for so long tried to reason with and win over.

In reading Ebadi through critical transnational and counterhegemonic feminist reading practices, I attempt to amplify what comes across so powerfully and often eloquently in her memoirs—that is, her very ordinariness as a citizen and activist. Given Ebadi's accomplishments and challenges, she is no doubt an extraordinary figure. Yet I want to humanize her and the immense, yet quotidian, labors of her activist life. Her memoirs-as-testimonies fold Muslim and Global South women's rights activists back into a history of decolonial world-making, a world-making so often attributed to "great" revolutionary men. In accentuating Ebadi's claim that the fulfillment of human rights requires an end to wars, and her critique of Western hegemony in its imperialist, Orientalist, and feminist forms, however, I do not wish to romanticize her as a perfect figure, inoculated against the contaminations of geopolitics. To be sure, her scathing critique of the Iranian government, particularly when made from her exiled status, makes her attractive to those who support the isolation of and/or Western intervention in Iran. But it is precisely her commitment to her beloved Iran, determined and shaped by her fellow citizens, that inspired her to "share [her] story on behalf of the many faceless Iranians, political prisoners and prisoners of conscience" (Ebadi 2015, 283). I wish to think with her about the importance of struggling against all militarized and patriarchal nationalisms as they play out on a complex global stage, a stage that often constrains our imaginations and our critiques.

WOMEN'S RIGHTS FROM THE HEART OF ISLAM

Ebadi's Nobel Peace Prize win ruptured the hegemonic storyline about Iran, particularly if read within the larger context of her life. The Nobel spotlight on her could function to produce new forms of (hyper)visibility and (mis) representation, potentially consolidating neocolonial and Orientalist discourses. For instance, on the one hand, Ebadi and Iranian women as a group could be understood as the "face" of the opposition, constructed as "good" (modern/women) citizens against "evil" (Islamist/male) states. On the other hand, if contextualized and returned from prizewinner to activist and citizen, Ebadi and her intensified visibility function to edify readers/viewers of the long history of Iranian women's political engagement and the centrality of women's rights activism to the reform movement.

Ebadi earned her law degree in 1969 from the University of Tehran and became Iran's first female judge. When the revolutionary government barred women from being judges, she was forced out of her job. In 1994 she helped establish an NGO, the Society for Protecting the Rights of Children, and litigated many high-profile cases involving human rights abuses. In 2000 she was arrested and jailed, along with lawyer Hojjatoleslam Mohsen Rahami, in connection with a case in which members of the establishment were alleged to have been involved in activities of the Partisans of the Party of God (Ansar-e Hezbollah), including the attempted murder of Hojjatoleslam Abdolla Nouri, former vice president and critic of the regime's conservative clerics (Monshipouri 2004, 5–6). Despite these particular challenges, Ebadi has remained a highly visible and outspoken activist for women's and children's human rights. She lent her support and notoriety to the OMSC and has maintained, despite her forced departure from Iran, an abiding, if heavily shaken, faith in the internal democratization process.

Ebadi's Nobel Prize was in part a culmination of her life's work as an activist for women's and children's rights and a Muslim feminist reformer. As a "driving force behind the reform of family laws in Iran by seeking changes in divorce and inheritance legislation" (*BBC World News* 2003), Ebadi and her win marking the achievement of Iranian feminists pushed the reform movement onto the world stage. Her work in reforming family law fits with what Ali Akbar Mahdi (2003) has called women's postrevolutionary activism. Skeptical of nationalist movements, which often sacrifice women's needs to the "greater good" of the patriarchal nation, feminist activists have focused on pragmatic social and political changes that can bring them more individual control and freedom—equal rights in divorce and child custody, for instance. In reflecting Mahdi's understanding of women's postrevolutionary activism, Ebadi's discourse also echoes the pragmatist reformist discourses of Islamicate feminisms and the OMSC. Seeking to make claims on the state and societal institutions, women's rights activists stress the harmonious relationship between individual rights and the collective good.

Ebadi capitalized on her award, using multiple opportunities to assert that Islam and human rights are compatible, to solicit support from the international community for the Iranian reform movement and to profile feminism within an Islamic framework. In her Nobel lecture, Ebadi (2003) asserted: "The discriminatory plight of women in Islamic states, too, whether in the sphere of civil law or in the realm of social, political and cultural justice, has its roots in the patriarchal and male-dominated culture prevailing in these societies, not in Islam. This culture does not tolerate freedom and democracy, just as it does not believe in the equal rights of men and women, and the liberation of women from male domination (fathers, husbands, brothers . . .), because it would threaten the historical and traditional position of the rulers and guardians of that culture."[1]

In disaggregating patriarchy from Islam, Ebadi distinguishes between patriarchal practices that serve to maintain male authority and control, and Islam, a discursive tradition that informs and accommodates principles of social justice. In a news report from the transnational feminist organization Women Living Under Muslim Laws (2003), Ebadi asserted: "My problem is not with Islam, it is with the culture of patriarchy. For twenty years I have been putting out the message that it is possible to be Muslim and have laws that respect human rights. Islam is not incompatible with human rights and all Muslims should be glad about this prize." Identifying patriarchy rather than Islam as the source of women's oppression, Ebadi disrupts the metonymic collapsing of Islam and patriarchy so prevalent in Islamophobic and Orientalist discourses. By pointing to a culture of patriarchy, she locates women's oppression within a structure that is neither inherent in, nor a product of, Islam.

Throughout her two memoirs Ebadi mobilizes religion as an ethical and legal resource, while arguing against the abuse of political power in the name of religion. She offers an alternative framework to the notion of the Iranian state as a static theocracy, incapable of changing because of some repressive apparatus inherent to Islam. In fact, Ebadi understands many of the poor legal outcomes for women in the courts as a product of the substandard religious education of legal jurists. Working on case after case, she "discovered that many judges in the Islamic Republic had little or no understanding of Islamic legal tenets" (Ebadi 2015, 7), tenets she insists should work in favor of women. In a passage from *Until We Are Free*, Ebadi (2015, 51) lamented her daughter's inferior legal training:

> When I had been a law student, in the 1960s, we had carefully studied key principles of Islamic sharia, despite the fact that the shah had instituted a secular criminal and civil code. After the revolution, one would have expected the universities to expand and enhance their teaching of sharia, since the new regime had replaced the shah's secular legal system with Islamic law. But Nargess was learning less than half of what I had learned about sharia principles in my own student days. Why was this the case? Essentially because the crafters of the Islamic Republic's education system did not want to teach students the subtleties of sharia law, philosophy, and tradition. Well-trained and erudite students would be equipped to argue for fresher and more modern angles and approaches to Islamic laws.

This lament captures the epistemological investment in Islamic law as a flexible and capacious instrument, an investment shared by many reformers and activists who sought to participate in a national debate about the meaning of sharia and persuade the state away from its narrow and often incorrect applications.

Implicit in Ebadi and other reformers' discourses is a critique of secularism and colonial modernity. Talal Asad (2003) has argued that the project of liberal secularism was to authorize itself as the rational counterpart to what it framed as the inherent fanaticism of religion. Asad critiques the notion that "secular arguments are rationally superior to religious ones . . . based on the belief that religious convictions are the more rigid." Like many of the religious reformers in Iran, Asad asserts the flexibility of religion to accommodate shifts in human understandings and strategies to make religion work for them. Assad reminds us that political extremists "come in all shapes and sizes among skeptics and believers alike—as do individuals of a tolerant disposition. As for the claim that among the religious, coercion replaces persuasive argument, it should not be forgotten that we owe the most terrible examples of coercion in modern times to secular totalitarian regimes—Nazism and Stalinism" (Asad 2003, 236). Feminists working in Islamicate contexts, like Ebadi, radically challenge the hegemony of secularism and disaggregate political repression from religion per se. In claiming Islam as the framework within which a just and egalitarian vision of gender can take root, Ebadi works against secular-liberal and Orientalist framings of Islam and Iran as inherently patriarchal.

Ebadi also echoes the strategies of those engaging *ijtehad*. "The legal keys that Shia religion has given us enable us to transform and act according to the times," she said (quoted in *Al Jazeera* 2003). Here Ebadi points to the interpretive tradition many women have been engaging with in Iran since the 1990s, both at the formal literary level and at the level of more informal everyday discourses. Paralleling key reform clerics who were part of this new wave, Ebadi makes a claim for human understanding of Islamic text to accommodate the present historical context in which it is read; she locates the alternative to patriarchal codifications of Islam within Islam itself. In a 2004 interview with Jacqueline Massey in *Herizons*, Ebadi argues against "erroneous interpretations of Islam" made by patriarchal authorities: "As an example, when we protest and say, 'Why should men be allowed to take four wives?' they say, 'Because this is the dictate of Islam.' So the answer would have to come out from the heart of Islam. And we should prove that Islam can be interpreted in another way." She positions her feminism from within the parameters of Islam, parameters set by the Islamization processes in the revolutionary and postrevolutionary periods. It is precisely these parameters that have enabled an alternative discourse, one that embraces women's equality, to emerge from the very "heart of Islam."

Iranians responded to Ebadi's Nobel Prize win with the hallmark enthusiasm that had heretofore marked other positive points of entry into the international spotlight for Iran.[2] Among the thousands of citizens who welcomed Ebadi on her return from Europe were relatives of then President Khatami and every female member of the Parliament. Beyond mere ceremonial formality, Ebadi's win, return, and reception, as Ziba Mir-Hosseini (2003) has argued, gave a much-needed boost to the reform movement in Iran. While certainly the Nobel Peace Prize functions strategically to call out repressive states by spotlighting exemplary individuals, Ebadi and other reformers recuperated the win to mark a collective indeed national process. Elaheh Koolaee (2003), a reformist MP at the time, claimed that Ebadi's win "shows the world that the democracy process in Iran is going forward."

Ordinary Iranians too sounded reformists' hopes while engaging in lively discussions about the meaning of Ebadi's win. Reflecting a desire for the international community to solidarize with Iran's internal struggle for democratization, Iranians pointed to Ebadi's social location as an Iranian, a Muslim, and a woman. In the popular Muslim online magazine *Muslim Wakeup!*, Omid Safi (2003) wrote: "This is huge. Is there a good way of talking about earthquakes and aftershocks? That might give you a sense of the impact of this award will have on the global Muslim community." Safi argued that Ebadi's award would affirm the majority of Muslims around the world "who simply want to live lives of quiet dignity." Pointing to the significance of Ebadi's social location as a "strong mother of two children, a judge, and an activist," Safi applauded how Ebadi breaks the "many stereotypes about being a Muslim and a woman, an Iranian and a woman . . . through the grace of her being." In a similar vein, *Payvand Iran News* reported that the crowd greeting Ebadi shouted such slogans as "Long Live Iranian Women, Long Live Shirin Ebadi" and "Dearest Ebadi, Hope of Iran" (Sayyah 2003).

When the Ayatollah Khomeini returned to Iran from his exile in France, an estimated five million people lined the streets of Tehran to greet him. In the Cemetery of Martyrs, twelve miles south of Tehran, Khomeini addressed 250,000 of his supporters, claiming, "From now on it is I who will name the government."[3] Once again bringing these two historic returns together, the parallels are outflanked by the difference that makes a difference. Ebadi and her supporters mobilized international attention to gesture toward the collective social sum of which she is but one part. Through her discursive responses to the award, Ebadi shot through other transnational discourses that stage Islam and feminism in opposition to each other, as mutually exclusive and antagonistic forces, and challenged her critics from within and outside Iran. Embedded in Ebadi's responses to her award, as well as those of Iranians inside Iran, was an implicit critique of the hegemony of secular-liberal notions of democracy and modern citizenship. It was an explicit call to the Iranian state to fully actualize the demands and desires of Iran's huge reform movement.

Ebadi further used her prize to challenge the justification of human rights abuses by the Iranian state vis-à-vis anti-imperialist discourses as well as the justification of human right abuses by Western powers, in this case the United States's actions at Guantanamo, in the name of "security."[4] By linking human rights abuses in two different but similarly repressive states, Ebadi critiqued human rights regimes that locate human rights violations within "religious cultures" yet are silent about such violations in putative liberal democracies. In challenging the civilizational discourses emerging in the post-9/11 period, and in holding both the Iranian state and the US government accountable, Ebadi drew out similarities between the repressive actions of Iran and the United States. In so doing, she carved out a discourse that is simultaneously antiwar, anti-interventionist, and critical of the Iranian state's internal repression. Ebadi resisted the poverty of choices put forward in response to US-Iran relations: one, a cultural relativist "anti-imperialist" politics (defending the Iranian state against the West), and the other, an interventionist politics ("protecting" the Iranian people from their government). Instead, throughout her lecture Ebadi (2003) mapped out an alternative politics, one that insists on transnational support for all "nations' right to determine their own destinies." This uncompromising politics of sovereignty, birthed through peaceful social movements, also runs throughout Ebadi's memoirs. Like Noushin Khorasani of the OMSC, Ebadi insists on prioritizing nonviolent, life-affirming movements for self-determination and democracy, embedded in a *longue durée* strategy of changing a highly militarized world order in which the United States and Iran are key players.

The Nobel award drew attention to Ebadi's lifelong work of reforming Iran from within an indigenous Iranian and Islamicate feminist framework. "In the last twenty-three years," she wrote in *Iran Awakening*, "from the day I was stripped of my judgeship to the years doing battle in the revolutionary courts of Tehran, I had repeated one refrain: an interpretation of Islam that is in harmony with equality and democracy is an authentic expression of faith." Shifting patriarchy from an essentialized religion to particular *political* leanings, Ebadi (2007, 204) argued that "it is not religion that binds women, but the selective dictates of those who wish them cloistered. That belief, along with the conviction that change in Iran must come peacefully and from within, has underpinned my work." Here, as in all of her writings, Ebadi insists on the necessity of change coming from within Iran as well as the legitimacy of mobilizing the social justice vision of Islam.

Pivoting on her win, Ebadi consistently holds accountable the conservative forces inside Iran that seek to discredit her but also, importantly, the secular fundamentalists outside Iran who position Islam in opposition to democracy. "I have been . . . threatened by those in Iran who denounce me as an apostate for daring to suggest that Islam can look forward and denounced outside my country by secular critics of the Islamic Republic, whose attitudes are no less dogmatic." What distinguishes Ebadi's 2007 memoir from other Iranian women's autobiographical narratives is her consistent and forceful denouncement of modes of politics and representation that secure Western secular-liberal hegemony. "Over the years, I have endured all manner of slights and attacks, been told that I must not appreciate or grasp the real spirit of democracy if I can claim in the same breath that freedom and human rights are not perforce in conflict with Islam," she wrote, calling out her detractors. "When I . . . heard my religion mentioned specifically alongside my work defending Iranians' rights, I knew at that moment what was being recognized: the belief in a positive interpretation of Islam, and the power of that belief to aid Iranians who aspire to peacefully transform their country" (Ebadi 2007, 204). Notably, when I spoke to OMSC activists, they commented that some diasporic Iranians criticized Ebadi for identifying herself as a Muslim first and an Iranian second.

Ebadi's emphasis on peaceful transformation from within captures a bottom-up, pragmatic, anti-imperialist politics that draws attention to and challenges Western hegemony over Iran. Her deep commitment to working for pragmatic feminist reform from within Iran enacts an important challenge to the regnant notion of Iran and the Iranian state as a priori resistant to change and as exceptionally repressive. The construction of Iran and the United States as exceptional states—one an intractable theocracy, the other the pinnacle of democracy—has remained relatively consistent through decades of different Iranian and US governments. While the West—the United States and Europe in particular—are places where Iranian citizens and activists have found themselves able to live and move about, temporarily or permanently, this is not a naturalized condition but one born of the politics of state violence. Iran is not alone in such violence, however. The sanctions regimes imposed by the past several US presidents have increased the economic and political hardship of Iranian citizens. Moreover, with Trump's Muslim ban, the ability of Iranians to move freely in (let alone enter) the United States ratchets up state violence to a new level. Frequently leaving this complexity aside, the genre of women's memoirs about Iran and/or the Muslim world often reinforces the dominant narrative of Iran/Islam as captivity and the United States/secularism as freedom. I read Ebadi against and along with this genre, arguing that she produces a critical counterhegemonic narrative of Iran by testifying to her own and other human rights work, work that calls us to a decolonial *for.*

IRAN/ISLAM AS PRISON

In her refusal to choose exile and flight from Iran, Ebadi works against the pervasive notion, produced by a host of Iranian women's memoirs, of Iran as a place always already foreclosing women's agency. The mere sketch of titles suggests that for Iranian women, living in Iran is equivalent to being held captive, imprisoned, with escape the only option: *Between Two Worlds: My Life and Captivity in Iran* (Saberi 2010); *Journey from the Land of No: A Girlhood Caught in Revolutionary Iran* (Hakakian 2004); *My Prison, My Home: One Woman's Story of Captivity in Iran* (Esfandiari 2009); *Even After All This Time: A Story of Love, Revolution, and Leaving Iran* (Latifi 2005); and *Prisoner of Tehran: A Memoir* (Nemat 2007). While the production of

Iran as captor is deeply troubling, what is equally problematic in these memoirs is the insistence of the West as the site of freedom, as the condition of freedom. The state of captivity is only resolved with leaving or fleeing for another (Western) society. This is evident in some of the titles above and also in memoirs whose titles constitute the West as the modern antidote to antimodern Iran, including the best known, *Reading Lolita in Tehran: A Memoir in Books* (Nafisi 2003). Although the memoirs themselves contain nuances and complexities, overall they often work to produce and secure representations of Iran as antithetical to freedom, and a space of containment and impossibility, and the West as the liberator.

Excellent scholarly work has critiqued many contemporary Iranian women's memoirs (Keshavarz 2007; Mahmood 2008; Rastegar 2006). Mitra Rastegar (2006) has analyzed the ways in which Azar Nafisi's critically acclaimed and hugely popular 2003 memoir, *Reading Lolita in Tehran*, reframes the Orientalist narrative "into one of promodern Iranians versus antimodern Iranians." She argues that the "representation of women as victims of state violence in Iran becomes a key component of asserting this binary," as Nafisi's putative modern women students seek out the "democratic ethos that she argues is implicit in the (Western) novel," while religious men seek to imprison them in a putative antimodern "mythical Islam" (Rastegar 2006, 108–9). As audiences in the West, for whom they were produced, read these memoirs in the post-9/11 climate, their suspicions about Iran and Iranian culture as an enormous prison for women are confirmed. Islam, staged as inherently patriarchal and inflexible, is the very imprisoning force in many of these interpretations.

The reception of Nafisi's memoir to critical acclaim and bestseller status in the West confirms the ease with which audiences outside of Iran consume such neo-Orientalist tales of antimodern Islam versus democratic West.[5] Indeed, Nafisi eloquently presents herself as an authority, facilitating the pleasure readers experience in her message. Both Nafisi's narrative and her reception by Western readers, Rastegar asserts, "legitimates the work as an 'authentic' and 'representative' view of postrevolutionary Iran. It is a story that rings true to the ears of its readers, posing few challenges to their preconceived notions and allowing them to maintain their flexible superiority as Westerners." While Nafisi tries to downplay her own authority, "her representation of *other* women and their interests and desires is read as 'authentic,' as is her account of the appropriate solutions" (Rastegar 2006, 111). Nafisi's text discursively sanctions widely circulating discourses about Iran, Islam, and women.

In the post-9/11 context memoirs like Nafisi's often reproduce the colonial narrative about Muslim societies as victimizers of women, but with a new lethality afforded by their "native" status. As Saba Mahmood has argued (2008, 84), the figure of the Muslim woman as both "insider and victim" is "a key subject within Orientalist understandings of women in Muslim societies." Unlike older Orientalist representations by Europeans, however, this time "it is the 'indigenous woman' herself who provides the ethnographic grist for this bloodied imagination, lending a voice of authenticity to the old narrative that a liberal ear, raised on a critique of colonial literature, can more easily hear and digest." Mahmood considers Nafisi's memoir alongside of Irshad Manji's *The Trouble with Islam: A Muslim's Call for Reform in Her Faith*, Carmen bin Laden's *Inside the Kingdom: My Life in Saudi Arabia*, and Ayaan Hirsi Ali's *The Caged Virgin: An Emancipation Proclamation for Women and Islam*, and other lesser known works by Muslim women. What is particularly troubling about this genre, Mahmood argues, is both the native informant status they take on as they circulate in this period but also the ways in which they present themselves and are received as representatives of feminist literature. As Mahmood (2008, 95) notes, Nafisi's book received warm praise from feminist writers, who appear "blind . . . to the larger political projects [such memoirs] facilitate."

The political projects to which Mahmood speaks aim to "reform" Islam, potentially through the eradication of Muslims, and secure Western hegemony—from occupation to war to secular-liberal discourses about Islam as static, irrational, antimodern, and inherently patriarchal to recruiting so-called good Muslims to surveil their own communities.[6] Mahmood (2008, 95) urges "feminist writers and cultural critics" to "learn to read such texts more critically, a reading that must ground itself in a familiarity with the complexities and ambiguities that attend even the much-spurned Iranian clerical regime and the politics of dissent it has spawned." Feminist writers, cultural critics, students, and everyday readers have devoured Nafisi. For several years her book was the sole explanatory referent to Iran for a whole range of people, familiar and not so familiar to me, who asked about my research.

The "intellectual exhaustion" (Mahmood 2008, 81) these encounters produce is overwhelming. Yet anyone engaged in producing knowledge about Iran or Islam must contend with such fraught terrain and work to detail and foreground the alternative narratives and activist projects of social actors who are crafting their own terms of social change. Through Ebadi's decolonial feminist voice, a different story emerges from Iran—a space providing the condition for feminist agency. Here I do not suggest Ebadi is a "more authentic" voice of Iranian women than Nafisi or anyone else. Amy Motlagh (2011) has persuasively argued that scholarly critiques of Iranian women's memoirs, which maintain that personal experience stands in for scholarly truth, often rest on the very tropes of authenticity and authority they are critiquing. As Motlagh reasons, exilic or diasporic Iranian scholars, in critiquing the memoir genre, unconsciously and consciously also mobilize personal experience, setting themselves up as more accurate interpreters of Iran. Instead of looking for the "real" Iran in Ebadi, I am interested in how she articulates the possibility of change from within Iran in ways that align with other reformist discourses. Her nuanced political analysis reflects a different political project than that of other transnational Iranian women memoirists who, in aggregate form, risk consolidating the narrative of Iran as a space of a priori and permanent impossibility.

Amy Malek (2006, 359–64) has argued compellingly that some Iranian women writers, in their desire to be career writers, have "veered" toward memoirs, given "the command of the market economy and the commercial inaccessibility of nonmemoir genres to Iranian women" in the period following 9/11. One example Malek gives is Azadeh Moaeveni's 2005 *Lipstick Jihad: A Memoir of Growing up Iranian in America and American in Iran.* Born in the United States, Moaeveni "returns" to Iran to explore the majoritarian population of contemporary Iran—youth. Malek considers how Moaeveni, a journalist by trade, sought to decenter her own story but ultimately felt funneled into the memoir genre by the American publishing industry. As Malek explains, memoir and film, as commercially viable genres, have been the dominant windows into Iran for Western viewers, at the exclusion of other artistic, literary, and scholarly modes. This limiting apparatus, she contends, has furthered Othered Iranians and shrunk the depth and breadth of the Iranian experience (Malek 2006, 359–64).

It is significant then that Ebadi wrote her first memoir with Moaeveni. US sanctions against Iran made the publication process of Ebadi's first memoir difficult. It could be that Moaeveni's name lent credibility and facility to the project. Ebadi states that her story is personal and not political, an attempt, perhaps, like Moaeveni's, to reframe a deeply political document into a "safer," more palatable "personal story" for Western readers. A serious engagement with the content and framework of Ebadi's memoirs, however, doesn't afford this safe experience. Indeed, it is precisely her complex rendering of the interplay between the personal, political, local, and global that make her a particularly important and undertheorized writer. Perhaps constrained by the memoir genre, Ebadi nonetheless does offer political analysis and a vision of the world that gives voice to decolonial feminist practices.

BEARING WITNESS

In reading Ebadi against more neo-Orientalist women's memoirs, I recognize that she is neither innocently removed from nor inoculated against the trappings of representational politics. Ebadi too wrote both of her memoirs for Western readers, thus entering the messy landscape of transnational reading and reception practices that might mobilize or position her against her own desires. But her clear aim is to challenge the parallel erasures—one from hardliners in the Iranian state, the other from secular dogmatists in the West—of everyday Iranians' capacities to affect changes from within their society. While Ebadi's memoirs are neither a comprehensive history of Iranian politics nor a complete account of women's movements, they offer historical complexity and nuance to questions of religion, gender, politics, modernity, and the state. For instance, in her first memoir, describing her mother's era, Ebadi writes critically about the compulsory deveiling policies of Reza Shah, recuperating this history to reveal that the state's biopolitical mode of power was operative long before the Islamic Republic's edict on mandatory hijab.

"Turning an expansive country of villages and peasants overnight into a centralized nation with railroads and a legal code was a complex task. Reza Shah believed it would be impossible without the participation of the country's women, and he set about emancipating them by banning the veil," Ebadi (2007, 7–8) writes. "Reza Shah was the first, but not the last, Iranian ruler to act out a political agenda—secular modernization, shrinking the clergy's influence—on the frontier of women's bodies." Considering the constraints and opportunities of women of Ebadi's mother's and grandmother's generations, Ebadi shows the ways in which a modernizing state consolidated its authority on and through the bodies of women. Moreover, Ebadi illustrates how a modernizing and secular state still barred women from educational opportunities. Her mother's ambitions to attend medical school were cut short by the demands on her to be married and raise a family. Ebadi's widowed grandmother, however, secured custody of her children and part of her deceased husband's assets through appeals to clerics in Qom, who often advocated on women's behalf.

This historical complexity runs throughout Ebadi's memoirs, as she painstakingly tries to sever the metonymic framing of Islam *as* patriarchy. Instead, she historicizes the constraints Iranian women have faced in the modern period as part of a complex web of patriarchal practices emerging from the family, society, and state. In many cases religion and religious clerics are often presented as allies to women, challenging secular state power and authority. As Ebadi details the rise of her career in *Iran Awakening*—she graduated from law school at age twenty-two and in 1970 became a judge at age twenty-three—she also chronicles her support for the growing opposition movement to the Shah. She frames rising support for Khomeini as part of the historic role religious leaders have had in democratizing society. "In 1906, for example, the mullahs lent their critical support to a movement that produced the Constitutional Revolution, which forced the reigning dynasty to decree a European-style constitution and legislative body into existence." Speaking to the importance of the mosque as a site of protest, she explains: "The mosque in particular offered a public gathering place where grievances against the moment's king could be freely aired and exchanged, behind the semiprotected walls of a holy building." Claiming religion as a crucial space of protest, Ebadi (2007, 32) argues that "it was neither shocking nor particularly foreboding to hear Ayatollah Khomeini raining invective down on the shah from exile."

Ebadi reframes the Islam/secularism binary by documenting how religious leaders were part of a broad opposition to the Shah that included "secular nationalists, socialists, and Marxists among its ranks." She remembers how "the clergy, whose network of mosques spread out across the country . . . had standing centers from which to raise their voices and organize," arguing that it wasn't "so alarming that the mullahs should take the lead" (Ebadi 2007, 33–34). Ultimately, the revolution fails Ebadi, as she is barred from her judgeship in its aftermath. But as she reflects throughout the remainder of her first memoir, her faith in Islam, and the democratic possibilities emanating from within its tenets, is never challenged.

In the aftermath of the revolution and the years of the Iran-Iraq War (1980–88), Ebadi witnessed the massive exile of her fellow Iranians. As she wrote in *Iran Awakening*, throughout the 1980s and 1990s roughly four million to five million Iranians left the country (Ebadi 2007, 78). When her friends and colleagues leave, it was particularly devastating: "One by one, my dearest friends deserted. They packed up their belongings, said their good-byes, and, in my eyes, turned their backs on Iran. Each time I wearily picked up a pen to cross out yet another name in my address book, my disappointment crushed me. I felt as though I were living in an abandoned house that was decaying by the day, in the company of ghosts" (Ebadi 2007, 79). Signaling the affective registers of political struggle, Ebadi's pain and disappointment become part of her political claim staking. Ebadi opens up space to critique, rather than normalize, chosen exile and speak to the political and emotional effects of such massive flights from Iran. "In the beginning," Ebadi writes (2007, 79, emphasis added), "I fought them. Each and every one of them, when they declared their intent to leave, faced my perhaps unfair flood of dissuasion and protest. I knew that the decision to leave was deeply personal. And, true, I didn't have sons. *But all the same, as an ethical and political stand, I didn't believe in leaving Iran.*" Ebadi (2007, 81) identifies this moment, more than any difficulties that followed, as the lowest point of her life. Notable is her willingness to critique chosen exile as political and ethical liability, and the commitment to staying as its antidote. This is striking when read against the genre of Iranian women's memoirs that dramatize their flight from Iran as the condition of their putative freedom. In laying claim to staying and working within Iran, Ebadi envisions a political and affective space beyond despair, fear, and cynicism, even as she faces disappointment.

By remaining in Iran, Ebadi becomes part of and helps shape the dynamic reform movement. As she is forced from her judgeship, she turns in the 1980s and 1990s to practicing law again, deciding to engage legal frameworks from within the parameters set up by the Islamic Republic. As with the OMSC activists who build on Ebadi's decades of work, Ebadi herself cultivates a pragmatic approach to changing what she identifies as outdated legal codes to reflect the social justice ethos of ordinary Iranians. She distinguishes between "the politico-religious worldview of . . . traditionalists" and those, like her, who began to "advocate for female equality in an Islamic framework" (Ebadi 2007, 118 and 122). "If I'm forced to ferret through musty books of Islamic jurisprudence and rely on sources that stress the egalitarian ethics of Islam," she writes, "then so be it. Is it harder this way? Of course it is. But is there an alternative battlefield" (Ebadi 2007, 122)? It is precisely this battlefield on which Ebadi and other feminist reformers staged their struggles.

A local activist, engaging the discursive framework of the state, Ebadi refused to be positioned as the native informant who becomes implicated in the political projects of Western hegemony. Her work helps legitimize the burgeoning Islamicate feminist and reform movements that exploded in Iran in the 1990s. As Ebadi notes in *Iran Awakening* (2007, 142), by the time of Khatami's first election in 1997, notions of "Islamic democracy" are emanating from all corners of Iran. Indeed, as Ebadi asserts, it was not Khatami who created the space for this discourse, but the work of everyday citizens and activists that made his election possible. "President Khatami deserves only a measure of credit for this shift. Really it was because my daughters' uncowed generation started fighting back and, through the force of their sheer numbers and boldness, made it unfeasible for the state to impose itself as before" (Ebadi 2007, 180). Although it is true that youth were (and still are) at the forefront of social change struggles in Iran, they have been emboldened in part by the work of Ebadi's generation, those who stayed in Iran to press for reforms.

In 2003, Ebadi worked with female MPs to draft a bill on family law. Ebadi (2007, 185) remembered her exchange with one MP: "'Write something that broadens women's rights, but in a way that's compatible with Islam,' she requested, 'so that we can defend it on the floor.'" Ebadi (2007, 186) drafted a law that "included everything we sought in terms of divorce rights, embedded in sharia in a way that was wholly defendable." The MPs approved it but asked Ebadi to conceal the fact that she was the bill's author, so as not to threaten the hardliners in parliament. However, when the female MPs weren't able to defend the bill's compliance with Islamic law, they asked Ebadi to do it, thus she was forced to confront hardline clerics in the parliament. This confrontation, in which Ebadi argued that the husband's consent is not required for a woman to divorce him, resulted in Ebadi being thrown out of the court. Ultimately the bill failed. This experience forced Ebadi to confront the limits of Islamic reform under a regime dominated by hardliners. But Ebadi located those limits in the political apparatuses of those constituencies in the state who use illegal tactics (in terms of both civil and Islamic laws) to crush dissent, not in the mechanism of *ijtehad* itself nor the possibility of gender equality in Islam. Although these limits seemed to her intractable at times, Ebadi refused to relinquish the pragmatic feminist reform strategies that have promised (and at times, delivered) critical victories over patriarchal and repressive codes.

FEMINIST RECONFIGURATIONS OF DUTY

Ebadi's second memoir, *Until We Are Free* (2015, 4, emphasis added), begins where *Iran Awakening* leaves off, with a declaration of commitment to her country:

> The story of Iran is the story of my life. Sometimes I wonder why I am so attached to my country, why the outline of Tehran's Alborz Mountains is as intimate and precious to me as the curve of my daughter's face, and why *I feel a duty to my nation that overwhelms everything else*. I remember when so many of my friends and relatives began leaving the country in the 1980s, disheartened by the bombs raining down from the war with Iraq and by the morality police checkpoints set up by the still new Islamic government. While I did not judge anyone for wanting to leave, I could not fathom the impulse. Did one leave the city where one's children had been born? Did one walk away from the trees in the garden one planted each year, even before they bore pomegranates and walnuts and scented apples?

In this powerful opening paragraph and throughout the book Ebadi narrates a life given to a national cause. But here, this cause is not bound by patriarchal codes that relegate women to either symbolic representation or gender-differentiated roles. Instead, national duty and pride are reimagined as a commitment to human rights and gender equality. The affective register here is not nostalgia for a romanticized past. Rather, Ebadi expresses a sense of duty and pride in connection with this struggle, and profound sorrow when, by force, she is severed from it.

Ebadi's 2015 memoir also strikes an increasingly skeptical tone, as she recounts the repression under Mahmoud Ahmadinejad. She details the years of intimidation and harassment by state intelligence officers, which became more potent and repressive after the 2009 elections and ultimately resulted in her forced exile. In contrast to her 2007 memoir, Ebadi draws more pessimistic conclusions about the possibility of reforming the state, a state she explicitly calls out as a police state. Yet she continues to bear witness to the struggle of Iranians to determine their own destiny, to see the fruits of their activist labor. As a political thinker and strategist, Ebadi argues that, even after the state's rightward turn with the 2005 presidential election of Ahmadinejad, she "was not an opponent of the state." As a "human rights defender," Ebadi (2015, 45) contends, "I based my criticisms of the state on legal grounds." This proclamation emblematizes the strategies of Ebadi and the OMSC activists, who sought a pragmatic and reformist approach to the law. They appealed to the state's vision of itself as just, as able to accommodate the rights of its citizens under Islamic law.

When the increasingly conservative state sought to shield itself from criticism under the guise that such criticism would weaken the Islamic

Republic, making it more vulnerable to imperial aggression from the West, Ebadi countered with an appeal to the state's own legal mechanism. Revealing a number of conversations with the particular state intelligence officer who frequented her office and home, *Until We Are Free* chronicles Ebadi's investment not simply in the law but in the long struggle to align the state with society's values and desires. When taking on cases of citizens, journalists, and activists, Ebadi did not hesitate to publicly criticize the state. The following exchange between Ebadi and the intelligence officer typifies one of many such conversations peppered throughout the book:

> "Khanoum Ebadi, you know what the problem is," he said, crossing his legs and looking at me intently. "America is our enemy, and it takes advantage of such criticisms."
>
> "But what I've said is perfectly true."
>
> "So you should come and tell these things directly to us. Don't go and tell the media. When you do that, the enemy exploits your words."
>
> It was a conversation we had had before, on several occasions. Each time Mahdavi made the same supplications, and I gave him the same replies.
>
> "If the state stops behaving badly, then I won't have anything to say. Then there will be no cause for anyone to exploit anything. But if what I say is being exploited, the root of the problem is the state's behavior."
>
> He looked at me that day with some disappointment. I shrugged, finding I had nothing to add. I had been a judge and was now a lawyer, and the law concerns itself with intent and the results of intent. If the state intended the best for its citizens, then it needed to demonstrate that in its behavior toward them. (Ebadi 2015, 56–57)

Ebadi is not naïve in her appeals to the intelligence officer. She knows they will most likely fall on deaf ears. Yet I point to this exchange as a way of distinguishing between a state-mandated anti-imperialism that constructs duty to the nation in authoritarian terms, and Ebadi's belief in the legal, pragmatic, and democratic transformation of society.

Duty-bound to this vision, Ebadi calls on the state to find strength and sovereignty by harmonizing its policies and practices with the needs and desires of Iranian citizens. A critic of both the repressive actions of the Iranian state and US or Western intervention into Iran, Ebadi represents a democratic, feminist, antiwar alternative grounded in discourses of Islamic democracy, feminism, and human rights. In many ways Ebadi refuses the position of native informant: in consistently arguing for reform within Islam, in reflecting desires of ordinary Iranians, and in claiming herself as one; in critiquing political power of repressive regimes at the same time as speaking as a Muslim and a feminist; and finally in rejecting the ontological status of captive subject. She offers an alternative subject position to native informants who become willing bedfellows of neo-Orientalist, imperialist projects.

Using the genre of memoir to elaborate her claims, Ebadi constructs what Julia Watson and Sidonie Smith (1992, xx) have called, in reference to women's memoirs from the Global South, "an alternative way of knowing." As "a process and product of decolonization," Ebadi's memoirs have "the potential to intervene in the comfortable alignments of power relationships," where the "self-representation and self-presentation" of the marginalized subject through autobiography are political acts (Watson and Smith 1992, xxi). They write: "Also in this alternative space, narrative itineraries may take different paths. For the colonial subject, the process of coming to writing is an articulation *through* interrogation, a charting of the conditions that have historically placed her identity under erasure" (Watson and Smith 1992, xx). While Ebadi is a particularly privileged subject in that she is highly educated and transnationally mobile, the geopolitical and cultural conditions that have produced not only her exile but also her marginality in the Iranian women's memoir genre have certainly worked to mute a narrative such as hers. On their own, but also in relation to the neo-Orientalist memoirs of exiled Iranian and Muslim women, Ebadi's memoirs function as autotheoretical accounts of decolonial feminism, constituted by and constitutive of a politics of nonviolence, sovereignty, and transnational engagement.

TABOOS AND TRANSNATIONAL CIRCULATIONS

To what extent and to what ends Ebadi is read and analyzed are certainly bound within the geopolitics of war and coloniality. To write about "democracy" and "democratization" in Iran and the Middle East within a global order defined by permanent war, Islamophobia, and a neocolonial ordering of people and nations risks essentializing Iran, the Middle East, and Muslims, thus reproducing colonial binaries. The US and European "democracy projects" in the MENA have in fact been in the service of imperialist occupation and war profiteering. President George W. Bush's rhetorical war against Iran helped consolidate the hardliners' rise to power in Iran and intensify the vast anti-Muslim sentiments circulating within the West.

Indeed, the war on the Muslim world has not been simply rhetorical, as the actual occupations show and as the United States, several administrations later, continues and intensifies its policies of isolation, containment, and sanctions toward Iran. Transnational circulation of "indigenous feminist" texts of Middle Eastern and Muslim women makes them vulnerable to misinterpretation by unintended or unwanted allies, who may seek to appropriate their texts for different kinds of means.

But unlike Nafisi, who has developed deep ties to such neoliberals as Bernard Lewis, Ebadi has had a very different transnational reception.[7] In fact, as Ebadi (2007, 210) wrote in *Iran Awakening*, "sanctions regulations in the United States, it turned out, made it virtually impossible for me to publish a memoir in America." The United States is never a site for unmitigated freedom for Ebadi, as her particular forms of knowledge and experience have, in the punitive sense, been sanctioned. In 2004 she sued the US Treasury Department and ultimately forced it to revise "its regulations on publications of works by citizens of embargoed nations" (Ebadi 2007, 213). One must ask if such practices of exclusion and erasure were enacted on Nafisi and other Iranian authors, and examine the range of effects flowing out from sanctions as well as the particular bodies and forms of knowledge production such sanctions target.

The aim of the earlier memoir, in Ebadi's words, was "to correct Western stereotypes of Islam, especially the image of Muslim women as docile, forlorn creatures" (2007, 210). While it's not possible to quantify her success, it is unclear how widely she has been read in the West. Compared to Nafisi, fewer Western readers recognize Ebadi's name, or the fact that she won the Nobel Prize for Peace in 2003.[8] Although I could not locate accurate sales data for *Iran Awakening*, the number of reviews and other citations of Ebadi's memoir between its release and 2015 in a LexisNexis search totaled 106, compared with 609 reviews and other citations of *Reading Lolita in Tehran* between 2003 and 2015. While Nafisi's book has been out longer, its citational frequency is more indicative of the popularity of its content and transnational reception.

Meanwhile, reviews of *Iran Awakening* have tended to be mixed. While some focused on Ebadi's commitment to using the discourses of Islam for democratic change from within (Aslan 2006), others focused on the particular tribulations she endured (Secor 2006). These divisions tend to fall along political lines: Aslan wrote for left-leaning *The Nation*, while Secor wrote for the more centrist *New York Times*. Also revealing is Ebadi's claim that in her travels since the Nobel Prize she has "realized that Iran is still unknown to the people of many countries. That is to say, inaccurate propaganda has portrayed Iran as worse or better than it actually is" (Ebadi 2007, 217). Representing an alternative story to that of the "secular dogmatists" outside Iran and the hardliners inside the regime, Ebadi's auto-theoretical account constitutes a decolonial feminist intervention into knowledge production about Iran.

Although it might be possible to read the transnational reception of Ebadi as playing into the ubiquitous framing of good (innocent) citizens of Iran pitted against bad (repressive) state, I find Lata Mani's (1990) ideas about "discrepant audiences" and the politics of location useful in applying transnational reading and reception practices that don't further silence Ebadi. If we are to understand and read Ebadi from her position as an Iranian Muslim woman writing from within Iranian spaces, but with the aim of greater elucidation for Western readers, how might we think about the ways in which her discourses are taken up by different readers? Recognizing that Ebadi too is mired in a particular political moment, where the production of knowledge about Iran and Islam and the transnational circulation and reception of such knowledge always risk complicity with dangerous discursive and material practices, is there an epistemic mode that does not attach to these dangerous practices or the equally dangerous mode of cynical abstentionism? Parts of the Iranian diaspora have disengaged from Iran, writing it off as an untenable space. Some sectors of the US left, particularly after the 2009 election fraud in Iran, enact another kind of disengagement, dismissing the Green Movement and defending then-president Mahmoud Ahmadinejad as an anti-imperialist. Both of these political and intellectual frameworks constitute an epistemic mode of silencing voices that are simultaneously anti-interventionist and supportive of bottom-up democracy in Iran.

Considering the processes and dilemmas of writing about debates on the practice of *sati*, or widow burning, in India, but more aptly about the politics of knowledge production in a postcolonial set of relations, Mani (1990, 26) takes stock of the ways in which feminists have theorized the "revolt of the particular against that masquerading as the general," or the situated knowledges of women and people of color against the disembodied, masculinist knowledge that poses as universal. She explores the way postcolonial feminists like Chandra Mohanty (1987) pushed some of these initial feminist discourses. Quoting Mohanty, Mani (1990, 26) points to the ways Mohanty argues for a more complex politics of location "characterized by multiple locations and nonsynchronous processes of movement 'between cultures, languages, and complex configurations of meaning and power.'" Mani applies Mohanty's ideas to her own project, writing that "this definition of the space of politics very nicely illuminates the dynamics of how my conception of a project on the debate on *sati* in colonial India bears the traces of movement between cultures and configurations of meaning." Pondering the ways that audiences in the United States, Britain, and India "seized on entirely different aspects of [her] work as politically significant," Mani (1990, 26–27) asserts: "These responses in turn have caused me to reflect on how moving between different 'configurations of meaning and power' can prompt different 'modes of knowing.' The experience has also required me squarely to confront a problem not adequately theorized in discussions of positionality or of the function of theory and criticism: the politics of simultaneously negotiating not multiple but discrepant audiences."

We must read Ebadi and the particular production of Islam, feminism, and democracy that she elaborates within the context of discrepant audiences. Reading Ebadi only within discourses of democracy and democratization emanating from neoliberals and neoconservatives in the West who support dangerous interventions in Iran elides the complex and painstaking ways in which Ebadi has struggled to elaborate discourses of feminism and democracy *internal* to Iran. Mani's (1990, 31) discussion is very particular to her experiences speaking to audiences in Britain, the United States, and India about the politics and history of *sati*, and her experience "dramatizes the dilemma of postcolonial intellectuals working on the Third World in the West." Her political landscape is different than Ebadi's, as her own position is, but Mani raises important questions that are useful as I consider the transnational triangulations of Ebadi, the One Million Signatures Campaign, and other kinds of Iranian feminist engagements with the West. Mani provides a way of thinking about complicities in colonial forms of knowledge production. As she asserts, many postcolonial intellectuals working in the Global North have come under attack for "inauthenticity or ideological contamination by the West" (Mani 1990, 31). Seeking a more complex and flexible analytical framework, Mani (1990, 31) argues that "assertions about ideological contamination are often shorthand allusions to genuine issues, such as asymmetries in the material conditions of scholarship in metropolitan and Third World contexts. Such problems are, however, not clarified by a moralistic formulation of the issue in terms of purity or pollution."

Mani attempts to confront real power relations, at the same time that she recognizes the different reading and reception practices of her discrepant audiences and the effects such practices might have on thinking about women's agency in colonial contexts. As Mani (1990, 32) found in discussing her work in both India and the West, audiences in the West tended to "aggrandize" colonialism as a force in thinking about *sati*, while audiences in India tended to minimize it, instead focusing on the Indian state. Instead of thinking of her work only as contaminated, Mani (1990, 32) found that she "inescapably participate[s] in multiple conversations, not all of which overlap." What is powerful in applying Mani's framework to how Ebadi's discourses become refracted through transnational reception and reading practices is the ways in which such practices might open up the possibility for thinking about complex modes of agency that come from Iranian women themselves. In other words, while looking at the ways in which scholars and activists are contaminated by and complicit in what is the most powerful at the global level—neoliberal regimes of Western economic, military, and ideological dominance—can be useful, it not only assumes there is an alternative space of purity, but it fails to capture other epistemic and political emphases.

Ebadi, as someone invested in the project of reforming Islamic law in favor of a gender justice perspective, might be read by some in the West as implicated in the projects of democratizing Iran and the Middle East vis-à-vis a retooling of Islam imposed by secular-liberal Western regimes. Her mere association with the genre of Iranian women's memoirs, and certainly the strong critique of the state in her second memoir and recent comments, leave her vulnerable to being interpreted as a native informant. For instance, in a 2017 conversation with Porochista Khakpour in *The Guardian*, Ebadi argued: "There is a system here, but in Iran there is no system. . . . The state and the citizen are very different. The government can be bad but the people are not like that. And this is why there are tensions in society. Because the culture of the people is higher than the culture of the government." Again, context is critical here. As Ebadi tells Khakpour, the aim of her second memoir was to testify to what she and so many activists have endured under an authoritarian state.

In *Until We Are Free*, Ebadi recounts in painful detail how the state tore apart her thirty-five-year marriage by orchestrating and filming a sexual encounter between her husband and another woman. Charged with adultery and possession of alcohol, her husband is imprisoned in Evin and ultimately forced to publicly denounce his wife as a puppet of the West. Ebadi told Khakpour (2017): "The reason I told the story so openly was that I wanted to show what the government in Iran is capable of. They have done what they did to my husband to many others. But more so, the talk of this in Iran is taboo, and I wanted to break the taboo. A government who can whip me on streets if strands of hair are revealed, and hires a sex worker for politics in the name of Islam?" In refusing to withhold critique of her government in the service of anti-imperialism, Ebadi does not a priori become a native informant. Rather, her deep commitments to human rights, peace, and justice necessitate that she breaks the silence, a silence imposed by the state but also by many activists and scholars who equate anti-imperialism with supporting an authoritarian, postcolonial state.

However, Ebadi's taboo breaking comes at a cost. By making visible the deployment of sexuality within the state's security apparatus, she risks reinforcing the notion of Iran and Islam as "backward," evidenced by the putative "taboo" of speaking about sexuality. Indeed, her personal injury seems here to have trumped a more nuanced discussion of sexual politics in Iran.[9] Unlike the detailed work she does in her 2007 memoir to provide historical and cultural context to women's rights practices, her 2015 memoir leaves behind an explication of the complexity of sexual discourses and practices. As scholars have shown, sexuality is deployed within neoliberal and security discourses in most corners of the globe.[10] Despite Ebadi's blind spots, she nonetheless does critical work in unsuturing the naturalized link between Islam and repression, exposing violence as the work of patriarchal states. Her lacunae point to the need for more scholar-activist explorations of sexuality in local contexts that do not reify the traditional/modern binary.

Reading Ebadi's memoirs and the discourses that surrounded her Nobel Prize within a politics of location that mediates discrepant audiences requires notions of agency internal to the historic context in which she writes. The hermeneutical and exegetical practices of rereading Islam within a gender justice framework that Ebadi and the One Million Signatures Campaign engage are enabled through the *ijtehad* tradition within Shia Islam. Ebadi, like the campaign, is part of the new publics who are accessing Islamic discourses through cyber and print culture, bringing their lived realities to bear on such discourses. Iranian reformers' success at the discursive (and at times institutional) level in reframing Islamic law to incorporate a perspective of gender justice reflected cultural shifts in Iranian society toward greater equality for women. Within the nexus of legal reforms and everyday discourses and practices over the past several decades in Iran emerged a movement of women's rights activists and a deep penetration of their vocabularies and aspirations into Iranian society. It is within this context that Iranian women's agency must be understood.

Using a "complex sense of agency" allows for the recognition of women's victimization and the possibility for struggling against it as located within the victim/agent herself (Mani 1990, 37–38). Without this complex sense of agency, Mani (1990, 38) argues, "we run the risk of producing a discourse which sets women up to be saved. This would situate women within feminist analysis in ways that are similar to their positioning within colonialist or nationalist discourse." The various forces at work, which mobilize discourses of saving Iranian and Muslim women, deserve critical attention and scrutiny. And yet there are other kinds of discourses emerging in ongoing and complex ways from Iranian women themselves, which may not be so recruitable by empire. While those of us doing anticolonial scholarship that engages local and global forces and actors in the post-9/11 era must contend with their own and their subjects' complicity in projects not of our making, we must not revictimize social actors by neglecting their projects or assuming they are useful only to empire. By recognizing the ways in which a figure like Ebadi interrupts the ideological toehold someone like Nafisi has had on the subject of "Iranian women," we might reveal a space of epistemic and political possibility.

THE FEMINIST FACE OF REFORM

As she entered the transnational stage, Shirin Ebadi became an emblematic figure of Islamicate feminism and democracy through her Nobel Prize. Now on a transnational stage, Ebadi translated the particular discourses around Islam, women's rights, and reform to a global audience. Her award resonated with Iranians around the world, and reformers inside Iran capitalized on her transnational recognition by continuing to push for reforms in Islamic law. In publishing her memoirs, Ebadi sought to continue that translation project, making a crucial intervention into global debates about Islam and democratic society. While a cautionary approach to the ways in which the transnational circulation and reception of her discourses could intersect with projects not of her making—particularly those of saving Iranian women and refashioning (eliminating) Muslims through military intervention by Western powers—is important, reading Ebadi only through this danger further silences the project of an indigenous and decolonial Iranian feminism. In foregrounding Ebadi's particular discourses through a counterhegemonic reading practice, I offer a framework for thinking about a decolonial feminism in practice in the small but significant spaces of intellectual and activist practices that might unravel the coloniality of knowledge production.

As this book is largely an attempt to consider how Iranian women's rights activists themselves auto-theorize the struggle to change their society, I assert that Ebadi should be read within a complex understanding of agency. The discourses surrounding her Nobel Prize win and her memoir can be read as cutting against the neo-Orientalist genre of Iranian and Muslim women's "freedom flights." Moreover, acknowledging that Ebadi's discourses travel to discrepant audiences, whose interests might signal emphases different than those of scholars and activists oriented only to the West, makes visible the epistemic and political projects of Iranian feminism that exceed the framework of entrapment. Ebadi's memoirs also contribute to production of hope and possibility that is implicit in and necessary for the kinds of women's rights activism considered here. A close examination of the discourses and practices of feminism, democratic participation, and Islam through the projects of Iranians like Ebadi, who enact an ethical and political commitment to working within Iran when possible, generates a different kind of knowledge project—one that might emphasize possibility over danger, local agency over global contamination. Like campaigns, discourses, politics, and bodies, hope and despair travel, and in their circulations they do certain kinds of work. Drawing on and extending the idea of "living proof" which Ethel Brooks (2007, 141–42), in her scholarship on garment workers, lays out as a methodological, epistemological, and political orientation, I suggest that Ebadi contributes to a decolonial feminist politics, offered in "women's testimony, women's witnessing, and women's telling of their histories" that "disrupt the maintenance of difference." Theoretical work that attends to the "living proof," or "offering of life stories, subjectivities, bodily materialities, and practices by women as acts of courage and political claim staking" (Brooks 2007, 138), can gesture toward epistemic paths worth pursuing in such fraught and perilous times.

To foreground Ebadi's own claim staking, I end this chapter as I began, with her return to Iran after receiving her Nobel Prize:

> The plane skidded to a stop on the tarmac, and the flight attendant asked me to disembark first, guiding me to the door of the plane. When it swung open, the first thing I saw was my mother's shining face. I took her soft, wrinkled hands in mine and pressed them against my lips. And then I leaned back and finally noticed the crowd, stretching out as far as I could see. . . . The crowd surged forward on all sides. . . . I inhaled a great breath and belted out the loudest *Allaho akbar!* I could manage. . . .

> . . . As we finally made our way to the car and slowly drove forward, the crowds parted to let us ahead, and through the window I watched the faces slide by, hopeful, serious, proud, but, most of all, so *alive*. Near the arched monument built by the shah in south Tehran now renamed Freedom Square, I caught sight of a woman with a child in one hand, a makeshift poster in the other, and the sight made my breath catch, for her sign read, "This is Iran." (Ebadi 2007, 205–8)

"Allaho akbar" (God is the greatest) was shouted from rooftops during the 1979 Iranian Revolution and the Green Movement thirty years later, signifying once again the place of religion in protest. As Ebadi claims this space of protest and her own rightful citizenship and belonging, she narrates a project of Islamic democracy and decolonial feminism, marked by the animated participation and presence of women as citizens and activists who are part of a complex and dynamic society they are making and remaking every day.

If the anticolonial thrust of revolutionary and postrevolutionary Iran has been narrated primarily through key male theorists and politicians—most significantly the key theorists of the Iranian revolution, Ayatollah Ruhollah Khomeini and Ali Shariati—decolonial scholarship tends to reproduce this male-centered voice through its often uncritical and romanticized engagement with Shariati as the sole anticolonial voice of Iran. This is not to diminish the importance of a figure like Shariati, who had a huge following among many women who supported the revolution. It is, instead, to point to the ways in which anticolonial resistance becomes equated with male revolutionaries, whose politics often sideline feminism or understand women's political investments in gender-differentiated terms. A skewed formulation then unfolds in which male leadership/masculinity stands in for the anticolonial voice, and Iranian women become "susceptible" to "foreign" influence—that is, feminism and human rights. Inviting attention to Ebadi as an anticolonial thinker in her own right, I have offered an alternative decolonial voice, characterized by decoloniality's very commitment to gendered experience and unrelenting in its challenge to binary ways of thinking.

Ebadi's narratives are living proof of her decades-long struggle to socialize a postcolonial nation-state into a vision and practice of sovereignty that does not sacrifice women's undifferentiated equality. Working within the parameters of Islam, human rights, and Islamic reformist strategies, Ebadi (like the OMSC activists) has articulated her work and vision as part of an indigenous project, one that can synthesize Islam, democracy, and women's rights. She insists that the desires and rights of women, their *sovereignty*, can and should strengthen rather than compromise the sovereignty of the nation, providing a conception of decoloniality that is decidedly feminist. Chapter 4 considers another life history and feminist practice, that of Mahboubeh Abbasgholizadeh. A longtime women's rights activist in Iran, Mahboubeh found herself exiled in the wake of the repression that followed the Green Movement. Like Ebadi and the OMSC activists, Mahboubeh conceptualizes self-determination from a feminist perspective and points to the pitfalls of and possibilities for working across multiple borders and boundaries.

CHAPTER 4

WE HAVE THE SAME JOURNEY, BUT NOT THE SAME DESTINY

> It is a place to start. And to start there would be to gather up some of what we might—or even once—knew.
>
> —GAIL LEWIS

IN OCTOBER 2011, MAHBOUBEH ABBASGHOLIZADEH, A LONGTIME women's rights activist in Iran, founded ZananTV, an independent, alternative Internet streaming channel in Farsi and English. Produced in studios in New York and London, the programs were created mostly by women's rights activists inside Iran. Mahboubeh launched ZananTV in Zuccotti Park in Manhattan, the heart of the Occupy Wall Street encampments and protests, crafting an affiliation between Iranian women's rights activists and the burgeoning Occupy Movement. An activist over many decades, Mahboubeh has spent years thinking about, among other things, how to build grassroots feminist networks and organizations in Iran, the complexities of geographical and social location, the relationship of the Iranian diaspora to Iran's social movements, and the ecosystem of new media platforms, activism, and social movements.

Imprisoned on three different occasions for her activism, Mahboubeh left Iran in early 2010. I came to know her shortly after that time, when I was living in New York, finishing my PhD, working at the Barnard Center for Research on Women and participating in Iranian feminist and solidarity work. I felt an immediate connection to Mahboubeh given our respective histories of feminist activism and nonprofit work. Although our activist projects had taken place in different locations and under different circumstances, we shared a deep investment in grassroots, intersectional, and decolonial feminist activism as well as a commitment to reflecting and theorizing feminism from the lives and labors of activists themselves. Mahboubeh and I met periodically, and our conversations always lasted for hours, usually over coffee or tea, fruit, and sweets. In 2014, in my capacity as associate director of the Barnard Center for Research on Women, I invited Mahboubeh to take part in a panel of scholars, writers, and activists who curate and participate in transnational digital feminist spaces to discuss how online engagement enables strategies for developing their work outside academic walls.[1] After moving to California, I occasionally met with Mahboubeh when back in New York, or on Skype, to catch up and to brainstorm potential collaborative projects. In June and September 2018, I did more structured interviews with her, asking about her upbringing, her development as an activist, and what it means to be an Iranian women's rights activist living in New York.

At many points during these interviews, Mahboubeh spoke of herself in the third person, delineating between the multiple parts of her identity. She would refer to herself, for example, as "Activist Leader Mahboubeh," or "Muslim Mahboubeh," or "Mom Mahboubeh," or "Lesbian Mahboubeh," or "Immigrant Mahboubeh." Some of these identities corresponded more coherently to one period in her life or another, but sometimes they would come together in interesting ways. As she told me, these personas would often debate or argue with each other. Sometimes, one persona would console the other. This chapter explores ZananTV and the life story of Mahboubeh Abbasgholizadeh herself as a way of opening up the limited categories of homeland versus diaspora, activist inside Iran versus activist outside of Iran. While these distinctions are often meaningful, they can also shrink the space for thinking more generatively about feminism as a world-making and boundary-breaking endeavor. Mahboubeh's reflections on her life and work, considered alongside the project of ZananTV, bring into sharp relief the importance of theorizing decoloniality from the lives, ideas, practices, and visions of activists who continue to build feminist projects within the complex geopolitical processes that delimit them.

A DIALECTICAL PERIOD

Mahboubeh was born in Khorramshahr, Iran, in 1958. Her family was *bazaari*, or merchant class, a historically significant sector of Iranian society. As Kevan Harris (2010) has written, the Pahlavi monarchy alienated many *bazaaris*, "preferring modern shopping centers and channeling financial support to heavy industry. . . . Disparate political tendencies of various bazaar merchants soon united against the shah's government. *Bazaaris* participated in and supported protests and demonstrations in the spring of 1977, well before most social groups—including the clergy—had joined the revolutionary surge." Compared with many working-class Arabs in her province, Mahboubeh felt relatively privileged but also different from many of her classmates, children of an elite class of gas engineers, whose families lived in "beautiful houses with beautiful gardens."[2] Until her teenage years Mahboubeh felt self-conscious about her traditional religious family. Her classmates' mothers, she recalled, were "beautiful and chic, with lipstick and things you see on TV," while her mother was "very traditional, with colorful chadors and hijab." When Mahboubeh was nine years old, her family moved to Tehran and settled in a neighborhood comprised of many military families. Again, she felt different from many of her more elite and Westernized classmates, self-conscious of her traditional family. "It was kind of, I think, a crisis of identity for me."

Conflicted from an early age, Mahboubeh struggled and fought many desires. She felt drawn to girls who appeared more Westernized in presentation, those she viewed as "independent and brave and open in sexuality." Yet she felt a distance from them, a gap between herself and these girls, represented by her mother's dress and her father's directives to "not watch TV and just focus on praying, and God. And cover yourself and have a scarf, and a long skirt, very modest things." But Mahboubeh "wanted to be beautiful, like, fresh and in fashion." By her early teenage years, well into the 1970s, Mahboubeh began reading voraciously. She recalls:

> Iranian society was very politicized, with different leftist and religious intellectuals. I had a tendency to read all of this literature. I felt different from other kids. They're more into parties, talking about celebrities. I wasn't into celebrities. Also, my older sister, she had a very nice influence on me because she was in Tehran University and many books and things came from her, to me. So I was attracted to the left. And then, it's mixed with my sexual orientation; that is another story. But I became more picky about being with different people, and then [thinking about] the concept of femininity. I [learned] about how "woman" is just a sexual object. And then, in my teenage years, I am finding that this is just colonialism, or neocolonialism. They just want to make us consumerist people, and this is about the new colonialism. My classmates, they are enjoying fashion and things. They are just, like, objects for this kind of lifestyle.

Mahboubeh felt increasingly distant from and critical of her Westernized counterparts. She used her budding intellectual capacities to conclude that she "didn't want to be like [them]," but also she didn't "want to be like [her] mom."

In her early teenage years, Mahboubeh and her friend started a political group at school. Inspired by their hero, Khoshrow Golesorkhi—a revolutionary poet, journalist, and critic of the Shah, whom the state accused of being an agent of Russia and executed under firing squad in 1974—the group, said Mahboubeh, did "funny actions." Before the school's morning exercise, students were made to pray about the Shah, chanting, "Javid Shah, Javid Shah" (Long live the King). "Our action was changing that slogan of 'Javid Shah' to 'Chaapid Shah,' 'Corrupted Shah.' He was stealing our resources!" Since the two phrases sound similar, Mahboubeh said, "nobody understood what we were saying, but we had a good feeling that we were saying 'Chaapid Shah' and just our friends could understand. I think we also took the picture of the Shah from the wall, and destroyed it."

After destroying the picture of the Shah, Mahboubeh recounted, they fled from the principal. "We escaped and hid ourselves in a small place for chickens, a very small yard. We hid ourselves there and my younger friends were crying, saying, 'If they find us, what's going to happen?' And I felt that, in that time, I am brave and I'm leading and I'm saying, 'No. What's going to happen? Nothing's going to happen.' I wasn't scared. So, from that time, I felt that I liked this challenge and making trouble for the Shah's regime. From that time, I always had like, an underground group." After this turning point, Mahboubeh began to understand her capacities for creativity and bravery, and feel less alienated from those around her as she came into her identity as an activist.

The next year, under the tutelage of a new teacher, a university student from the left, Mahboubeh experienced a crisis. She was drawn to this teacher, who took seriously Mahboubeh's little underground group and further trained them in leftist thought.

> I think there was always this connection between a beautiful woman, a strong woman, politics and action. So, we were kind of her followers. And she taught us that, "Okay, if you want to be leftists, you should ignore your tradition. You should see that God does not exist." And I felt that this is too much. I felt confused. This kind of attitude was very, very hard for me to understand. . . . She gathered a small group one day, and invited us to go to her home. And when we went inside, her grandma was sitting

> in the hall. She didn't say "hello" to her grandma, and then when her grandma said something, she said, "Ah, don't care about her." And it was very sad for me. I felt that a good person should be a kind person to everyone. For me, she was like a hero, but why is she doing this? . . . She told me that I should change, that I shouldn't believe in God. It was too much for me. It was kind of like, ideological brainwashing for me. I feel that now. . . . It was difficult. So one night, I talked with myself and I said, "Okay, there is a dialectic thing happening. So, you are from a traditional family. You are not ready to accept that God does not exist. You need some process, some period of dialectic. So, until that time, you can believe in God."

Mahboubeh and I both laughed as she said this, the endearing image of a young Mahboubeh wrestling with Hegelian dialectics very much alive with us in the room.

But this moment of levity ended quickly, as Mahboubeh talked about this struggle, this pull to be a "modern" leftist thinker, without abandoning her history, her family, and her religion. She came to tears when she relayed how much pressure she felt to choose one identity over the other, describing the intensity of the ideological battles that shaped the revolutionary period in Iran. Buckling under this political pressure and the pressure of her schoolwork, Mahboubeh failed that school year and had to repeat it. She was quite emotional talking about this, as a very smart student capable of academic success. As the educational system was shifting, she was forced to change schools in order to repeat her grade. In her new and much larger school, Mahboubeh met many new people, different from her old neighborhood, more socially rebellious. She became "numb about politics," she recalled. "I would hang out with the boys, and hang out with the girls, go to the bar, drink beer. My parents didn't understand what was happening. But my older sister did."

For the next couple of years, Mahboubeh's political rebellion morphed into a kind of withdrawal from intellectual life, hanging out with students who didn't care about books or family, just enjoying themselves. They seemed superficial to Mahboubeh, but she was angry about politics, about the intense sectarianism that defined the era. Escaping from school, she hung out with boys and went to bars. After a boyfriend broke up with her, Mahboubeh was so angry with him, but she was also in crisis because she didn't know who she was, if she was a lesbian or not. Her sexual involvement with boys, she recounted, was a kind of escape from the possibility that she might be lesbian. After dodging a number of classes, the school threatened to tell her parents about her absenteeism. Mahboubeh pleaded with her sister to not tell her parents and to come to the school to intervene.

At the time, Mahboubeh's sister was a leader of the Muslim student movement in her university and a follower of Ali Shariati. She came to talk to the school about Mahboubeh, dressed in a long chador and *maghnaeh*, the type of veil worn by many university students and women working in public institutions. "The principal was scared of her, this 'Islamic Marxist,'" Mahboubeh said. "And all of my friends said, 'Your sister is an Islamist Marxist?!' I said, 'You don't understand this thing.' And then the principal said, 'Of course, she is different and she is the leader of this group, so just take your sister and go out of this school!'" Mahboubeh was forced to enroll in night school, in the middle of the school year, where she continued for the next couple of years. "Still, I was in the mood of, 'I don't care about politics.'"

When Mahboubeh was at her old school, her sister had given her a copy of Shariati's book *Fatima Is Fatima* (Fatima Fatima Ast). She familiarized herself with the book.

> I don't know what happened about religion, but in night school, I find that I am tired from everything. I started to read *Fatima Fatima Ast*, and I started to listen [to] Shariati's speech. And it was like, for me it was like a renaissance. Like you are tired about privileged people. You are tired about like, many types of people and then, someone coming to you and talking from your heart. And that speech about *Fatima Fatima Ast*, it was like "You are the woman that you can . . ." [she trailed off, tearing up] "You are not like your mom. And you are not like this consumist [*sic*], Westernized woman. You have a voice for yourself."

I conveyed to Mahboubeh that I agree that the book is incredibly powerful. "It is. Wow, it *is*," she said with great emotion. "And it was, for me, it was like, 'Oh my God, this is from my heart,' you know?"

Drawing on the founding period of Islam, Ali Shariati, an Iranian sociologist and revolutionary, argued that women should emulate Fatima, the Prophet Muhammad's daughter. Shariati put forth an ideal of womanhood that challenged what he saw as "the inherited mold" of traditionalist patriarchy and "the imported novelty" of European or Western feminism. "The one which is imposed upon her in the name of tradition which she inherits, is not related to Islam at all," he wrote, "but is related to ethnic customs of the period of paternalism and even slavery. And the one which is imported from the West is not science, not humanity, not freedom and not liberty. It is not based on sanctity and respect for women at all. Rather it is based on the low tricks of the bourgeoisie—stupefying consumerism and mindless self-indulgence" (Shariati 1996, 66). Shariati framed the new Muslim woman as an "authentic" response to older, pre-Islamic forms of patriarchy and "foreign" ideas that attached women's freedom to her role as a sexual object and consumer of Western goods. Shariati offered an alternative to secular communism, one that asked activists, as Mahboubeh's teacher did, to abandon religion and cultural traditions.

Part of Shariati's appeal was his emphasis not just on the new Muslim woman as an antidote to the putative liberated Western woman but on Islam as that which liberated women from the misogynist pre-Islamic cultures of the Arab world. Using the story of Fatima, Shariati built a strong case for the ways in which Islam granted women dignity, agency, and rights previously unknown to them. As the youngest child of Muhammad and his first wife, Khadija, Fatima was chosen, along with her father, to revolutionize the society to which she was born. Islam "revolutionizes the position of women" (Shariati 1996, 159) because in pre-Islamic, patriarchal Arabia, where daughters are not valued as sons are, Fatima's fate was supposedly determined. Muhammad's two sons died in their early childhood, and his three daughters with Khadija—Zaynab, Ruqiya, and Umm Kulthum—died before Muhammad did. When Khadija became pregnant later in life, they eagerly anticipated a son. "But once again, a daughter. They named her Fatima" (Shariati 1996, 156). As Shariati explained: "Now, a daughter became the owner of the values of her father, the inheritor of all the honors of her family." Fatima became the "final link in this chain of divine justice . . . the last daughter of a family who had anticipated a son. . . . Muhammad had known what the hands of fate had in store for him. And Fatima, also, had known who she was. Yes! A woman, in this religion, was freed like this. Isn't this the religion of Abraham and of them, his heirs?" (Shariati 1996, 159–60).

Through the story of Fatima and the important role she played in her family, Shariati evoked a sense of pride in women's contributions to building a new society. Fatima studied, worked, and fought alongside her father, became his confidant and also comforted him. She was known as "the mother of her father" (Shariati 1996, 164) because of her capacity to nurture and take care of Muhammad through the many difficulties of his life.

Contrasting Iran's prerevolutionary period with Islam's early period through the story of Fatima, Shariati offered a discursive structure through which many women, including Mahboubeh, found resonance.

Offering these details of Mahboubeh's narrative, I invite attention to the intimate reaches of colonial hegemony, which, as Walter Mignolo (2018, 142) has asserted, "circumscribes the progression of modernity within all the domains used to categorize and classify the modern world: political, economic, religious, epistemic, aesthetic, ethnic/racial, sexual/gender subjective." The recognition Mahboubeh found in Shariati's words quieted, at least for a period, the sense of conflict, anger, and alienation she felt as a burgeoning intellectual and activist. Shariati was an eloquent and brilliant theorist in conversation with other revolutionary traditions and thinkers. As Roxanne Varzi (2006, 7–8) has explained, "Shariati's work was much influenced by and in conversation with Frantz Fanon, whose work on Algeria and colonialism focused on identity and self-knowledge—in short, the importance of keeping one's cultural and national identity and self-awareness in the face of racist colonial policies that aimed at assimilating 'natives.'" Shariati elaborated a conception of justice and sense of Muslim women's contributions to society on their own terms. "We are Muslims, women of a society, who wish to make decisions through reason and choice and to relate them to a history, religion and society which received its spirit and basis from Islam. A woman in this society wants to be herself. She wants to build herself, 'herself.' She wants to be reborn. In this re-birth, she wants to be her own midwife" (Shariati 1996, 83). Inspired by Shariati's writings, Mahboubeh joined her sister in the Muslim student movement, finding an identity and a community that felt genuine, culturally resonant, and self-directed.

FROM MUSLIM REVOLUTIONARY TO MUSLIM MAHBOUBEH

The figures of Fatima and also Forough Farrokhzad, the legendary Iranian poet who wrote about women's experiences in a patriarchal society, provided Mahboubeh with a language of feminism. "It wasn't about theory of feminism," she told me. "It was talking about how you can be an empowered woman and revolutionary. . . . It gave me an identity. It gave me, like, a feeling that I can put my life in this way." With time, Mahboubeh's politics shifted, incorporating other conceptual frameworks. But, she claimed, "that woman who finds herself in Forough or in Fatima, [she] is always with me. Just struggling, in a different time, in a different way." Moving between her history and her present, between her multiple versions of herself, Mahboubeh reflected, with a kind of tender criticality, on her Muslim revolutionary persona: "Many of my friends, when they [found] they [were] Muslim revolutionaries, it was the end of their journey. Many women, from my generation, we had the same journey. But they just freeze in that stage, or in that version. But that version, for me, it was like, just for a period of time. I think the thing that made me more critical was my sexuality. When you have different contexts, it makes you think different. We have the same journey, but not the same destiny."

This is a gentle critique, rather than a repudiation, but a powerful one. Like the OMSC activist Maryam (profiled in chapter 2) and Shirin Ebadi, Mahboubeh participated in the effervescent Iranian revolution. And, like Maryam, Ebadi, and countless women of her generation, she found the ideological purity and exclusionary apparatus of the postrevolutionary state troubling, but nonetheless she was committed to the spirit of the revolution and its promise to transform society. Mahboubeh received her BA in theology from Tehran University, a BA in Islamic sciences from Islamic Azad University in Tehran, and a master's in communication sciences from Allameh Tabatabaee University in Tehran. She became interested in feminist readings of the Qur'an, and in 1986 she cofounded the Institute of Women's Studies and Research (IWSR). Mahboubeh from 1993 to 2003 was editor of the institute's journal, *Farzaneh* (Wise woman), which explored feminist engagements with the discursive tradition of Islam. In her article "The Experience of Islamic Feminism in Iran," Mahboubeh wrote: "Islamic feminism is more a social movement than an ideology or social theory. . . . Islamic feminism in Iran has a history of more than three decades. This movement has tried to fill the social gaps resulting from the semi-traditional and quasi-modern character of Iranian society by insisting on the independent identity of Muslim women" (Abbasgholizadeh 2000). Her emphasis on social movement over ideology and theory underscores the distinction of Islamicate feminisms from patriarchal Islam but also responds to the ways in which, driven by the lives and experiences of Muslim women, Islamicate feminism cannot be contained within the epistemic boundaries of academia, even if it is a contested term within it.

Mahboubeh was arrested for the first time in 2004. She had just returned from a Beijing +10 Campaign on Discriminatory Laws conference in Bangkok, Thailand, where, as director of the Non-Governmental Organization Training Center (NGOTC)—a civil society capacity-building project—she gave a speech about the diversity of feminism in Iran.[3] It was the first time, she remarked, that the Beijing conferences were *officially* thinking and talking about the relationship between secular and Muslim feminisms. Arrested by *sepah*, the notoriously brutal Revolutionary Guard Corps founded by Khomeini, Mahboubeh was accused of being a "bridge" between "foreign agents" and reformist parties in Iran; she was kept in an anonymous jail site with imprisoned journalists for four weeks. Of her three arrests, she later said, this was the hardest, one of the lowest points in her life. She endured "white torture"—a form of torture based on isolation and sensory deprivation. In solidary confinement she was denied fresh air and visits from her family; she was interrogated regularly. Her interrogators accused her of being a bad Muslim, trying to get her to "confess" that she had sex with well-known reformers and therefore was a "bad" Muslim or not really a Muslim at all. Mahboubeh implored them to understand that she was indeed devout. After a couple of weeks of extreme torture, she "confessed."

But Mahboubeh insisted that in her "confession," she had taken back some power. Whereas Shirin Ebadi gave little nuance to her experience in either of her memoirs, Mahboubeh explained to me how the language of sexual "immorality" is used to insult and shame women within a particular discursive structure that defines them through traditional gender roles and places value on modesty. Fatima, said Mahboubeh, became transformed in the postrevolutionary period from a revolutionary figure to a humble, sexually modest, and more traditionally gendered woman. Mahboubeh points to the similarities between shame and insult as discursive torture tactics and the colonial discourse in prerevolutionary Iran that defined "modern" women through their sexual object status—the very discourse that the figure of Fatima challenged. As Mahboubeh described, internalizing the shame and insult would have legitimated the power her interrogators had over her. She "confessed" but maintained a sense of self and agency defined on her own terms.[4]

During this period of extreme torture, Mahboubeh told me, "I felt I had died. I was not totally functioning, in between conscious and unconscious states." It was then that she reconnected with her brother, a martyr in the Iran-Iraq War. As scholars have detailed, the increasingly conservative postrevolutionary state conceptualized a gendered notion of male martyrdom, consolidated during the Iran-Iraq War, as national duty (Moallem 2005; Varzi 2006). The war took an estimated one million lives all told, with greater casualties on the Iranian side, including Mahboubeh's brother. "I asked my brother to support me, to make me strong and to give me power," she said. "After that, I could change the context of *azaan* [call to prayer] from jail to Tajrish bazaar.[5] I can see, during *azaan*, Tajrish and smell the different spices. I can journey, by the song of the *azaan*, to my freedom. I began to separate from political Islam and feel Islam as a way I can rebuild my strength and beliefs. It gave me an identity. So the next time [my interrogator] said that I am not a Muslim, not a good woman, I have my spirituality, my memory, my culture."

In this and in many difficult and lonely moments after her departure from Iran, living in the United States as an immigrant, Mahboubeh drew on the affective nexus of religion/memory/culture, not simply as a mode of comfort but as a way of integrating her various identities, contexts, histories, and lives. She never disavowed her Muslim revolutionary self. Rather, as she had been doing from a very young age, Mahboubeh sought to reconcile her many personal and political aspirations. The reconfiguration of her Muslim self was not about privatizing religion as much as it was about disassembling it from its patriarchal and heteronormative instrumentalization by the state. In one sequence of Mahboubeh's 2014 film, *Tunnel*—an exploration of women's rights activism by those inside and outside of Iran—activists gather on June 18, 2010, in Toopkhaaneh Square in Tehran for a vigil to mark the one-year anniversary of those murdered in the Green Movement uprisings in 2009. They chant, "One, two, three . . . Oh my martyred sister, I will take back your vote" (Abbasgholizadeh 2014b). They reference Neda Agha-Soltan, who was shot dead on June 20, 2009, while walking to her car after the protests. In Mahboubeh's dreamlike connection with her brother and in the chants of activists seen in the film, women decolonize an exclusionary Islam, constructed through a postcolonial and patriarchal vision that would frame them as outside the bounds of their religion and nation.

OCCUPYING THE SPACE OF THE OTHER

Mahboubeh was jailed on two other occasions. In 2007 she was arrested with other women's rights activists during a peaceful demonstration in front of Tehran's Revolutionary Court. They were there to support OMSC activists who were on trial for the June 2006 demonstration that inspired their campaign. This time Mahboubeh was put in Evin Prison for three weeks, systematically interrogated by the Information Ministry. Her interrogators sought a confession for feeding the women's movement through international donor funding. As Mahboubeh narrated this particular moment, she explained: "There was an actual dilemma there." As director of the NGOTC, she had secured funding from Hivos People Unlimited, a

Dutch development aid organization that supports, among other things, women's empowerment, during the reform period and the expansion of civil society organizations throughout Iran. Mahboubeh felt like she was wearing two hats—one as a women's rights activist and the other as a professional nonprofit worker. "Now I can say, it was a big mistake," she told me. "When you are an organizer, you want to minimize risk." But at the time, she sought to use the grant money to build women's organizational and personal capacities, and to provide financial stability for women's movements and herself.

Before working at the NGOTC, Mahboubeh was in the private sector, working in publishing and advertising. Experiencing sexism in the workplace led her to pursue activism and writing within feminist circles. Her work on the journal *Farzaneh* and other activism, she said, was always like a parallel job. Like so many activists in the United States who have parlayed their experience in the grassroots into stable jobs, Mahboubeh felt like she could both build the NGOTC and be an activist. She had balanced multiple roles and identities before. "I learned to divide and balance being a mother and a lesbian, underground, a manager of a publishing house and at the same time, a Muslim feminist, being in Muslim feminist gatherings," she said, tearing up. "It didn't make me confused. As long as you believe, as long as you are in the field, the whole thing about being a woman, that pure feminism—for me, it was love." Mahboubeh expressed her sadness at losing this proximity to the terrain of women's rights activism and organizations inside of Iran.

As the NGOTC was repeatedly targeted by Ahmadinejad's government and shut down in 2007, Mahboubeh cofounded Meydaan Zanan (Women's field), a coalition of online and on-the-ground campaigns, each targeting a very specific issue, like gender discrimination in education or attacks by the morality police. Like the OMSC, Meydaan used real and virtual space to mobilize for women's rights. Mahboubeh was arrested again in 2009, as she was traveling to Qom by bus to attend the funeral of senior cleric Grand Ayatollah Hossein Ali Montazeri. A leader of the Iranian revolution who was once poised to become Khomeini's successor, Montazeri became increasingly critical of the rightward turn of the postrevolutionary state, resulting in his house arrest. He was a strong supporter of the sovereignty of Muslim nations, deeply committed to citizens rights. Outspoken against the Iranian government's crackdown on demonstrators in the aftermath of the contested June 2009 presidential elections, he died in December 2009.

His death was intensely felt by different generations of Iranian citizens and activists. The authorities accused Mahboubeh of making a film about women prisoners and confiscated her laptop.

Although she was released within twenty-four hours, Mahboubeh knew her computer contained personal information that would make her vulnerable to *sepah*, including arguments with her then girlfriend. In the wake of the intense crackdowns on the Green Movement, it was an extremely dark time for her. "When I came back to Tehran," she recounted, "the city was so empty. Most friends were in jail. We were depressed. We didn't have that collective feeling. I was so tired, so stressed, I couldn't focus on what is dangerous, what isn't. When they took my laptop, it was the final clampdown." Mahboubeh and her girlfriend broke up, and she left Iran in January 2010, splitting her time in London and Malaysia, to be with her daughters.

It was in Malaysia that Mahboubeh planned ZananTV as a way of staying connected to the field of women's rights activism in Iran. Her experience with what she calls "backpack activism," or in-the-street and online citizen journalism and activism, during the repressive Ahmadinejad years could be mobilized from exile.[6] The aims of ZananTV were, according to Mahboubeh, to "provide an alternative space for women to meet, interact and organize in cyberspace, enable the sharing of trustworthy information by women for women, and build women's capacity to develop their own video and audio contributions." She aspired to make women's voices and feminist analysis more visible in the Iranian opposition movement.

Shortly after Mahboubeh moved to New York, just over two years after the Green Movement, the Occupy Wall Street Movement erupted. The first time I went to the encampment in Zuccotti Park, I burst into tears. I had been in New York for more than eight years by this time and had participated in many activist events, marches, and demonstrations both in New York and in my twenty previous years in Portland, Oregon. But I had seen nothing like the Occupy encampment. I was overcome by the sense in which people were working together, day after day, making signs and food together, singing and taking care of children, forming a human microphone—in which a speaker's words are repeated by the crowd to the crowd—so that everyone could hear in the absence of an wired microphone. The human microphone functioned as utilitarian but also as a larger metaphor for the movement's horizontal and democratic ethos.

Mahboubeh was deeply moved, too. "The experience of being a women's rights activist, of going to Zuccotti Park, gave me a place," she told me.

"Coming from my experiences as an activist, and then in jail, and then exile, I felt the process of evolution, how you can find new versions of yourself. All my years, American feminists were not my people, but I felt here they are my people. I can connect with them." She recounted: "The loneliness I felt in jail, all the pressure, the sadness in exile" were eased by this connection to other activists. In one of the first segments to air on ZananTV, at the launch in Zuccotti Park, Mahboubeh speaks to Occupy activists and then directly to the camera. The following excerpts are from the transcript of this segment, worth quoting at length:

> *You've come here to occupy this space and now I've come to occupy your space.* [Turning toward the camera] I've come here because I feel that this is the best place to launch ZananTV and to announce the kickoff of this station as an alternative, visual outlet in cyberspace. . . . One reason to announce our launch here is to emphasize that ZananTV considers itself a successor to the sites of various, preceding women's movements. In particular, we follow in the steps of media outlets begun in recent years such as Zanan-e Iran (Women of Iran) and the Feminist Tribune, and then sites that followed those, including Change for Equality, Maydaan'eh Zanan (Women's Arena), the School of Feminism, and Law for an Equal Family. Truly, these sites were platforms, environments in which various women's actions and reactions could be organized and generate dialogue. To that extent, these sites were able to greatly influence the Iranian democratic movement. ZananTV is a successor to these sites because it is also a part of the women's movement. Our hope is that as a visual extension of the women's movement, ZananTV can create a space for the strengthening and enriching of ongoing debates and can incorporate existing exchanges as well as consolidate communication within and around pro-democracy advocacy in various groups and active campaigns.[7]

By launching in the heart of the Occupy Movement, ZananTV built links between Iranian feminism and grassroots movements outside of Iran and offered a pedagogical moment to activists in the United States experimenting with new organizational forms.

In "occupying" Zuccotti Park as the launchpad of ZananTV, Mahboubeh made a decolonizing move. Indeed, Occupy Wall Street was about taking back space, resources, and discourses, occupied and pilfered by neoliberalism.[8] It was a networked and horizontal movement, sharing characteristics with the OMSC, Meydaan, the Green Movement, the Arab Spring, and the many mediated movements that would follow. The presence of a colonial subject, an Iranian women's rights activist, in a space being decolonized by the Occupy Movement, a space inside a country with a long history of colonial hegemony over Iran, is a powerful double occupation/decolonization. Mahboubeh did not occupy Occupy as a benighted savior who knows better, an Iranian woman coming to save Americans, but as fellow activist, building connections to other citizens and activists in an effervescent moment that would shatter many social, political, ideological, and geographical borders.

Extending the backpack activism framework to this new encampment, Mahboubeh continues:

> We also seek to develop relationships between transnational action groups, such as the Occupy Wall Street movements in the US and Europe, and dynamic contemporary movements inside Iran. There are many similarities between our work and the virtual networks of Occupy Wall Street in the US and the various areas they occupy in different cities. In the Occupy Wall Street movement, Americans or Europeans or anyone who wants to state their demands show up in an urban area and occupy that space. Multifarious groups gather and create a base camp. They talk amongst themselves and discuss their issues. *Each person has their own sort of tent, each person has their own claim, each party comes and creates their own agenda and consolidates their teamwork, and then they begin building a movement.* Such folks are called "movement-makers" here [in Iran]. Both the physical, urban spaces and the virtual spaces where pro-democracy advocates gather—especially activists who were involved in the women's movement begun many years ago—are similar in terms of social networking apparatus. And if a space doesn't exist, whether that space is a structure or an institution, then people cannot assemble, they cannot state their issues, they cannot generate dialogue, and they cannot produce content. Therefore, there must be an arena where groups can collaborate and make their voices heard.[9]

The utilitarian and symbolic uses of backpacks, tents, and encampments created, in a sense, a home away from home for Mahboubeh. While she traveled away from her beloved country and activist terrain, enduring the crushing loneliness and difficulties of exile, she created a place in ZananTV that enabled her to become more than an exiled activist. Drawing on her own rich history, she became a fellow traveler, a backpacker, a camper in her own tent, among other backpackers, campers, and tents. In the microcosm of the Occupy Movement, the world became her home.

(RE)LOCATING WOMEN'S RIGHTS, AGAIN

Six years after Occupy, in early 2017, women again took to the streets. Signs of "Women's Rights are Human Rights" popped up in major cities and towns all over—all over the United States, that is. Donald Trump had been elected to the presidency, and many sectors of American society—some for whom protest is old hat and some for whom it is new—protested the patriarchal discourses, actions, and policies of Trump. It turns out that women in the United States need their rights, too. The election of Trump and the accusations against movie mogul Harvey Weinstein and countless other men in positions of power brought the #MeToo movement, founded by survivor, activist leader, and community organizer Tarana Burke over a decade ago, to national and international visibility. In late 2018 a national drama unfolded over the nomination of Judge Brett Kavanaugh to the US Supreme Court. Accused by Stanford research psychologist Christine Blasey Ford of sexual assault when they were in high school, Kavanaugh and Ford each testified before the Senate Judiciary Committee on September 27, 2018. The hearings captivated the entire nation and exposed the profound misogyny of political, cultural, economic, and social life in the United States. Women in the United States have seized the opportunity to jump into the deep learning curve of what it means to live and organize under extreme conditions. Iranian feminists, who've organized over many decades without giving up or giving in, may be helpful here.

When feminist scholar and women's rights activist Homa Hoodfar was imprisoned in Iran, she told *The Guardian*, her interrogators repeatedly asked if she was a feminist. "They kept asking me if I was a feminist. And I asked them to define what is a feminist—we spent quite a lot of time discussing feminism and the history of feminism in Iran." Laying claims to feminism as an indigenous project of Iran, Hoodfar sought, as have many women's rights activists within and outside of Iran, to socialize those in power to the realities and significance of feminist ideas. The accusations that she was interfering with the presidential elections as an outsider, a Western-backed enemy of the state, crushed Hoodfar. "I'm heartbroken. I know I'm a Canadian as well and I lived most of my time outside, but I was born there and brought up there and I never felt I was an outsider," she said.

"But they treated me like an enemy and that hurt more than the fact that I was in jail" (quoted in Kassam 2016).

The discourses Hoodfar uses and the affective registers she strikes here resonate with several others explored throughout this book. For many years and through many different iterations of the state, Iranian women's rights activists have insisted on the viability of a more democratic and feminist national politics. They take seriously and personally the accusations that they are working against the state, and they push back against this notion by making demands on the state and authorities to accommodate their ideas and desires, which they frame as beneficial to and emerging from Iranian society. Iranian women's rights activists have intimate conversations with their interrogators, with security forces, with those who punish and even torture them. I return to the comment from Fakhri in the heat of the Green Movement protests. "All the time I see these women standing and talking to the military people, talking to the *basijis*," she said, "trying in a very sophisticated, peaceful way to say, we're the ones who are going to live together. You are like my son." In laying claims to their belonging through the discursive and material practices of everyday life and politics, women—as activists and citizens inside Iran as well as throughout the diaspora—have fashioned a presence that cannot be ignored.

In its most active period, ZananTV covered topics from Afghan immigrants in Iran to cross-dressing strategies for girls that enable them to enter soccer matches, as well as feminist and other political events outside Iran. One segment covered a demonstration outside of the United Nations in 2013. President Hassan Rouhani had just been elected for the first time, generating a wave of hope and possibility among activists. He was at the UN to give his speech to the General Assembly, and diasporic Iranian activists were there to make demands on Rouhani and Obama. Among the activists' concerns were sanctions and political repression:

> We have two messages here today. One is for President Obama. We are, as we have for many years now, asking him to unilaterally lift the sanctions that are causing collective punishment and suffering for the Iranian people. We are asking him to stop threatening Iran with war. We are asking him to lead nuclear disarmament by disarming America's nuclear weapons first. That would be a wonderful way to lead the world toward nuclear disarmament. We have these messages and these demands for President Obama. At the same time, we have some questions and demands for President Rouhani. We're very excited that there's so much

> hope now among activists and our friends and people we know. Young people and people of all ages in Iran who voted for Rouhani are very hopeful that things could actually change. We've seen the release of some political prisoners. That's a good sign, but we really want to keep the pressure on. Rouhani has raised expectations, but there's so much that needs to be done. So we're here demanding that all political prisoners be released. We're here demanding that the attacks on women's rights to education be rescinded, that women be allowed equal access to all fields of higher education. We're here to demand that all the students who were kicked out of school for political reasons be allowed to return, and really to demand a serious economic program in Iran—job creation, which would have to start with discontinuing the persecution of trade union activists who are protesting for back wages and against factory closure. So there's a huge array of economic, political, and social demands that people in Iran have, and we're here to amplify those demands and put pressure on Rouhani to do what he was elected to do.[10]

By holding state leaders from both Iran and the United States accountable, as these activists do, and in making links between new social movements, the networked projects of Iranian feminists have underscored what Maylei Blackwell has called a "geopolitics of location: a way in which to forge solidarity projects that recognize the radically uneven terrains of power and imperial geopolitics that exist between us" (Blackwell, Briggs, and Chiu 2015, 6).

The Obama-Rouhani era saw the easing of some sanctions and the shaky brokering of the Iran Nuclear Deal. But Obama left many of the sanctions in place and an already deeply troubling Trump-Rouhani era is unfolding with alarming speed and shifts on a daily basis. In May 2018, Trump pulled out of the Iran Nuclear Deal, and by August, reinstated a horrific sanctions program that has exacerbated a failing economy and high inflation. We must keep a close watch on this geopolitical standoff as it determines the lives and livelihoods of so many. Yet we must also keep our eyes on spaces and our ears attuned to voices that are perhaps more difficult to see and hear, obscured by a world politics gone mad. In telling a small part of the story of Iranian women's rights activists, I have sought to think with them about politics and social change, about ethical and fertile transnational affiliations that are feminist, democratic, and anti-imperialist, about the possibilities for a decolonized feminism.

In the course of my conversation with Mahboubeh, she reflected: "In the last few years, I find myself as a transnational feminist. This is new for me. I never could connect with that term." By way of explanation, she said:

> Being a transnational Iranian activist is different from transnational Filipina or Latina activist. "Transnational Iranian activist" in the New York context is different than in Los Angeles or in the academy. I feel like I can put all the Mahboubeh Abbasgholizadeh versions together and feel that it has meaning for me. For me, being transnational in New York, the main indicator is the conflict between the Iranian regime and the American state. Tomorrow, President Hassan Rouhani is talking at the UN.[11] Many from the Iranian opposition are protesting, demanding things from regime change to small changes. For me, first, I want to talk about the effects of sanctions on Iranian women inside Iran, but also in my life in New York. What is the effect on my life? How am I surviving here? How is it for me when I don't have the privileges of other Americans? How can we survive when one thousand dollars six months ago was equal to four million *tomans*, and now one thousand dollars is equal to fifteen million *tomans*? How can my family provide fifteen million *tomans* to buy one thousand dollars and send to me or my daughters? This is not just me, but many women in middle age from Iran who are still depending on home, resources, and family. They are going to have lots of changes in their lives here because they are in middle age, and can't just go get a job. Every day you can't enjoy that the regime is failing because of Trump and sanctions.

Challenging the weapon of sanctions that impoverishes so many, Mahboubeh exposes the relentless poverty of choices that so many activists come to accept in this standoff between Iran and the United States.

Human rights and sanctions are weaponized by colonial powers, and some activists, understandably dismayed by decades of repression by the Iranian government, fall prey to the idea the sanctions will target the Iranian government without hurting people. Or they accept that the further immiserization of Iranians is the price to pay for pressuring the state. On the other side are those who believe that solidarity means saying nothing about the Iranian government and focusing only on the neocolonial machinations of the United States. While Rouhani's charge of "economic terrorism" against the United States is compelling, it cannot be the only flag that solidarity activists fly.[12] Like the OMSC activists, like Shirin Ebadi, like so many activists not represented in this book, Mahboubeh links women's rights to Iranian sovereignty, a sovereignty born of peace and democracy, an end to sanctions, and a full-scale deescalation of tensions between Iran and the United States.

AUTONOMY AS SOLIDARITY

When I visited her at the ZananTV offices in Brooklyn in the spring of 2015, Mahboubeh told me she wasn't sure if she would keep the project going. She was tired of the donor game. I talked to her more about this in September 2018. Initially funded with a small grant from Hivos, Mahboubeh said: "As long as ZananTV was small, it made sense. The mistake was when I wanted to develop it, to mix it between media and a workshop inside of Iran." In 2013, ZananTV became more than just a media project. She explained this transition:

> In 2013 it became a mix between ZananTV and NGOTC. Registered as nonprofit, I could get a grant for training and development inside Iran. SIDA [Swedish International Development Cooperation Agency] became interested in working with us, especially about the development section inside Iran. It seemed like it would help my vision of mixing between visual and real space. We wouldn't just be working in the field, but also we would transfer the micro level to mainstream by media, making it visible. But it was a mistake to combine. As long as we had small, humble, media organization, it was a good idea. But it was a mistake—this very fast and I think, fake, development.

I asked her what she meant by "fake." She said: "I was scared after I left Iran. How can I survive in a foreign country with no job, no identity? My identity was my activism. I wanted to create the same thing here that I had in Iran. But it was a shadow of what I had there."

As she continued along these lines, it became more clear why the different versions of herself met so often in loud and conflictual conversations in her head. "I was also scared because now, I was an immigrant. I wanted security. I wanted to support my two daughters, one a student, one in transition. And why not? I was a good nonprofit manager, a good business woman." But, she reflected, "it was not just about a job, but it could give me the same privileges I had as a women's rights activist. 'Look at me. This is my organization, my staff, my work in Iran, in London, in Malaysia. I'm very successful.' I could send a message to the regime. 'You think I am loser; no, I am good.' And message for my ex-girlfriend. 'I have a good life.'"

But the biggest factor that contributed to "fake development" was the funding game, embedded not just in bureaucracy but in colonial hegemony. She explained:

> It was the Obama time, a time for pro-democracy projects funded by international organizations, Hivos, SIDA, the US State Department. We didn't take money from the State Department, but they are all connected. When they make decisions, they say, "Who is good in women's empowerment in Iran? Come, we have money for you." SIDA came to me and said, "We have a budget. The minimum is five hundred thousand dollars per year. But you need to have an organization." We had ZananTV, but okay, we needed capacity, administration. I thought: This is our money, our petrol money![13] We take it back! Our people deserve that! There were so many activists inside Iran with so much talent, but no income. So I got this money and I sent them money. My job was getting that money, getting it to activist friends, saying, What do you want to do? I never said, This is the program, and you are my agents.

Mahboubeh's use of the term "agents" reflects the accusations leveled against her and countless others arrested, imprisoned, and exiled for their activism on trumped-up charges of threatening national security with the help of foreign agents. But it also contains an acknowledgment of the ways in which donors, as she says, used her, and how in hindsight she became complicit in their game.

Mahboubeh read critiques of the nonprofit industrial complex from US-based activists. As she put it:

> The reason we had this administration and reporting here was not strong enough to hold this bureaucracy. Trying to take money and transfer it to Iran, and play by their rules. It was a big mistake. I had problems with the language. I could not argue with the donors. They always needed someone for reporting. My personal life was not stable. I'm suffering from post-trauma, my family is far away, I am lonely. I was not happy working with the grant. I couldn't fit. It was not my character. From Occupy Wall Street to being in the office, working all the time, having meeting after meeting. They are shaping me, telling me, "If you want to do that, work

> on your accounting system, change your board, have your system to fit with our regulation."

The ways in which donor-driven agendas affect nonprofit groups is well documented by activists themselves.[14] Hoping to scale up their grassroots efforts, many activists like Mahboubeh have sought the structure and funding of a nonprofit to have a wider reach and greater effect, only to find their original missions shifting or disappearing with the money.

More disturbing is the entanglement of such putatively progressive funders with forces that seek more dangerous interventions in the Global South, including Iran and the Middle East. "Pro-democracy funding didn't work. Now the funders are changing to other programs and it is clear they are supporting 'regime change.' They are looking to make different puppets," Mahboubeh said. "I was not happy to change my friends in Iran from real activists to being involved in this system." When asked for accounting information by SIDA that would compromise the security of activists in Iran in 2015, Mahboubeh had to think hard about "choosing the grant, continuing this game." But, she said, it's always the "same game. The donors don't see me as an activist. They just see me as an agent. I felt that and it was shocking for me. Their master plan is part of colonial history, especially in the Middle East. I just don't trust them." As scholars have pointed out (Grewal 1999; Basu 2000; Saunders 2002), and as Mahboubeh experienced firsthand, development and empowerment projects, like human rights, can strengthen neocolonial ambitions, ultimately undermining autonomous women's rights projects. As she recounted to me, SIDA's "new accounting procedures" and the audit they demanded of her felt more like an interrogation of her politics. It was confusing and decidedly disempowering for Mahboubeh. "At least with my interrogators in jail in Iran, I knew them, knew where they were coming from. And I had community around me for support. With SIDA, I felt vulnerable and alone." Explaining how she took back her agency, Mahboubeh said, "I could choose to be their puppet or not. So I chose to leave professional, donor-funded activism."

In her newfound identity as a transnational Iranian activist living in New York, Mahboubeh hopes to resuscitate ZananTV, on hold now for several years. "There are other Iranian women feeling the same way that I do," she told me. "Women from my generation, people like me in different cities, who have the same motivation. What is this? This is a movement." As she continued, I could see as her face lit up how energized she was. She was excited to return to activism, but to do it and think about it differently. The movement she feels connected to is "not inside of Iran, but outside. We have the same demands, the same critique, the same vision and we see here first and then we see Iran. We see Iran from the American context. Our main challenge is with Trump, not Hassan Rouhani. Yes, the reason we are here is because of the regime, but I am here now and my conflict is with Trump." Mahboubeh's face and voice bespoke an inner peace, a peace she has been looking for in her long journey to reconcile the many parts of her. "I feel happy because I don't have to make any reports to foreign donors or grants," she said. "I don't have to say I am so against the regime. I am so happy now. I feel independent and happy. ZananTV can be for creating discussion on different issues, like the effects of sanctions on women's rights. We don't need money because we can use media."

In associating happiness with independence, Mahboubeh underscores the importance of autonomy, a theme that runs throughout the narratives explored in this book. As I have argued elsewhere, autonomy—"the relative control by local actors of their political demands, messages, and methods for communicating their struggles to the rest of the world"—is a necessary component of any coalitional and transnational solidarity politics (Sameh 2017, 188). Within the structures of development and transnational "support" for democracy in the Middle East and elsewhere, colonial practices undermine such autonomy. In addition, when revolutionary politics and social transformation are framed in more masculinist terms, women's autonomy is invariably traded for the "good" of the collective. Not only in Iran but also in revolutionary and anticolonial uprisings everywhere, the new collective (nation, government, community, group) has consistently reproduced patriarchal and hierarchical structures for ordering political, civic, and personal life.

In her evolution as an activist and human being, Mahboubeh, like the other activists considered in this book, has maintained a robust anticolonial politics. Refusing the impoverished choices of wholly criticizing or wholly defending the Iranian government, Mahboubeh firmly rejects colonialist interventions in Iran *and* continues to struggle for the self-determination of Iranian women. Exiled for nearly a decade now, she continues to be a keen observer of local and global politics as well as the ways in which different conceptions of feminism and resistance can shore up power differences and relations of domination. Here too autonomy has been an important concept and lived practice, as Mahboubeh's experience with development organizations and agendas has made abundantly clear. Characteristically intrepid, she persists in finding ways to synthesize her different identities, commitments, experiences, and desires—an endeavor that politics, in its temporal urgencies, and intellectual thought, in its disciplining tactics, can often be hostile to. Mahboubeh's life story offers examples of synthetic and expansive decolonial feminist politics and thinking, often born within different contexts of repression and domination. Born also in dreams, memories, hopes, and visions. Indeed, hers is a story of and for our time.

EPILOGUE

> Feminism in the twenty-first century is a beleaguered project. The intersectionality of gender, race and religion is a combustible mix. Understanding these issues demands complex and nuanced analyses that are irreducible to the conventional binaries of right/left or secular/religious. But, by the same token, feminism is needed more than ever. We need to be mindful of all that potentially divides us, so as to work through strategies to foreground all that we hold in common and that holds us together.
>
> —AVTAR BRAH

THROUGHOUT THIS BOOK I HAVE ANALYZED THE DISCOURSES, practices, methods, organizational cultures, and transnational networks of Iranian women's rights activists in Iran and the United States. Examining online, print, and oral accounts of women's rights work, I have attended to the relations and processes that make up everyday activist life. Although activism often culminates in the grand gestures and important acts of public protest, of revolt and revolution, its more mundane and modest labors, its intimacies if you will, are rarely made visible or theorized. I have brought the efforts of Iranian women's rights activists into view with the hope of expanding how we conceptualize a number of issues. While women's rights activists have been unable to comprehensively overturn Iran's discriminatory legal structure, they have nonetheless compelled those in power to, at the minimum, take them seriously as a constituency. In moments of uptick and hope, they have found their demands and desires for full equality reflected on the national stage. Far from insignificant has been their vocal participation in imagining a society capacious enough to synthesize national sovereignty and women's self-determination.

This leads to questions of how we theorize success and failure in the political realm. There certainly has been much to mourn in the past several decades. The unwillingness of the highest bodies of authority to secure women's full legal equality, and the framing of such a political demand as foreign interference, is a huge blemish on the face of a postcolonial nation that has improved women's life chances and opportunities immensely. I finished writing this book as the fortieth anniversary of the Iranian revolution approached. Barely into my teen years in 1979, I witnessed my father glued to the television day after day, watching Iranians throw off a dictatorship that had exacerbated class divisions, repressed political debate and protest, and jailed and killed countless numbers of its opponents. Seared into my memory are images of the revolution and the deep emotion on my father's face as an effervescent, proud, and broad swath of Iranians overthrew their much-despised monarchy.

Perhaps the most important legacy of the revolution was the creation of a vast social welfare state with programs and services that dramatically increased literacy rates and life expectancy for women and men, reduced the birth and fertility rates of women, and increased the percentage of women in universities. Louise A. Halper (2010, 3–4) has offered the following compendium of data, worth quoting at length, as it illustrates the vast material improvements in women's lives in the postrevolutionary period:

> With respect to literacy, illiterates as a percentage of Iranian women 15 to 24 declined from over a third in 1980 to less than 10 percent in 2000. Over the same period, the illiteracy rate for the entire population of adult women was cut in half, from about 60 percent to about 30 percent. As for education, the number of women in secondary school as a percentage of the eligible age group more than doubled from about 30 percent to almost 80 percent. As of 1999, for every 100 boys in primary school, 96 girls were enrolled, indicating that boys and girls were almost equally likely to be learning basic literacy and numeracy skills. In 2000, half of all Iranian university students were women, as were 60 percent of entering students, who were selected on the basis of a difficult nationwide exam. Twenty-seven percent of working-age women were in the labor force as of 2000, up from 20 percent in 1980. In terms of health, life expectancy went up by 11 years between 1980 and 2000 for both Iranian men and women. With respect to family planning, "levels of childbearing have declined faster than in any other country" [Roudi-Fahimi 2002], going from 5.6 births per woman in 1985 to 2.0 in 2000, a drop accomplished by a voluntary, but government-sponsored, birth-control program.

These changes reflect the "redistributive character of the Islamic Republic," which "readjusted the share of national wealth going to lower-income quintiles" (Halper 2010, 4). The introduction of "schools, medical clinics, roads, electricity and piped water into the countryside" (Abrahamian 2009, 13) further contributed to the overall improvement in life conditions and opportunities for Iranian women.

But, of course, the legacy is mixed. The discursive structures that offered women equality in "different but equal" terms has translated into women's secondary status under the law. In addition, Supreme Leader Ayatollah Khomeini and his successor, Ayatollah Khamenei, continued the repression, imprisonment, and execution of those, including many clerics and scholars wholly committed to the revolution, who critiqued this legal discrimination and the postrevolutionary government's authoritarianism and curtailment of democracy. We can never tally the gains of the revolution without taking into account the horrific repression of activists and citizens that unfolded at different periods over the next forty years, or the fact that the autonomy and freedom of women and others was traded away to "secure" a postcolonial nation. Within this larger history of an anticolonial revolution gone south, however, there are other stories we must also tell. Less grand narrative and more a modest record from below, this book has considered the everyday acts of women's rights activists as they have written themselves into the history of Iranian resistance, transnational feminism, and decolonial feminist world-making.

In building local and transnational networks, campaigns, projects, and discourses, the Iranian women's rights activists profiled here reimagine notions of sovereignty within their national, transnational, and feminist locations. In an interview with Marcelle Maese-Cohen, Paola Bacchetta claimed that the *de* in decolonial feminism represents "the labor at the site of the intimate, an ongoing process." The decolonial, she argues, is inseparable from coalition work. "One cannot build coalitions," Bacchetta (2010, 182) asserts, "unless the subjects of the coalitions can recognize themselves and each other as subjects." This book has demonstrated how Iranian women's rights activists labor at many sites of the intimate in a decolonial and coalitional world-making project that insists on their recognition as self-determining subjects, unwilling to be defined through patriarchal nationalisms and colonial feminisms.

Within transnational feminist scholarship, we need more studies of how women from Muslim and Middle Eastern contexts challenge the discursive and material structures of coloniality that run through geopolitics and feminist movements alike. I hope that I have offered something in that direction. In amplifying the voices of Iranian women's rights activists, and their experiences within both patriarchal and feminist spaces, I urge us to think about how the tools of critique often excise some women right out of history. There is no question that the human rights instrument has been weaponized to maintain geopolitical domination and colonial relations. But we must not revictimize Muslim and Middle Eastern women by ignoring how human rights discourses, when traced through the various sites where activists ignite them, can prove flexible. In the authoritarian moment the United States finds itself in, women's rights discourses are being reconfigured once again, as American women look in their own backyard to confront a misogynistic culture and its patriarchal institutions. While I would never wish misogynistic authoritarianism on anyone, let us use this moment to remember that there are no normative and essential rights-bearing nor rights-needing subjects.

When Shirin Ebadi (2003, emphasis added) reminded the world in her Nobel Prize acceptance speech that "[a] quest for new means and ideas to enable the countries of the South, too, to enjoy human rights and democracy, while maintaining their *political independence and territorial integrity* of their respective countries, must be given top priority," she evoked the long history of colonial powers using human rights and women's rights as part of an arsenal to manage, control, and occupy countries and regions. Iranian women's rights activists confront this history in the present when entering into political projects with and within the West. Considering the ways in which they shift attention away from their "oppression" and toward the different local patriarchies that affect all women, I have shown how Iranian women's rights activists position themselves as insightful and savvy social and political actors with something to teach and offer American feminists and feminism writ large.

In looking at Iran through the network of activists in Iran and the diaspora, I gesture toward methods of thinking about "inside" and "outside" that take seriously different national contexts, politics, and borders, while imagining notions of home, community, and belonging in new ways. In conversation with the excellent and influential feminist scholarship analyzing how women negotiate their complex relationships to Iran and the diaspora, I have drawn attention to how an examination of gendered experience is generative for understanding patriarchal nationalisms, be they imperialist or postcolonial, and global politics. I suggest that the activists considered here are doing and thinking sovereignly *beyond* the nation. Of course, a big focus of their work has been in conversation with the state, which holds the power to give and deny them their legal rights. Yet this pragmatic approach has not muted a larger narrative about how to reimagine and remake a world free from injustice, war, patriarchy, and domination, a world decolonized. In romancing the decolonial, I have pushed it to accommodate the particular labors of love considered here. We need more generous, capacious, and useful language to think about decoloniality less as a final utopian destination and more as the many relationships, practices, and processes created through thinking of and being with each other.

APPENDIX 1

Statement on the Occasion of the June 2009 Presidential Elections in Iran

THE COALITION OF THE IRANIAN WOMEN'S MOVEMENT FOR VOICING THEIR DEMANDS IN THE ELECTION

Over the years, we, as part of the Iranian women's movement and civil rights advocates with diverse backgrounds—NGOs, political parties, various campaigns, media, trade unions, and individuals—had tried various methods and, when necessary, had walked in unison to pursue our demands.

On the occasion of the forthcoming presidential elections in Iran, we are determined to form another broad coalition in order once again to put forward these essential demands. Our goal is to present our demands to the candidates. We neither support any specific candidate, nor interfere with the rights of citizens to participate or reject the elections.

The coalition of the women's movement aims:

- To divert the dominant state-machismo discourse towards a more conciliatory tone in order to address the needs of civil society, especially women's demands.
- To attract the attention of the authorities to their responsibilities to the public, especially the most underprivileged and marginalized sectors.
- To notify the presidential candidates that if they require the votes of women, students, teachers, and other social groups, the candidates' platforms must include their needs and demands.
- To show that even under harshest social and political conditions it is possible to be an effective and responsible citizen and press for a better and just society.

Credit: From Noushin Ahmadi Khorasani, *Iranian Women's One Million Signatures Campaign for Equality: The Inside Story* (Bethesda, MD: Women's Learning Partnership, 2009).

- To achieve these goals, we women must prove that we have the ability and the courage to seek all peaceful and civil avenues. Our past experiences demonstrated that whenever a window of opportunity has opened for women, misogynists have interfered and women have faced further discrimination, limitations, and inhumane violence.

WHAT DO WE WOMEN WANT?

Equal rights and the elimination of all forms of gender, ethnic, religious, and class discrimination are the essence of women's collective demands. Iranian women of all social backgrounds share this common belief that social strata construct and affect gender relations. Hence, to achieve democracy, civil liberties, and citizens' rights, women have long fought shoulder to shoulder with men. Today, as in the past and along with social groups, and aside from our specific demands as women, we demand:

- The recognition of people's freedoms as specified in the Constitution, including freedom of speech and assembly, among others.
- To end pressures on women, students, teachers, workers, ethnic and religious minorities, and individuals.

We are well aware that gender equality is a pre-condition to democracy, sustainable development and the creation of a society which is void of violence, poverty, and injustice. Hence, we urge the presidential candidates to include our two main demands which we summarize as follows:

1. To actively pursue the ratification of the Convention on the Elimination of all Forms of Discrimination against Women (CEDAW). We are aware that this proposal was submitted to the Sixth parliament in the Seventh government (the first cabinet of Mohammad Khatami) and ratified by the members, but was rejected by the Council of Guardians. This proposal was later presented to the Expediency Council, of which the president was a member. We urge the presidential candidates to put this proposal at the top of their priorities with respect to the principles of equality and non-discrimination of citizens.
2. We endeavor to eliminate discriminatory laws against women, specifically Articles 19, 20, 21, and 115 of the Constitution with respect to the principle of unconditional gender equality. We are aware that the president has no power to change laws, but we are also aware that

> if the government is committed to the principle of equality and views it as its responsibility, it is able to utilize its capabilities to encourage the parliament to include the principle of equality in the Constitution.

WHAT WILL WE DO IN THE FUTURE?

In order to explain and expand our demand, we will take whatever action is necessary to reach the three levels: general public, civil society, and the presidential candidates. The forthcoming elections have offered an opportunity for us to promote our demands in favour of women.

HOW CAN WE DO THAT?

Through our peaceful and collective actions, we will determine the future of this broad coalition and will invite and encourage groups and individuals to join us and to shape the future of this coalition.

APPENDIX 2

Shirin Ebadi's Nobel Lecture

In the Name of the God of Creation and Wisdom

December 10, 2003

Your Majesty, Your Royal Highnesses, Honourable Members of the Norwegian Nobel Committee, Excellencies, Ladies and Gentlemen,

I feel extremely honoured that today my voice is reaching the people of the world from this distinguished venue. This great honour has been bestowed upon me by the Norwegian Nobel Committee. I salute the spirit of Alfred Nobel and hail all true followers of his path.

This year, the Nobel Peace Prize has been awarded to a woman from Iran, a Muslim country in the Middle East.

Undoubtedly, my selection will be an inspiration to the masses of women who are striving to realize their rights, not only in Iran but throughout the region—rights taken away from them through the passage of history. This selection will make women in Iran, and much further afield, believe in themselves. Women constitute half of the population of every country. To disregard women and bar them from active participation in political, social, economic and cultural life would in fact be tantamount to depriving the entire population of every society of half its capability. The patriarchal culture and the discrimination against women, particularly in the Islamic countries, cannot continue forever.

Honourable members of the Norwegian Nobel Committee! As you are aware, the honour and blessing of this prize will have a positive and far-reaching impact on the humanitarian and genuine endeavours of the people of Iran and the region. The magnitude of this blessing will embrace every freedom-loving and peace-seeking individual, whether they are women or men.

I thank the Norwegian Nobel Committee for this honour that has been bestowed upon me and for the blessing of this honour for the peace-loving people of my country.

Today coincides with the 55th anniversary of the adoption of the Universal Declaration of Human Rights; a declaration which begins with the recognition of the inherent dignity and the equal and inalienable rights of all members of the human family, as the guarantor of freedom, justice and peace. And it promises a world in which human beings shall enjoy freedom of expression and opinion, and be safeguarded and protected against fear and poverty.

Unfortunately, however, this year's report by the United Nations Development Programme (UNDP), as in the previous years, spells out the rise of a disaster which distances mankind from the idealistic world of the authors of the Universal Declaration of Human Rights. In 2002, almost 1.2 billion human beings lived in glaring poverty, earning less than one dollar a day. Over 50 countries were caught up in war or natural disasters. AIDS has so far claimed the lives of 22 million individuals, and turned 13 million children into orphans.

At the same time, in the past two years, some states have violated the universal principles and laws of human rights by using the events of 11 September and the war on international terrorism as a pretext. The United Nations General Assembly Resolution 57/219, of 18 December 2002, the United Nations Security Council Resolution 1456, of 20 January 2003, and the United Nations Commission on Human Rights Resolution 2003/68, of 25 April 2003, set out and underline that all states must ensure that any measures taken to combat terrorism must comply with all their obligations under international law, in particular international human rights and humanitarian law. However, regulations restricting human rights and basic freedoms, special bodies and extraordinary courts, which make fair adjudication difficult and at times impossible, have been justified and given legitimacy under the cloak of the war on terrorism.

The concerns of human rights' advocates increase when they observe that international human rights laws are breached not only by their recognized opponents under the pretext of cultural relativity, but that these principles are also violated in Western democracies, in other words countries which were themselves among the initial codifiers of the United

Nations Charter and the Universal Declaration of Human Rights. It is in this framework that, for months, hundreds of individuals who were arrested in the course of military conflicts have been imprisoned in Guantanamo, without the benefit of the rights stipulated under the international Geneva conventions, the Universal Declaration of Human Rights and the [United Nations] International Covenant on Civil and Political Rights.

Moreover, a question which millions of citizens in the international civil society have been asking themselves for the past few years, particularly in recent months, and continue to ask, is this: why is it that some decisions and resolutions of the UN Security Council are binding, while some other resolutions of the council have no binding force? Why is it that in the past 35 years, dozens of UN resolutions concerning the occupation of the Palestinian territories by the state of Israel have not been implemented promptly, yet, in the past 12 years, the state and people of Iraq, once on the recommendation of the Security Council, and the second time, in spite of UN Security Council opposition, were subjected to attack, military assault, economic sanctions, and, ultimately, military occupation?

Ladies and Gentlemen, allow me to say a little about my country, region, culture and faith.

I am an Iranian. A descendent of Cyrus The Great. The very emperor who proclaimed at the pinnacle of power 2500 years ago that "he would not reign over the people if they did not wish it." And [he] promised not to force any person to change his religion and faith and guaranteed freedom for all. The Charter of Cyrus The Great is one of the most important documents that should be studied in the history of human rights.

I am a Muslim. In the Koran the Prophet of Islam has been cited as saying: "Thou shalt believe in thine faith and I in my religion." That same divine book sees the mission of all prophets as that of inviting all human beings to uphold justice. Since the advent of Islam, too, Iran's civilization and culture has become imbued and infused with humanitarianism, respect for the life, belief and faith of others, propagation of tolerance and compromise and avoidance of violence, bloodshed and war. The luminaries of Iranian literature, in particular our Gnostic literature, from Hafiz, Mowlavi [better known in the West as Rumi] and Attar to Saadi, Sanaei, Naser Khosrow and Nezami, are emissaries of this humanitarian culture. Their message manifests itself in this poem by Saadi: "The sons of Adam are limbs of one another, having been created of one essence."

"When the calamity of time afflicts one limb, the other limbs cannot remain at rest."

The people of Iran have been battling against consecutive conflicts between tradition and modernity for over 100 years. By resorting to ancient traditions, some have tried and are trying to see the world through the eyes of their predecessors and to deal with the problems and difficulties of the existing world by virtue of the values of the ancients. But, many others, while respecting their historical and cultural past and their religion and faith, seek to go forth in step with world developments and not lag behind the caravan of civilization, development and progress. The people of Iran, particularly in the recent years, have shown that they deem participation in public affairs to be their right, and that they want to be masters of their own destiny.

This conflict is observed not merely in Iran, but also in many Muslim states. Some Muslims, under the pretext that democracy and human rights are not compatible with Islamic teachings and the traditional structure of Islamic societies, have justified despotic governments, and continue to do so. In fact, it is not so easy to rule over a people who are aware of their rights, using traditional, patriarchal and paternalistic methods.

Islam is a religion whose first sermon to the Prophet begins with the word "Recite!" The Koran swears by the pen and what it writes. Such a sermon and message cannot be in conflict with awareness, knowledge, wisdom, freedom of opinion and expression and cultural pluralism.

The discriminatory plight of women in Islamic states, too, whether in the sphere of civil law or in the realm of social, political and cultural justice, has its roots in the patriarchal and male-dominated culture prevailing in these societies, not in Islam. This culture does not tolerate freedom and democracy, just as it does not believe in the equal rights of men and women, and the liberation of women from male domination (fathers, husbands, brothers . . .), because it would threaten the historical and traditional position of the rulers and guardians of that culture.

One has to say to those who have mooted the idea of a clash of civilizations, or prescribed war and military intervention for this region, and resorted to social, cultural, economic and political sluggishness of the South in a bid to justify their actions and opinions, that if you consider international human rights laws, including the nations' right to determine their own destinies, to be universal, and if you believe in the priority and superiority of parliamentary democracy over other political systems, then you cannot think only of your own security and comfort, selfishly and contemptuously. A quest for new means and ideas to enable the countries of the South, too, to enjoy human rights and democracy, while maintaining their political independence and territorial integrity of their respective countries, must be given top priority by the United Nations in respect of future developments and international relations.

The decision by the Nobel Peace Committee to award the 2003 prize to me, as the first Iranian and the first woman from a Muslim country, inspires me and millions of Iranians and nationals of Islamic states with the hope that our efforts, endeavours and struggles toward the realization of human rights and the establishment of democracy in our respective countries enjoy the support, backing and solidarity of international civil society. This prize belongs to the people of Iran. It belongs to the people of the Islamic states, and the people of the South for establishing human rights and democracy.

Ladies and Gentlemen, in the introduction to my speech, I spoke of human rights as a guarantor of freedom, justice and peace. If human rights fail to be manifested in codified laws or put into effect by states, then, as rendered in the preamble of the Universal Declaration of Human Rights, human beings will be left with no choice other than staging a "rebellion against tyranny and oppression." A human being divested of all dignity, a human being deprived of human rights, a human being gripped by starvation, a human being beaten by famine, war and illness, a humiliated human being and a plundered human being is not in any position or state to recover the rights he or she has lost.

If the 21st century wishes to free itself from the cycle of violence, acts of terror and war, and avoid repetition of the experience of the 20th century—that most disaster-ridden century of humankind, there is no other way except by understanding and putting into practice every human right for all mankind, irrespective of race, gender, faith, nationality or social status.

In anticipation of that day.
With much gratitude
Shirin Ebadi

NOTES

INTRODUCTION

Epigraphs: Fakhri (a pseudonym), interview with the author, October 22, 2009; Mahboubeh Abbasgholizadeh, interview with the author, June 14, 2018.

1 Mahboubeh Abbasgholizadeh, interview with the author, June 14, 2018.

2 I have used pseudonyms for all of the California OMSC activists. Sahar, interview with the author, October 23, 2009.

3 In his "9/11 Address to the Nation," delivered on September 11, 2001, President George W. Bush stated: "America and our friends and allies join with all those who want peace and security in the world, and we stand together to win the war against terrorism." In an "Address to a Joint Session of Congress Following 9/11 Attacks," delivered on September 20, 2001, Bush claimed: "Our war on terror begins with al Qaeda, but it does not end there. It will not end until every terrorist group of global reach has been found, stopped, and defeated." Soon after, the phrases "war on terror," "war on terrorism," and "the global war on terror" (GWOT) became interchangeable. GWOT still functions as the overriding military, ideological, and discursive apparatus of the day.

4 Alavi 2005; Amir-Ebrahimi 2008; Bunt 2009; Godazagar 2009; Khiabany and Sreberny 2007; Semati 2009; and Shakhsari 2011.

5 The #saynotothememo movement erupted in response to the Trump administration's move to define gender as a biological, immutable category, rolling back protection for transgender people.

6 Castells 2015; Dixon 2014; Mottahedeh 2014; and Zayani 2015.

7 This photo circulated on Facebook and the Occupy website, generating lots of confusion. Although the exact source is unclear, most Iranian activists I've spoken with agree that the photo looks like a government-staged rally along the lines of the many government-staged "Down with the USA" rallies used as anti-West propaganda.

8 Taravati as quoted in Thomas Erdbrink, "Rouhani Wins Re-election in Iran by a Wide Margin," *New York Times*, May 20, 2017.

9 Afary 1996; Paidar 1995; Sanasarian 1982; and Tohidi 2010.

10 In more recent work Najmabadi (2005) explores how Iranian modernity hinged on the production of a heterosocial world that disavowed homosociality, homoeroticism, and same-sex affectivity. Heterosociality and its complementary heterosexuality become naturalized through the assignation of a gender binary to "modern" men and women. Najmabadi further argues that women's claims

for equality also did the cultural work of disavowing homosociality and reproducing the ideal of heterosociality and heterosexuality. As a gendered project, the construction of a modern nation legitimized ideas about women's equality but "harnessed this project to the heteronormalizing dynamic of Iranian modernity" (Najmabadi 2005, 231). This critical work uncovers the violence contained within the state's modernizing project and women's complicity in such a project.

11 Bacchetta 2010; Maese-Cohen 2010; Pérez 2010; Mendoza 2015; Icaza 2017; and Mignolo and Walsh 2018.

12 Included with other writings in *Shariati on Shariati and the Muslim Woman* (1996).

13 Abu-Lughod 2002; Ahmed 1992; Mohanty 1991; Puar 2007; Razack 2008; and Spivak 1988.

14 Alexander and Mohanty 1997; Grewal and Kaplan 1994; and Mohanty, Russo, and Torres 1991.

15 These feminist scholars include Karim 2006; Karim and Khorrami 1999; Malek 2006, 2015; Moallem 2005; Motlagh 2011; Naghibi 2016; and Rahimieh 2007.

16 Afshar 1998; Hoodfar 1999; Moghadam 2002, 2003; and Paidar 2002.

17 By "formal" I mean at the level of electoral and parliamentary politics. At the grassroots, civil society level, the reform or opposition movement has ebbed and flowed in the post-2005 period.

18 Other publications include *Farzaneh*, *Zan*, *Badjens*, *Zan-e Rouz*, *Payam-e Zan*, and *Payam-e Hajjar*.

19 See Alidou 2011; Basarudin 2016; Deeb 2006; Hafez 2011; Kassam 2010; Mernissi 1987; and Salime 2011 for examples outside Iran.

20 Bayes and Tohidi 2001; Hoodfar 1999; Mahdi 2003; Moghadam 2002; Moghadam 2003; Paidar 2002; and Tohidi 2002.

21 In deploying the term "Western feminism," I draw attention to its particular hegemonic forms critiqued in this book. I recognize within Western feminism there are many feminisms, including those that destabilize the term itself.

CHAPTER 1. WE SANG THE SONGS OF EQUALITY

Epigraphs: Bayat, 2007, 15; Ebadi, Change for Equality website; Sahar, interview with the author, October 23, 2009.

1 Pardis, interview with the author, October 24, 2009.

2 Women have been disqualified from running for president through a literal interpretation of the articles of the Constitution that refer to the president as "he."

3 Sahar and Zahra, interview with the author, October 23, 2009.

4 Between 98 and 99 percent of the Iranian population is Muslim (Association of Religion Data Archives n.d.). Of course, among Muslims there are several different religious and political identifications: secular Muslim, Islamist, Islamic feminist, etc. (see the Introduction).

5 Asad 1993, 2003; and Mahmood 2001, 2005.

6 I too use this understanding of culture, acknowledging there are multiple cultures within any society. But here I'm exploring the ever-shifting practices and discourses about gender that permeate most corners of society.

7 In 2008 the International Campaign for Human Rights in Iran reported that, since August 2006, activists in the OMSC "faced harassment and obstruction of their peaceful efforts by security forces. They have been systematically denied space for convening meetings. Additionally, activists have been arrested while colleting signatures in support of the Campaign's petition . . . for convening meetings and for writing on the Campaign's website. As of 2008, 44 members of the Campaign have been arrested for alleged violations in relation to their peaceful activities in support of women's rights." In addition to harassment of campaigners, the website was frequently blocked by government authorities.

8 The Family Protection Bill failed to be ratified by the full Parliament in September 2008. Among other discriminatory provisions, the Family Protection Bill would have put a tax on *mehr* (dowry paid to the wife), authorized polygamous marriages without the consent of the first wife, and made divorce for women even more difficult to obtain. A coalition of feminist activists, including the campaign, was instrumental in its defeat.

9 The state continues to inflict corporeal punishment, sometimes in public, despite its legal obligations to forbid such acts as a signatory to the International Covenant on Civil and Political Rights. Authorities justify corporeal punishment for activists and journalists who are accused of "publicly lying" or "threatening national security" and for citizens accused of "immorality," by referring to Islamic law.

10 Pardis, interview with the author, October 24, 2009.

11 Sahar, interview with the author, October 23, 2009.

12 Mitra, interview with the author, October 22, 2009.

13 Sahar, email interview with the author, August 7, 2018.

14 Fakhri, email interview with the author, July 25, 2018.

15 See the "Statement on the Occasion of the June 2009 Presidential Elections in Iran," from the Coalition of the Iranian Women's Movement for Voicing Their Demand in the Election, reproduced in Appendix 1.

16 Mitra, interview with the author, October 22, 2009.

CHAPTER 2. WITHOUT THOSE BRANCHES, THIS CANNOT BE A TREE

Epigraphs: Dabashi 2016, 188; Rahimieh 2007, 225.

1 According to US census data from 2000, of the 338,266 Iranians living in the United States, 159,016 lived in California. According to US census data from 2010, 463,552 Iranians were living in the United States. Numbers for California were unavailable.

2 Here I'm referencing the 2009 postelection Green Movement.

3 Vashti and Fakhri, interview with the author, October 22, 2009.

4 See chapter 3 for more about women's creative writing and, in particular, the genre of memoir.

5 Pardis, interview with the author, October 24, 2009.
6 Pardis, interview with the author, October 24, 2009.
7 Sahar, interview with the author, October 23, 2009; emphasis added.
8 Sahar, interview with the author, October 23, 2009.
9 Zahra, interview with the author, October 23, 2009.
10 Sahar, interview with the author, October 23, 2009.
11 Sahar, interview with the author, October 23, 2009.
12 Maryam, interview with the author, October 24, 2009.
13 Sahar, interview with the author, October 23, 2009.
14 Zahra, interview with the author, October 23, 2009.
15 Zahra, interview with the author, October 23, 2009.
16 Maryam, interview with the author, October 24, 2009.
17 Maryam, interview with the author, October 24, 2009.
18 Maryam, interview with the author, October 24, 2009.
19 Maryam, interview with the author, October 24, 2009.
20 Maryam, interview with the author, October 24, 2009.
21 Maryam, interview with the author, October 24, 2009.
22 Zahra, interview with the author, October 23, 2009.
23 See Shalakany 2007 for a case study of troubling human rights intervention in Egypt.
24 In 2007 campaigner Parvin Ardalan was awarded the Olaf Palme Award, and in 2008 campaigner Nasrin Sotoudeh was awarded the International Human Rights Award of Italy (Moghadam and Gheytanchi 2010).
25 Maryam, interview with the author, October 24, 2009.
26 Abu-Lughod 2013; Amar 2013; Bernal and Grewal 2014; Eisenstein 2007; Farris 2017; Grewal 2017; and Puar 2007.
27 Mitra, interview with the author, October 22, 2009.
28 Mitra, interview with the author, October 22, 2009
29 For an example of how this functions in the context of transnational labor organizing, see Brooks 2007, specifically chapter 3.
30 Pardis, interview with the author, October 24, 2009.
31 Mitra, interview with the author, October 22, 2009.
32 Pardis, interview with the author, October 24, 2009.
33 Pardis, interview with the author, October 24, 2009.
34 Mitra, interview with the author, October 22, 2009.
35 Pardis, interview with the author, October 24, 2009; emphasis added.
36 Fakhri, interview with the author, October 22, 2009.
37 Farhadi's films, among other Iranian cinematic representations, give nuance and texture to intimate and everyday life in Iran. See, for instance, Rahimieh 2009 for an analysis of representations of divorce in Iranian cinema.
38 I was active in this collective for many years, including at the time of this report, and contributed, as we all did, to the collective analysis put forward here.

CHAPTER 3: HUMAN RIGHTS WORK IS AN ACT OF WORSHIP

Epigraphs: Ebadi 2003; Ebadi 2015, 277.

1 See Appendix 2 for Shirin Ebadi's full Nobel lecture.

2 Examples before 2003 include Khatami's presidential wins in 1997 and 2001 and Iran's defeat of the United States in World Cup Soccer in 1998.

3 Khomeini returned to Iran on February 1, 1979. The Shah had been forced into exile in January and Prime Minister Shahpur Bakhtiar was leading the government. Khomeini's remarks were aimed at Bakhtiar; http://news.bbc.co.uk/onthisday/hi/dates/stories/february/1/newsid_2521000/2521003.stm (accessed August 20, 2017).

4 In her Nobel lecture, Ebadi (2003) said: "The concerns of human rights' advocates increase when they observe that international human rights laws are breached not only by their recognized opponents under the pretext of cultural relativity, but that these principles are also violated in Western democracies, in other words countries which were themselves among the initial codifiers of the United Nations Charter and the Universal Declaration of Human Rights. It is in this framework that, for months, hundreds of individuals who were arrested in the course of military conflicts have been imprisoned in Guantanamo, without the benefit of the rights stipulated under the international Geneva conventions, the Universal Declaration of Human Rights and the [United Nations] International Covenant on Civil and Political Rights." For the full lecture, see Appendix 2.

5 As Rastegar (2006, 109) has noted: "As of October 2005, the memoir had sold more than nine hundred thousand copies in the United States (*National Sales*) and was approaching its second year on the *New York Times* best sellers list ('Paperback Best Sellers,' 2005)."

6 For an elaboration of the latter, see the forthcoming work by Azza Basarudin and Khanum Shaikh.

7 Nafisi has been linked in intellectual partnership and friendship to Lewis, a well-known British historian and Orientalist.

8 This claim is based on many, many casual conversations I've had about my book, which, on the mention of Iran and women, often turn toward a discussion of Nafisi. When describing my project as one that includes an analysis of Ebadi, few people—from academics to laypeople—are as familiar with Ebadi.

9 For different kinds of discussions of sexuality in Iran, see Najmabadi 2005; Satrapi 2009; Mahdavi 2009; and chapter 4, note 4 in this book.

10 Amar 2013; Farris 2017; Grewal 2017; and Puar 2007.

CHAPTER 4: WE HAVE THE SAME JOURNEY, BUT NOT THE SAME DESTINY

Epigraph: Lewis 2017, 16.

1 The panel was part of a conference on transnational feminisms, marking the twentieth year since the 1994 publication of the field-generating book by Inderpal Grewal and Caren Kaplan, *Scattered Hegemonies: Postmodernity and Transnational Feminist Practices*. The recorded session is available at

http://bcrw.barnard.edu/videos/digital-engagement-in-transnational-feminisms/.

2 Mahboubeh's life history and direct quotes from her in this chapter come from interviews with the author in New York on June 14 and over Skype on September 25, 2018.

3 The Beijing conference is part of the UN World Conferences on Women that have convened every five years since 1975.

4 An exploration of the complexities of sexuality within Muslim contexts and Iran is beyond the scope of this book. But, as I signal in chapter 3, the framing of Islam and Muslim societies and communities as "sexually backward" or inherently hostile to non-normative sexualities is part of a colonial framework that divides the world between "modern/superior" and "backward/inferior" societies. As many scholars have explored, the colonial discourse that cast MENA cultures as sexually exotic and *unrepressed* in the eighteenth and nineteenth centuries is reversed in the twentieth and twenty-first centuries to frame Muslim societies as fundamentally sexually *repressive* (Massad 2002; Puar 2007; Hélie 2012; Shakhsari 2012). Recent scholarship considers the ways in which modernity disciplined non-normative gendered and sexual desires and affiliations (Najmabadi 2005; De Sondy 2013).

5 An old bazaar in northern Tehran.

6 See "Digital Engagement in Transnational Feminisms," Barnard Center for Research on Women, http://bcrw.barnard.edu/videos/digital-engagement-in-transnational-feminisms/.

7 "ZananTV Launches in the Heart of Occupy Wall Street," https://zanantv.net/en/2011/12/01/zanan-tv-launches-heart-occupy-wall-street/ (accessed July 23, 2012), emphasis added.

8 I acknowledge the imperfections and limits of the Occupy Movement and the ways in which it mobilized the word "occupy" while not always recognizing the earlier occupations of Native American lands.

9 "ZananTV Launches in the Heart of Occupy Wall Street," https://zanantv.net/en/2011/12/01/zanan-tv-launches-heart-occupy-wall-street/ (accessed July 23, 2012), emphases added.

10 "Obama and Rouhani: A Call to Action," https://zanantv.net/en/2013/09/25/obama-rouhani-call-action/ (accessed February 18, 2014).

11 The 73rd Session of the United Nations General Assembly. Rouhani spoke September 26, 2018.

12 Rouhani made this comment in his speech at the UN General Assembly.

13 Mahmoud Ahmadinejad won the 2005 presidential elections on a platform that promised to bring oil money to people's dinner tables.

14 For examples, see INCITE! 2007; Munshi and Willse 2016.

EPILOGUE

Epigraph: Brah and Clini 2017, 167.

REFERENCES

Abbasgholizadeh, Mahboubeh A. 2000. "The Experience of Islamic Feminism in Iran." *Farzaneh* 5, no. 10 (Winter): 7–14.

———. 2014a. "'To Do Something We Are Unable To Do in Iran': Cyberspace, the Public Sphere, and the Iranian Women's Movement." *Signs* 39, no. 4 (Summer): 831–40.

———. 2014b. *Tunnel*. Produced and directed by Mahboubeh Abbasgholizadeh. www.youtube.com/watch?v=tpHcm5OLCXA (accessed September 30, 2018).

Abrahamian, Ervand. 1982. *Iran Between Two Revolutions*. Princeton, NJ: Princeton University Press.

———. 2009. "Why the Islamic Republic Has Survived." *Middle East Report* no. 250 (Spring): 10–16.

Abugideiri, Hibba. 2002. "Hagar: A Historical Model for 'Gender Jihad.'" In *Daughters of Abraham: Feminist Thought in Judaism, Christianity, and Islam*, ed. Yvonne Yazbek Haddad and John Esposito, 81–107. Gainesville: University Press of Florida.

Abu-Lughod, Lila. 2002. "Do Muslim Women Really Need Saving? Anthropological Reflections on Cultural Relativism and Its Others." *American Anthropologist* 104, no. 3 (September): 783–90.

———. 2011. "The Active Social Life of 'Muslim Women's Rights.'" In *Gender and Culture at the Limit of Rights*, ed. Dorothy Hodgson, 101–19. Philadelphia: University of Pennsylvania Press.

———. 2013. *Do Muslim Women Need Saving?* Cambridge: Harvard University Press.

Afary, Janet. 1996. *The Iranian Constitutional Revolution, 1906–1911: Grassroots Democracy, Social Democracy, and the Origins of Feminism*. New York: Columbia University Press.

———. 2009. *Sexual Politics in Modern Iran*. New York: Cambridge University Press.

Afshar, Haleh. 1998. *Islam and Feminisms: An Iranian Case Study*. New York: St. Martin's Press.

Ahmed, Lila. 1992. *Women and Gender in Islam: Historical Roots of Modern Debate*. New Haven: Yale University Press.

Alavi, Nasrin. 2005. *We Are Iran*. London: Portobello Books Ltd.

Alexander, M. Jacqui, and Chandra Talpade Mohanty, eds. 1997. *Feminist Genealogies, Colonialist Legacies, Democratic Futures*. New York: Routledge.

Alidou, Ousseina D. 2011. "Muslim Women, Rights Discourse, and the Media in Kenya." In *Gender and Culture at the Limit of Rights*, ed. Dorothy Hodgson, 101–19. Philadelphia: University of Pennsylvania Press.

Al Jazeera. 2003. "Nobel Winner Urges Freedom for Dissidents." *Al Jazeera*. October 10. www.aljazeera.com/programmes/oneonone/shirin_ebadi (accessed November 28, 2003).

Alvarez, Sonia. 1999. "Advocating Feminism: The Latin American Feminist NGO Boom." *International Journal of Feminist Politics* 1, no. 2: 181–209.

———. 2009. "Beyond NGO-ization? Reflections from Latin America." *Development* 52, no. 2: 175–84.

Amar, Paul. 2013. *The Security Archipelago: Human-Security States, Sexuality Politics, and the End of Neoliberalism*. Durham, NC: Duke University Press.

Amirahmadi, Hooshang, and Shahir Shahidsale. 2012. "The Ninth Iranian Parliamentary Elections." American Iranian Council, February 13.

Amir-Ebrahimi, Masserat. 2008. "Blogging from Qom, Behind Walls and Veils." *Comparative Studies of South Asia, Africa and the Middle East* 28, no. 2: 235–49.

Asad, Talal. 1993. *Genealogies of Religion: Discipline and Reasons of Power in Christianity and Islam*. Baltimore, MD: Johns Hopkins University Press.

———. 2003. *Formations of the Secular: Christianity, Islam, Modernity*. Stanford, CA: Stanford University Press.

Aslan, Reza. 2006. "Review of *Iran Awakening: A Memoir of Revolution and Hope*, by Shirin Ebadi with Azadeh Moaveni." *The Nation*, May 29.

Association of Religion Data Archives. N.d. Iran. www.thearda.com/internationalData/countries/Country_110_2.asp (accessed June 5, 2010).

Bacchetta, Paola. 2010. "Decolonial Praxis: Enabling Intranational and Queer Coalition Building." *Qui parle* 18, no. 2 (Spring–Summer): 147–92.

Badran, Margot. 2006. "Islamic Feminism Revisited." *Counter Currents*. October 2. www.countercurrents.org/gen-badran100206.htm (accessed 23 October 2008).

———. 2009. *Feminism in Islam: Secular and Religious Convergences*. Oxford: Oneworld Publications.

Bahkru, Tanya. 2008. "Negotiating and Navigating the Rough Terrain of Transnational Feminist Research." *Journal of International Women's Studies* 10, no. 2: 198–216.

Barlas, Asma. 2002. *"Believing Women" in Islam: Unreading Patriarchal Interpretations of the Qur'an*. Austin: University of Texas Press.

Barlow, Tani. 2000. "International Feminism of the Future." *Signs* 25, no. 4 (Summer): 1099–1105.

Bar On, Bat-Ami. 1993. "Marginality and Epistemic Privilege." In *Feminist Epistemologies*, ed. Linda Alcoff and Elizabeth Potter, 83–100. New York: Routledge.

Basarudin, Azza. 2016. *Humanizing the Sacred*. Seattle: University of Washington Press.

Basu, Amrita, ed. 1995. *The Challenge of Local Feminisms: Women's Movements in Global Perspective*. Boulder, CO: Westview Press.

———. 2000. "Globalization of the Local/Localization of the Global: Mapping Transnational Women's Movements." *Meridians: Feminism, Race, Transnationalism* 1, no. 1: 68–84.

Batliwala, Srilatha. 2002. "Grassroots Movements as Transnational Actors: Implications for Global Civil Society." *Voluntas: International Journal of Voluntary and Nonprofit Organizations* 13, no. 4 (December): 393–409.

Bayat, Asef. 2007. *Making Islam Democratic: Social Movements and the Post-Islamist Turn.* Stanford, CA: Stanford University Press.

———. 2013. *Life as Politics: How Ordinary People Change the Middle East.* Stanford, CA: Stanford University Press.

Bayes, Jane H., and Nayereh Tohidi, eds. 2001. *Globalization, Gender, and Religion: The Politics of Women's Rights in Catholic and Muslim Contexts.* New York: Palgrave.

BBC News World Edition. 2003. "Shirn Ebadi's Peace Prize Citation." October 10. http://news.bbc.co.uk/2/hi/middle_east/3180486.stm (accessed November 28, 2003).

Bernal, Victoria. 2014. *Nation as Network: Diaspora, Cyberspace and Citizenship.* Chicago: University of Chicago Press.

Bernal, Victoria, and Inderal Grewal. 2014. *Theorizing NGOs: States, Feminisms, and Neoliberalism.* Durham, NC: Duke University Press.

Blackwell, Maylei, Laura Briggs, and Mignonette Chiu. 2015. "Transnational Feminisms Roundtable." *Frontiers: A Journal of Women's Studies* 36, no. 3: 1–24.

Brah, Avtar, and Clelia Clini. 2017. "Contemporary Feminist Discourses and Practices within and across Boundaries: An Interview with Avtar Brah." *Feminist Review* 117: 163–70.

Brooks, Ethel C. 2007. *Unraveling the Garment Industry: Transnational Organizing and Women's Work.* Minneapolis: University of Minnesota Press.

Bunt, Gary R. 2009. *iMuslims: Rewiring the House of Islam.* Chapel Hill: University of North Carolina Press.

Bush, George W. 2001a. "Address to a Joint Session of Congress Following the Attacks of 9/11." *American Rhetoric.* www.americanrhetoric.com/speeches/gwbush911jointsessionspeech.htm (accessed February 20, 2012).

———. 2001b. "9/11 Address to the Nation." *American Rhetoric.* www.americanrhetoric.com/speeches/gwbush911addresstothenation.htm (accessed February 20, 2012).

Castells, Manuel. 2000. *The Information Age: Economy, Sociology, and Culture.* 2nd ed. Oxford: Blackwell.

———. 2015. *Networks of Outrage and Hope: Social Movements in the Internet Age.* Cambridge, MA: Polity Press.

Change for Equality. 2006a. "About 'One Million Signatures Campaign Demanding Changes to Discriminatory Laws.'" August 28. www.campaignforequality.info/english/spip.php?article18 (accessed October 23, 2008).

———. 2006b. "The Effect of Laws on Women's Lives." August 28. www.campaignforequality.info/english/spip.php?article41 (accessed October 23, 2008).

———. 2006c. "Interview with Simin Behbahani by Mansoureh Shojaee: The Million Signatures Campaign is an Ultimatum." December 17. www.campaign forequality.info/english/spip.php?article6 (accessed October 23, 2008).

———. 2006d. "Launching of the One Million Signatures Campaign Demanding Changes to Discriminatory Laws." August 27. www.campaignforequality.info /english/spip.php?article20 (accessed October 23, 2008).

———. 2006e. "Petition: International Support for Women's Campaign." August 27. www.campaignforequality.info/english/spip.php?article19 (accessed October 23, 2008).

———. 2006f. "Shahla Lahiji: Signature Drives are the Most Civic of Activities." December 10. www.campaignforequality.info/english/spip.php?article4 (accessed October 23, 2008).

———. 2007a. "Cultures Create Civil Laws: Interview with Taghi Rahmani." July 6. www.campaignforequality.info/english/spip.php?article109 (accessed October 23, 2008).

———. 2007b. "Interview with Jelve Javaheri: From a Reading Group to the Campaign for One Million Signatures." December 30. www.campaignforequality.info /english/spip.php?article196 (accessed October 23, 2008).

———. 2007c. "Interview with Sara Loghmani: The Campaign for One Million Signatures: A Grassroots Effort." January 6. www.campaignforequality.info /english/spip.php?article28 (accessed October 23, 2008).

———. 2008a. "Esha Momeni: A Different Experience." www.campaignforequal ity.info/english/spip.php?article374 (accessed October 23, 2008).

———. 2008b. "Interview with Shirin Ebadi: Illegal to Publicly Announce Charges before Trial and Conviction." January 6. www.campaignforequality.info/en glish/spip.php?article201 (accessed October 23, 2008).

———. 2009. "Sussan Tahmasebi: If Alieh Belongs in Prison, Then All Women Should Be Imprisoned." February 10. www.campaignforequality.info/english /spip.php?article466 (accessed February 23, 2009).

Charlesworth, Hilary. 1994. "What Are 'Women's International Human Rights?'" In *Human Rights of Women: National and International Perspectives*, ed. Rebecca J. Cook, 59–84. Philadelphia: University of Pennsylvania Press.

Cheah, Pheng. 1997. "Posit(ion)ing Human Rights in the Current Global Conjuncture." *Public Culture* 9: 233–66.

Clough, Patricia. 1998. *The End/s of Ethnography: From Realism to Social Criticism*. New York: Peter Lang.

Connolly, William E. 1999. *Why I Am Not a Secularist*. Minneapolis: University of Minnesota Press.

Dabashi, Hamid. 2016. *Iran without Borders: Towards a Critique of the Postcolonial Nation*. London: Verso.

Deeb, Lara. 2006. *An Enchanted Modern: Gender and Public Piety in Shi'i Lebanon*. Princeton, NJ: Princeton University Press.

Desai, Manisha. 2005. "Transnationalism: The Face of Feminist Politics Post-Beijing." *International Social Science Journal* 57, no. 184: 319–30.

De Sondy, Amandullah. 2013. *Islamic Masculinities*. London: Bloomsbury.

DeVault, Marjorie. 1999. *Liberating Method: Feminism and Social Research.* Philadelphia: Temple University Press.

Dixon, Chris. 2014. *Another Politics: Talking across Today's Transformative Movements.* Oakland: University of California Press.

Ebadi, Shirin. 2003. "In the Name of the God of Creation and Wisdom." Nobel Lecture, December 10. www.nobelprize.org/nobel_prizes/peace/laureates/2003/ebadi-lecture-e.html (accessed March 2, 2004).

———. 2007. *Iran Awakening: One Woman's Journey to Reclaim Her Life and Country.* With Azadeh Moaveni. New York: Random House.

———. 2015. *Until We Are Free: My Fight for Human Rights in Iran.* New York: Random House.

Ehsani, Kaveh, and Norma Claire Moruzzi. 2014. "Mahsa Shekarloo." *Middle East Report* no. 272 (Fall): 48.

Eickelman, Dale F., and Jon W. Anderson. 2003. "Redefining Muslim Publics." In *New Media in the Muslim World: The Emerging Public Sphere*, ed. Dale F. Eickelman and Jon W. Anderson, 1–18. Bloomington: Indiana University Press.

Eisenstein, Zillah. 2007. *Sexual Decoys: Gender, Race, and War in Imperial Democracy.* London: Zed Books.

Esfandiari, Haleh. 2009. *My Prison, My Home: One Woman's Story of Captivity in Iran.* New York: Harper Collins.

Farhadi, Ashgar. 2011. *A Separation.* Directed by Ashgar Farhadi.

———. 2012. Quoted in Gazelle Emami. "Asghar Farhadi, Golden Globe Winner for 'A Separation,' Talks Getting Past the Censors in Iran." *Huffington Post,* January 17.

———. 2017. Quoted in Tracy Brown, "Full Statement from Foreign-language Film Winner Asghar Farhadi, Who Refused to Go to the Oscars in Protest." *Los Angeles Times,* February 26.

Farhang, Sara. 2009. "Iran: Women at the Forefront of Popular Defiance." July 1. www.sign4change.info/english/spip.php?article544 (accessed September 15, 2009).

Farris, Sara R. 2017. *In the Name of Women's Rights: The Rise of Femonationalism.* Durham, NC: Duke University Press.

Gladstone, Rick. 2012. "Election Fears and Economic Woes Pose New Challenges For Iran's Leaders." *New York Times,* January 2.

Glenn, Evelyn Nakano. 1992. "From Servitude to Service Work: Historical Continuities in the Racial Division of Paid Reproductive Labor." *Signs* 18, no. 1 (Autumn): 1–43.

Godazagar, Hossein. 2009. "Attitudes Towards the Internet in an Iranian University." *Viewpoints* special edition "The Iranian Revolution at 30." Middle East Institute: 70–73.

Greiner, Clemens, and Patrick Sakdapolrak. 2013. "Translocality: Concepts, Applications, and Emerging Research Perspectives." *Geography Compass* 7, no. 5: 373–84.

Grewal, Inderpal. 1999. "'Women's Rights as Human Rights': Feminist Practices, Global Feminism, and Human Rights in Transnationality." *Citizenship Studies* 3, no. 3: 337–54.

———. 2005. *Transnational America: Feminisms, Diasporas, Neoliberalisms.* Durham, NC: Duke University Press.

———. 2017. *Saving the Security State: Exceptional Citizens in Twenty-First-Century America.* Durham, NC: Duke University Press.

Grewal, Inderpal, and Caren Kaplan. 1994. "Transnational Feminist Practices and Questions of Postmodernity." In *Scattered Hegemonies: Postmodernity and Transnational Feminist Practices*, ed. Inderpal Grewal and Caren Kaplan, 1–36. Minneapolis: University of Minnesota Press.

Grosfoguel, Ramon. 2010. "Epistemic Islamophobia and Colonial Social Sciences." *Human Architecture: Journal of the Sociology of Self-Knowledge* 8, no. 2 (Fall): 29–38.

Grosz, Elizabeth. 1990. "Contemporary Theories of Power and Subjectivity." In *Feminist Knowledge: Critique and Construct,* ed. Sneja Gunew, 59–120. New York: Routledge.

Hafez, Sherine. 2011. *An Islam of Her Own: Reconsidering Religion and Secularism in Women's Islamic Movements.* New York: New York University Press.

Haj, Samira. 2008. *Reconfiguring Islamic Tradition: Reform, Rationality, and Modernity.* Stanford, CA: Stanford University Press.

Hakakian, Roya. 2004. *Journey from the Land of No: A Girlhood Caught in Revolutionary Iran.* New York: Crown.

Halper, Louise A. 2010. "Law and Iranian Women's Activism." In *Women and Islam*, ed. Zayn R. Kassam, 3–18. Santa Barbara, CA: Praeger Publishers.

Haraway, Donna. 1988. "Situated Knowledges: The Science Question in Feminism and the Privilege of Partial Perspective." *Feminist Studies* 14, no. 3 (Fall): 575–99.

Hardt, Michael, and Antonio Negri. 2004. *Multitude: War and Democracy in the Age of Empire.* New York: Penguin Books.

Harris, Kevan. 2010. "Iran Primer: The Bazaar." PBS.org. October 26. www.pbs.org/wgbh/pages/frontline/tehranbureau/2010/10/iran-primer-the-bazaar.html.

Hartmann, Heidi. 1979. "The Unhappy Marriage of Marxism and Feminism: Towards a More Progressive Union." *Capital & Class* 3, no. 2, 1–33.

Hélie, Anissa. 2012. "Risky Rights? Gender Equality and Sexual Diversity in Muslim Contexts." In *Sexuality in Muslim Contexts: Restrictions and Resistance*, ed. Anissa Hélie and Homa Hoodfar, 294–334. London: Zed Books.

Hodgson, Dorothy. 2011. "Gender and Culture at the Limit of Rights." In *Gender and Culture at the Limit of Rights*, ed. Dorothy Hodgson, 101–19. Philadelphia: University of Pennsylvania Press.

Hoodfar, Homa. 1999. *The Women's Movement in Iran: Women at the Crossroads of Secularization and Islamization.* Grebels Cedex, France: Women Living Under Muslim Laws.

Hussain, Muzammil M., and Sonia Jawaid Shaikh. 2015. "Three Arenas for Interrogating Digital Politics in Middle East Affairs." *International Journal of Middle East Studies*, no. 47: 366–68.

Icaza, Rosalba. 2017. "Decolonial Feminism and Global Politics: Border Thinking and Vulnerability as a Knowing Otherwise." In *Critical Epistemologies of Global*

Politics, ed. Mark Woons and Sebastian Weier, 26–45. Bristol: E-International Relations Publishing.

Ignatieff, Michael. 2001. "Human Rights as Moral Imperialism." Paper presented for the Conference on Rethinking Human Rights, New York. November 8–9.

INCITE! Women of Color Against Violence. 2007. *The Revolution Will Not Be Funded: Beyond The Non-Profit Industrial Complex.* Boston: South End Press.

International Campaign for Human Rights in Iran. 2008. "Equal Rights Denied: The Systematic Repression of the Women's Rights Movement in Iran." May 5. www.iranhumanrights.org/2009/01/repression-women (accessed March 12, 2009).

Iran's Nuclear Program. 2012. *New York Times.* Times Topics. http://topics.nytimes.com/top/news/international/countriesandterritories/iran/nuclear_program/index.html (accessed February 20, 2012).

Islam, Naheed. 2000. "Research as an Act of Betrayal: Researching Race in an Asian Community in Los Angeles." In *Racing Research, Researching Race*, ed. France Winddance Twine and Jonathan W. Warren, 35–66. New York: New York University Press.

Kaplan, Caren. 1994. "The Politics of Location as Transnational Feminist Practice." In *Scattered Hegemonies: Postmodernity and Transnational Feminist Practices*, ed. Inderpal Grewal and Caren Kaplan, 137–52. Minneapolis: University of Minnesota Press.

Karim, Persis. 2006. *Let Me Tell You Where I've Been: New Writing by Women of the Iranian Diaspora.* Fayetteville: University of Arkansas Press.

Karim, Persis, and Mohammad Mehdi Khorrami. 1999. *A World Between: Poems, Short Stories, and Essays by Iranian-Americans.* New York: George Braziller.

Kassam, Ashifa. 2016. "Canadian-Iranian Professor: I Survived Imprisonment by Studying My Captors." *The Guardian*, October 10.

Kassam, Zayn R. 2010. *Women and Islam.* Santa Barbara: Praeger Press.

Keddie, Nikki R. 2003. *Modern Iran: Roots and Results of Revolution.* New Haven, CT: Yale University Press.

Keshavarz, Fatemeh. 2007. *Jasmine and Stars: Reading More than* Lolita *in Tehran.* Chapel Hill: University of North Carolina Press.

Khakpour, Porochista. 2017. "Shirin Ebadi: 'Almost a Fourth of the People on Earth Are Muslim. Are They Like Each Other? Of Course Not.'" *The Guardian*, April 25.

Khiabany, Gholam. 2015. "Technologies of Liberation and/or Otherwise." *International Journal of Middle East Studies*, no. 47: 348–53.

Khiabany, Gholam, and Annabelle Sreberny. 2007. "The Politics of/in Blogging in Iran." *Comparative Studies of South Asia, Africa and the Middle East* 27, no. 3: 563–79.

Khomeini, Imam. 1985. *Islam and Revolution: Writings and Declarations.* Trans. Hamid Algar. London: Routledge.

Khorasani, Noushin Ahmadi. 2009. *Iranian Women's One Million Signatures Campaign for Equality: The Inside Story.* Bethesda, MD: Women's Learning Partnership.

Koolaee, Elaheh. 2003. "Iranian Reformists Happy over Nobel Win." Dawn .com. http://archives.dawn.com/2003/10/11/int5.htm (accessed December 11, 2003).

———. 2009. "New Challenges for Iranian Women." *Viewpoints*. Special edition, "The Iranian Revolution at 30." Middle East Institute: 58–61.

Landler, Mark. 2011. "United States and Its Allies Expand Sanctions on Iran." *New York Times*, November 21.

Latifi, Afschineh. 2005. *Even After All This Time: A Story of Love, Revolution, and Leaving Iran*. New York: Harper Collins.

Lewis, Gail. 2017. "Questions of Presence." *Feminist Review* 117: 1–19.

Longino, Helen. 1993. "Subjects, Power, and Knowledge: Description and Prescription in Feminist Philosophies of Science." In *Feminist Epistemologies*, ed. Linda Alcoff and Elizabeth Potter, 83–100. New York: Routledge.

Lugones, Maria. 2007. "Heterosexualism and the Colonial/Modern Gender System." *Hypatia* 22, no. 1: 186–209.

———. 2010. "Toward a Decolonial Feminism." *Hypatia* 25, no. 4: 742–59.

Maese-Cohen, Marcelle. 2010. "Toward Planetary Decolonial Feminisms." *Qui parle* 18, no. 2: 3–17.

Mahdavi, Pardis. 2009. *Passionate Uprisings: Iran's Sexual Revolution*. Stanford, CA: Stanford University Press.

Mahdi, Ali Akbar. 2003. "Iranian Women: Between Islamicization and Globalization." In *Iran Encountering Globalization: Problems and Prospects*, ed. Ali Mohammadi, 47–72. London: Routledge.

Mahmood, Saba. 2001. "Feminist Theory, Embodiment, and the Docile Agent: Some Reflections on the Egyptian Islamic Revival." *Cultural Anthropology* 6, no. 2: 202–36.

———. 2005. *Politics of Piety: The Islamic Revival and the Feminist Subject*. Princeton, NJ: Princeton University Press.

———. 2006. "Retooling Democracy and Feminism in the Service of New Empire." *Qui Parle* 16, no. 1: 117–43.

———. 2008. "Feminism, Democracy, and Empire: Islam and the War of Terror." In *Women's Studies on the Edge*, ed. Joan Wallach Scott, 81–114. Durham, NC: Duke University Press.

Malek, Amy. 2006. "Memoir as Iranian Exile Cultural Production: A Case Study of Marjane Satrapi's *Persepolis* Series." *Iranian Studies* 39, no. 3: 353–80.

———. 2015. "Claiming Space: Documenting Second-generation Iranian Americans in Los Angeles." *Anthropology of the Middle East* 10, no. 2: 16–45.

Mani, Lata. 1990. "Multiple Mediations: Feminist Scholarship in the Age of Multinational Reception." *Feminist Review* 35: 24–41.

Maoulidi, Salma. 2011. "Between Law and Culture: Contemplating Rights for Women in Zanzibar." In *Gender and Culture at the Limit of Rights*, ed. Dorothy Hodgson, 32–54. Philadelphia: University of Pennsylvania Press.

Marcotte, Roxanne. 2010. "Muslim Women's Scholarship and the New Gender Jihad." In *Women and Islam*, ed. Zayn R. Kassam, 131–62. Santa Barbara, CA: Praeger Publishers.

Massad, Joseph. 2002. "Re-Orienting Desire: The Gay International and the Arab World." *Public Culture* 14, no. 2: 361–86.

Massey, Jacquelinc. 2004. "A Nobel Cause: Shirin Ebadi Leads the Charge for Human Rights in Iran." *Herizons*, October 1.

Melucci, Alberto. 1996. *Challenging Codes: Collective Action in the Information Age*. Cambridge: Cambridge University Press.

Mendoza, Breny. 2015. "Coloniality of Gender and Power: From Postcoloniality to Decoloniality." In *The Oxford Handbook of Feminist Theory*, ed. Lisa Disch and Mary Hawkesworth, 100–121. New York: Oxford University Press.

Mernissi, Fatima. 1987. *The Veil and the Male Elite: A Feminist Interpretation of Women's Rights in Islam*. New York: Basic Books.

Mignolo, Walter D. 2018. "The Invention of the *Human* and the Three Pillars of the Colonial Matrix of Power." In *On Decoloniality: Concepts, Analytics, Praxis*, ed. Walter D. Mignolo and Catherine E. Walsh, 153–76. Durham, NC: Duke University Press.

Mignolo, Walter D., and Catherine E. Walsh. 2018. *On Decoloniality: Concepts, Analytics, Praxis*. Durham, NC: Duke University Press.

Mir-Hosseini, Ziba. 1999. *Islam and Gender: The Religious Debate in Contemporary Iran*. Princeton: Princeton University Press.

———. 2003. "Shirin Ebadi's Nobel Peace Prize Highlights Tension in Iran." *Middle East Report Online*, October 27.

———. 2006a. "Is Time on Iranian Women Protesters' Side?." June 16. www.merip.org/mero/mero061606.html (accessed August 1, 2006).

———. 2006b. "Muslim Women's Quest for Equality: Between Islamic Law and Feminism." *Critical Inquiry* 32, no. 4: 629–45.

Mir-Hosseini, Ziba, and Kim Longino. 1998. *Divorce Iranian Style*. Directed by Ziba Mir-Hosseini and Kim Longino.

Moaeveni, Azadeh. 2005. *Lipstick Jihad: A Memoir of Growing up Iranian in America and American in Iran*. New York: Perseus.

Moallem, Minoo. 1999. "Transnationalism, Feminism, and Fundamentalism." In *Between Woman and Nation: Nationalisms, Transnational Feminisms, and the State*, ed. Caren Kaplan, Norma Alarcon, and Minoo Moallem, 320–48. Durham, NC: Duke University Press.

———. 2005. *Between Warrior Brother and Veiled Sister: Islamic Fundamentalism and the Politics of Patriarchy in Iran*. Berkeley: University of California Press.

Moghadam, Valentine M. 2002. "Islamic Feminism and Its Discontents: Toward a Resolution of the Debate." In *Gender, Politics, and Islam*, ed. Therese Saliba, Carolyn Allen, and Judith A. Howard, 15–51. Chicago: University of Chicago Press.

———. 2003. "Global Feminism and Women's Citizenship in the Muslim World: The Cases of Iran, Algeria, and Afghanistan." Paper prepared for the Conference on Citizenship, Borders, and Gender: Mobility and Immobility, New Haven, CT, May 8–10.

———. 2005. *Globalizing Women: Transnational Feminist Networks*. Baltimore, MD: Johns Hopkins University Press.

Moghadam, Valentine, and Elham Gheytanchi. 2010. "Political Opportunities and Strategic Choices: Comparing Feminist Campaigns in Morocco and Iran." *Mobilization: An International Journal* 15, no. 3: 267–88.

Moghadam, Valentine, and Fatemeh Haghighatjoo. 2016. "Women and Political Leadership in an Authoritarian Context: A Case Study of the Sixth Parliament in the Islamic Republic of Iran." *Politics and Gender* 12, no. 1: 168–97.

Mohanty, Chandra Talpade. 1991. "Under Western Eyes." In *Third World Women and the Politics of Feminism*, ed. Chandra Talpade Mohanty, Ann Russo, and Lourdes Torres, 51–80. Bloomington: Indiana University Press.

———. 2003. *Feminism without Borders: Decolonizing Theory, Practicing Solidarity.* Durham, NC: Duke University Press.

Mohanty, Chandra Talpade, Ann Russo, and Lourdes Torres, eds. 1991. *Third World Women and the Politics of Feminism.* Bloomington: Indiana University Press.

Monshipouri, Mahmood. 2004. "The Road to Globalization Runs through Women's Struggle: Iran and the Impact of the Nobel Peace Prize." *World Affairs* 167, no. 1 (Summer): 3–14.

Mostofi, Nilou. 2003. "Who We Are: The Perplexity of Iranian-American Identity." *The Sociological Quarterly* 44, no. 4 (Autumn): 681–703.

Motlagh, Amy. 2011. "Autobiography and Authority in the Writings of the Iranian Diaspora." *Comparative Studies of South Asia, Africa and the Middle East* 31, no. 2: 411–24.

Mottahedeh, Negar. 2014. *#iranelection: Hashtag Solidarity and the Transformation of Online Life.* Stanford, CA: Stanford University Press.

Munshi, Soniya, and Craig Willse, eds. 2016. "Navigating Neoliberalism in the Academy, Nonprofits, and Beyond" (special issue). *The Scholar and Feminist Online* 13, no. 2 (Spring).

Naficy, Hamid. 1993. *The Making of Exile Cultures: Iranian Television in Los Angeles.* Minneapolis: University of Minnesota Press.

Nafisi, Azar. 2003. *Reading Lolita in Tehran: A Memoir in Books.* New York: Random House.

Naghibi, Nima. 2016. *Women Write Iran: Nostalgia and Human Rights from the Diaspora.* Minneapolis: University of Minnesota Press.

Najmabadi, Afsaneh. 1998. *The Story of the Daughters of Quchan: Gender and National Memory in Iranian History.* Syracuse, NY: Syracuse University Press.

———. 2005. *Women with Mustaches and Men without Beards: Gender and Sexual Anxieties of Iranian Modernity.* Berkeley: University of California Press.

Naples, Nancy. 2003. *Feminism and Method: Ethnography, Discourse Analysis, and Activist Research.* New York: Routledge.

Narayan, Uma. 1997. *Dislocating Cultures: Identities, Traditions, and Third World Feminism.* New York: Routledge.

Nemat, Marina. 2007. *Prisoner of Iran: One Woman's Story of Survival Inside an Iranian Prison.* New York: Free Press.

Osanloo, Arzoo. 2006. "Islamico-Civil 'Rights Talk': Women, Subjectivity, and Law in Iranian Family Court." *American Ethnologist* 33, no. 2: 191–209.

———. 2009. *The Politics of Women's Rights in Iran*. Princeton, NJ: Princeton University Press.

Paidar, Parvin. 1995. *Women and the Political Process in Twentieth-Century Iran*. Cambridge: Cambridge University Press.

———. 2002. "Encounters between Feminism, Democracy and Reformism in Contemporary Iran." In *Gender Justice, Development and Rights*, ed. Maxine Molyneux and Shahra Razavi, 239–76. Oxford: Oxford University Press.

Parreñas, Rhacel Salazar. 2008. *The Force of Domesticity: Filipina Migrants and Globalization*. New York: New York University Press.

Pérez, Laura E. 2010. "Enrique Dussel's *Etica de la liberacion*, U.S. Women of Color Decolonizing Practices, and Coalitionary Politics Amidst Difference." *Qui parle* 18, no. 2: 121–46.

Puar, Jasbir. 2007. *Terrorist Assemblages: Homonationalism in Queer Times*. Durham, NC: Duke University Press.

Raha Iranian Feminist Collective. 2011. "Solidarity and Its Discontents." *Jadaliyya*, February 19. www.jadaliyya.com/pages/index/683/solidarity-and-its-discontents (accessed March 3, 2011).

Rahimieh, Nasrin. 2007. "Border Crossing." *Comparative Studies of South Asia, Africa and the Middle East* 27, no. 2: 225–32.

———. 2009. "Divorce Seen through Women's Cinematic Lens." *Iranian Studies* 42, no. 1: 97–112.

Rastegar, Mitra. 2006. "Reading Nafisi in the West: Authenticity, Orientalism, and 'Liberating' Iranian Women." *Women's Studies Quarterly* 34, nos. 1 and 2 (Spring–Summer): 108–28.

Razack, Sheren H. 2008. *Casting Out: The Eviction of Muslims from Western Law and Politics*. Toronto: University of Toronto Press.

Reed, Jean-Pierre, and John Foran. 2002. "Political Cultures of Opposition: Exploring Idioms, Ideologies, and Revolutionary Agency in the Case of Nicaragua." *Critical Sociology* 28, no. 3: 335–70.

Roskos, Laura H. 2004. "From the Center to the Margins: The Radicalization of Human Rights in the United States." *Meridians: Feminism, Race, Transnationalism* 4, no. 2: 129–67.

Roudi-Fahimi, Farzaneh. 2002. *Iran's Family Planning Program: Responding to a Nation's Needs*. Washington, DC: Population Reference Bureau.

Saberi, Roxanne. 2010. *Between Two Worlds: My Life and Captivity in Iran*. New York: Harper Collins.

Safi, Omid. 2003. "What Shirin Ebadi's Nobel Means to Progressive Muslims." *Muslim WakeUp!*, October 11. www.muslimwakeup/pages/index/shirinebadi (accessed November 28, 2003).

Said, Edward. 1978. *Orientalism*. New York: Vintage Books.

Salime, Zakia. 2011. *Between Feminism and Islam: Human Rights and Sharia Law in Morocco*. Minneapolis: University of Minnesota Press.

Sameh, Catherine. 2017. "Solidarity." In *Gender: Love*, ed. Jennifer C. Nash, 181–95. Farmington Hills, MI: Macmillan Reference USA.

Sanasarian, Eliz. 1982. *The Women's Rights Movement in Iran: Mutiny, Appeasement and Repression from 1900 to Khomeini.* New York: Praeger Publishers.

Sanger, David E., and William J. Broad. 2011. "U.N. Agency Says Iran Data Points to A-Bomb Work." *New York Times*, November 8.

Satrapi, Marjane. 2006. *Chicken with Plums.* New York: Penguin.

Saunders, Kriemild. 2002. *Feminist Post-Development Thought: Rethinking Modernity, Post-Colonialism and Representation.* London: Zed Books.

Sayyah, Syma. 2003. "Shirin White Roses: Shirin Ebadi Is with Us and She Is One of Us!" *Payvand Iran News*, October 15. www.payvand.com/news/03/oct/1095.html (accessed November 28, 2003).

Schulman, Barbara. 2004. "Effective Organizing in Terrible Times: The Strategic Value of Human Rights for Transnational Anti-Racist Feminisms." *Meridians: Feminism, Race, Transnationalism* 4, no. 2: 102–7.

Secor, Laura. 2006. "Review of *Iran Awakening: A Memoir of Revolution and Hope*, by Shirin Ebadi with Azadeh Moaveni." *New York Times Book Review*, July 16.

Semati, Mehdi. 2008. *Media, Culture, and Society in Iran: Living with Globalization and the Islamic State.* New York: Routledge.

Shakhsari, Sima. 2011. "Weblogistan Goes to War: Representational Practices, Gendered Soldiers and Neoliberal Entrepreneurship in Diaspora." *Feminist Review* 99, no. 1: 6–24.

———. 2012. "From Homoerotics of Exile to Homopolitics of Diaspora: Cyberspace, the War on Terror, and the Hypervisible Iranian Queer." *Journal of Middle East Women's Studies* 8, no. 3: 14–40.

Shalakany, Amr. 2007. "Sexual Rites/Human Rights: Corruption and Repression from Queen 52 to a Queer-Postcolonial Agenda." Unpublished manuscript.

Shariati, Ali. 1996. *Fatima Is Fatima.* In *Shariati on Shariati and the Muslim Woman*, ed. Laleh Bakhtiar, 75–214. Chicago: ABC Group International, Inc.

Shekarloo, Masha. 2005. "Iranian Women Take on the Constitution," July 21. www.merip.org/mero/mero072105.html (accessed August 1, 2006).

Sherkat, Shahla. 2015. "Zanan-e Emrooz." *Journal of Middle East Women's Studies* 11, no. 3: 376–79.

Smith, Andrea. 2004. "Beyond the Politics of Inclusion: Violence Against Women of Color and Human Rights." *Meridians: Feminism, Race, Transnationalism* 4, no. 2: 120–23.

Soroush, Abdolkarim. 2000. *Reason, Freedom, and Democracy in Islam: Essential Writings of Abdolkarim Sorush.* Oxford: Oxford University Press.

Spivak, Gayatri. 1988. "Can the Subaltern Speak?" In *Marxism and the Interpretation of Culture*, ed. Lawrence Grossberg and Cary Nelson, 271–316. Urbana: University of Illinois Press.

Sreberny, Annabelle. 2015. "Women's Digital Activism in a Changing Middle East." *International Journal of Middle East Studies*, no. 47: 357–61.

Tallbear, Kim. 2014. "Standing with and Speaking as Faith: A Feminist-Indigenous Approach to Inquiry." *Journal of Research Practice* 10, no. 2, article N17.

Tohidi, Nayereh. 2002. "The Global-Local Intersection of Feminism in Muslim Societies: The Cases of Iran and Azerbaijan." *Social Research* 69, no. 3 (Fall): 851–87.

———. 2010. "The Women's Movement and Feminism in Iran: A Glocal Perspective." In *Women's Movements in the Global Era: The Power of Local Feminisms*, ed. Amrita Basu, 375–414. Boulder, CO: Westview Press.

Twine, France Winddance. 2000. "Racial Ideologies and Racial Methodologies." In *Racing Research, Researching Race: Methodological Dilemmas in Critical Race Studies*, ed. France Winddance Twine and Jonathan W. Warren, 1–34. New York: New York University Press.

United States Census Bureau. 2000. American Community Survey. www.census.gov.

United States Census Bureau. 2010. American Community Survey. www.census .gov.

Varzi, Roxanne. 2006. *Warring Souls: Youth, Media, and Martyrdom in Post-Revolution Iran*. Durham, NC: Duke University Press.

Wadud, Amina. 1992. *Qur'an and Woman: Rereading the Sacred Text from a Woman's Perspective*. New York: Oxford University Press.

Walsh, Catherine E. 2018a. "The Decolonial *For*: Resurgences, Shifts, and Movements." In *On Decoloniality: Concepts, Analytics, Praxis*, ed. Walter D. Mignolo and Catherine E. Walsh, 15–32. Durham, NC: Duke University Press.

———. 2018b. "Insurgency and Decolonial Prospect, Praxis, and Project." In *On Decoloniality: Concepts, Analytics, Praxis*, ed. Walter D. Mignolo and Catherine E. Walsh, 33–56. Durham, NC: Duke University Press.

Watson, Julia, and Sidonie Smith. 1992. "De/Colonization and the Politics of Discourse in Women's Autobiographical Practices." In *De/Colonizing the Subject: The Politics of Gender in Women's Autobiography*, ed. Sidonie Smith and Julia Watson, xiii–xxxi. Minneapolis: University of Minnesota Press.

Women Living Under Muslim Laws. 2003. "Iran: Congratulations to Shirin Ebadi." October 19. www.wluml.org/node/1192 (accessed November 28, 2003).

ZananTV. 2011. "ZananTV Launches in the Heart of Occupy Wall Street." December 1, 2011. https://zanantv.net/en/2011/12/01/zanan-tv-launches-heart-occupy -wall-street/ (accessed July 23, 2012).

———. 2013. "Obama and Rouhani: A Call to Action." September 25, 2013. https:// zanantv.net/en/2013/09/25/obama-rouhani-call-action/ (accessed February 18, 2014).

Zayani, Mohamed. 2015. *Networked Publics and Digital Contention: The Politics of Everyday Life in Tunisia*. New York: Oxford University Press

INDEX

DECOLONIZING FEMINISMS

Piya Chatterjee, Series Editor

Humanizing the Sacred: Sisters in Islam and the Struggle for Gender Justice in Malaysia, by Azza Basarudin

Power Interrupted: Antiracist and Feminist Activism inside the United Nations, by Sylvanna Falcón

Transnational Testimonios: The Politics of Collective Knowledge Production, by Patricia DeRocher

Asian American Feminisms and Women of Color Politics, edited by Lynn Fujiwara and Shireen Roshanravan

Unruly Figures: Queerness, Sex Work, and the Politics of Sexuality in Kerala, by Navaneetha Mokkil

Resisting Disappearance: Military Occupation and Women's Activism in Kashmir, by Ather Zia

Tea and Solidarity: Tamil Women and Work in Postwar Sri Lanka, by Mythri Jegathesan

Axis of Hope: Iranian Women's Rights Activism across Borders, by Catherine Z. Sameh